THE
RECIPE

Spontaneous Praise from Couples-Counseling Clients of Dr. Rick Blum

"In this envelope please find a picture of our new baby, which was born because of you and your help to my husband and me."
— Baby announcement, 1987

"We went from both thinking there was no way it would work to now planning on renewing our vows. I feel as if I'm in a new marriage, and I like the man I'm married to a lot more — only I didn't have to get divorced to find him, because I was already married to him."
— Counseling session, 1990

"I'm writing to let you know that, after the events that I shared with you, I never thought I'd have the kind of closeness and love that we now have in our lives together. I thought you should know how grateful I am."
— Letter, 1998

"To update you, we:
- Are doing incredibly well
- Have built up our "reserves" so that little things really don't rock the boat
- Have rediscovered our love for one another
- Have actually been intimate on multiple occasions
- Are on the same page about the situation with our son
- Are really enjoying our time together, making dates, and becoming happy with each other

Who to thank? Rick Blum. Thank you, thank you, thank you."
— Email, 2015

How to Use this Book

The Recipe covers the entire spectrum of finding and keeping a loving relationship. One psychologist, hearing about the scope of the book, commented that it might be the "bible of relationship books." It is really three books in one, and it provides the recipe for love, no matter where you find yourself today.

❖ If you are single, Parts I and II are for you. Of course, you can read Parts IV and those after if you want a preview of coming attractions!

❖ If you are not single but wondering if you should be because you seem to be in it alone, Parts II and III are for you. Part II will strengthen you and prepare you. Then, Part III will not tell you whether to break up, but will show you how to make the decision. After following those steps, you will eventually be ready for the singlehood instructions in Part I, or the relationship guidance below.

❖ If you are in a viable relationship, both of you can learn to prepare the love-recipe in Parts IV, V, VI, and VII.

After reading the introduction, jump to the section you find most appropriate.

THE
RECIPE
Love Made Simple

By Dr. Rick Blum

AN ARTHUR KURZWEIL BOOK
New York/Jerusalem

AN ARTHUR KURZWEIL BOOK
11 Bond Street #456
Great Neck, NY 11021

First edition

Please visit www.dr-rick.com.

Cover concept by Naomi Glickman.
Interior and back cover design by Judith M. Tulli.

Dr. Rick Blum
The Recipe
Love Made Simple

ISBN: 978-0-9855658-9-3

To Arielle
To Alana
To Daniel
To Adam
Each of you is a continual lesson in love.

Acknowledgments

My first thanks are to my clients. You have shaped and supported my work, explicitly and consistently. You are my true collaborators on this book.

Tom Sargent: My original psychotherapy mentor and long-time friend. My acknowledgment of your contribution is too profound for this page and overflows into the rest of this work. Through it, may your contribution surpass your time among us.

Dency Sargent, Cathy Sargent, and Bernadette Kelley: Along with Tom, you provided the insight, inspiration, and confidence for everything that came later. Thank you.

Arthur Kurzweil: My friend, *chevrusa*, guide, buddy, and now publisher, I could never begin to describe the meaning of your company along my path. Years ago, you told me that I could write. I copied down what you said and trusted you.

Wendy Bernstein, my editor: You combined your vision and enthusiasm for my work with your wisdom on how to best present it. You made it happen.

Larry Blum, my brother: My relationship with you is the first emotionally intimate one of my life. I learned from you that love is all that matters, all that even begins to matter.

Terry Kole, my mother, and her true love, Marty Kole, my stepfather: You both taught me what a true marriage looks like, by having the best one I have ever seen.

Arielle, Alana, Daniel, and Adam Blum: My love for each of you is infinity divided by four. I wrote in the hope that your learning curve is a lot faster than mine.

Binyamin Zomberg and Zev Butler: Your arrival added an essential missing ingredient to our recipe.

Micha, Naomi, Hanna, Evan, and Seth: Please take this book as a testimonial to the greatest hero you and I know — your mother. She makes loving look simple.

Shoshana: My best friend and my love. Without you, no one would be holding this book. It would have been a bit too theoretical for me to have written it.

Finally, I want to thank you, the person who is reading this. Reaching you is the reason I have made time for writing. I have already been inspired by some readers through kind comments on my Facebook page and on the "Blum Blog" on my website, dr-rick.com. While writing this book, I have thought continually of you, your quest to love deeply and long-term, the barriers you may have overcome to hope for this, and the good you will make out of the opportunity to trust the right mate.

Table of Contents

Preface

How to Put Love on the Menu

Fact number one: All you need is love.

Fact number two: It seems to be the most elusive condition to both find and keep.

There is a reason for this, and it is one of the saddest features of the human condition: Whether we are searching for a mate or already in a long-term term relationship, *it is hardest to be our best selves when it matters most!*

I became a psychologist mostly to solve this puzzle and learn the recipe for giving people (including myself) the choice to have vibrantly loving relationships. Since then, I have enjoyed decades of the precious privilege of counseling singles and couples. My clients have taught me what works and what does not. Sometimes they revised what I had learned in my training, and they frequently reversed what the surrounding culture was telling me. Gradually, *The Recipe* for loving relationships became crisp and golden.

As it turns out, love is a choice. It is a choice you can make, once you know how. In this guide, you will learn precisely how to find the right person and how to get over the wrong one. I will share the easy-to-follow recipe, using simple steps to build the love of your life and keep that relationship nourished forever.

Introduction

Just How Hungry Are You?

What happens when you hear a love song? If some music is accessible, play a starry-eyed melody now and see what it does to you. The tunes are easy to find. Most pop music consists of ballads celebrating or lamenting tender attachments. Many movies are love stories or include one, often accompanied by romantic music to help the arrow hit that vulnerable place in our chests.

Whether you are listening now or remembering your long history of such listening, here's my question: What does it do to you? Where does it take you? To whom does it take you?

❖ Are you newly in love, your heart beating along with the song, but hoping that your relationship doesn't turn out like most of those around you?

❖ Are you feeling betrayed by the promise of the song — the illusion that love lives happily ever after, when everyone knows it always fades?

❖ Is someone special in the starring role of your love song, but you're not so sure you're playing that part in his or hers?

❖ Are you married to someone who has long ceased being in your love song at all, but you are hoping he or she cannot tell?

❖ Are you thinking of an old but not forgotten love, the one chance you had, but lost?

❖ Do you think you've entirely missed the parade, so perhaps others can dance down the street to the beat of that song, but never you?

❖ Do you and someone special think of each other when such songs play, but something about daily life seems to make you both forget?

Wherever listening to a love song takes you, would you be astonished if its fantasy could come true for you? Would you want to be married to the person who pops in your head when you hear a song like that? How glad would you be if you believed your relationship could actually strengthen with time instead of fading? One more question: What if the recipe for having such a soul-stirring, heart-snatching, smile-stretching love of your life were *simple*?

In the chapters to follow, we will explore just such a recipe together, including the steps for cooking it up and the strategies for serving up a delicious outcome. These steps anticipate several different life circumstances. As a result, not all the parts will apply to you. You will be able to skip some parts, unless you are curious about them. As I next describe them, you will recognize immediately which chapters do apply to you.

For example, the first part is about seeking the right person. Obviously, this is an important step for many. On the other hand, if you are currently married or in a relationship, shopping for a new mate is not where you will be starting. (In the third part, we'll talk about what to do if you started shopping before you were single.) Yet, if you are in a troubled relationship, you might be glad to have this first part in reserve, just in case you ever need it. We will consider the steps to finding the right someone: the difference between a desperate search and an inspired search, two special ingredients that will motivate your search, and three "spices" that will maximize your results. We will deal with the frightening question of how long this search could take or if it would ever succeed. Finally, we will develop your palate through evaluation strategies that help you select the *right* person rather than settle for the *next* person.

The second part might surprise you within the context of this book, because it is not about relationships with others. It consists of the steps to produce the first member of the couple you hope to be part of — and that first member is *you*. We know that it is necessary to be happy with oneself before being ready to find a fulfilling relationship. In this part, we will learn measures to help that happen, including managing loneliness, eliminating hindrances from the past, and building three kinds of love that you can have before even walking out of the kitchen door.

Part III is the most challenging to read. It is also potentially the most helpful in lessening the pain you may be living with. It explains what you can do if you are not sure whether you are with the right person. Our goal is to either restart happily with the person who is already in your life, or reset your life anew without that person. We will include how to evaluate a current relationship, how to deal with love addiction, how to manage distant or anger-prone partners, and how to do a remarkable experiment to discern the potential of the relationship. We will also explore the methods that couples can use if they are endeavoring to come back from betrayal. Finally, we will learn how to get over a broken heart, if that becomes necessary.

The next part (IV) prepares you to anticipate and even enjoy three typical challenges to a happy relationship. All three are nearly universal; yet if couples do not recognize that fact, they are more likely to blame the relationship and fear they are not meant to be together. Chapter 16 explores the influence of gender dynamics, differences that often lead to huge misunderstandings. The 17th chapter will show you the one and only argument the two of you have and how to stop it. Chapter 18 reveals and corrects a very surprising and unrecognized problem for most couples, not having to do with differences but with similarities!

After we have learned about how to find and evaluate relationships and how to manage the three widespread pitfalls above, we will learn how to cook up the Gold Medal Recipe. Part V contains the simple plan for a continually regenerating and passionate love. This recipe is fully intuitive — yet we each tend to have bad cooking habits that convince us to try to make love out of the wrong ingredients.

Building on Part V, the sixth part shows us how to determine whether we are on track together and what to do if we veer off course. In this section, we will learn how to lessen conflict, how to resolve it, and how to keep arguments from setting the kitchen on fire!

Finally, Part VII brings the insights from the previous chapters into the intimate arena of the bedroom, as we learn how to keep the thrill thriving and how to find it again if it has been lost.

Simple methods can bring blessings to those who practice them, and sometimes these advantages are not only love-saving but also life-saving. Looking at an example of the latter, the twelve-step programs — especially Alcoholics Anonymous — also supply simple formulas, in their case for recovery from substance addiction. One of their recipes includes the abundant use of slogans, and one of the best is K.I.S.S., which is sometimes explained as "Keep It Short and Simple," but with typical AA humor is more frequently rendered "Keep It Simple, Stupid!"

While the AA recipe is about restoring lives and ours is about restoring love, a common element is the simplicity. Another commonality is that, in both cases, you have to show up. Even the most elegantly simple magic trick has to be practiced in order to dazzle us.

As any AA sponsor will tell you, *simple* and *easy* are two different notions. The principles of recovery are straightforward and understandable, but recovery takes attention and follow-though. Accordingly, another AA saying goes, "It works if you work it; so work it, you're worth it."

Our recipe also calls for attention and follow-through in order to cook it up, just as the recovery programs do. *Talking the talk* has to lead to *walking the walk*. Yet, even for this requirement of follow-through, there are ways to increase motivation. In the first chapter, we will explore the steps to tap into your desire for a loving relationship and to create realistic hope for a successful outcome, even if you may not yet know the person whom you are seeking.

PART I

Essential Ingredients

CHAPTER 1

Why Go Looking?

In his masterwork *Man's Search for Meaning*, Viktor Frankl described his love for his wife as an endless reservoir of strength. The bond between them was pervasively powerful, such that thoughts of her carried him

Beginning at the end point

through an intensely hellish journey inside a series of death camps during World War II. He described how the experience of his profound love for her stayed with him, providing an indestructible resoluteness to survive for her. Then, he wrote the next astonishing point: Even had he known at the time that the murderers had already killed her, it would not have changed the effect that her love had upon him. Their relationship enabled him to prevail physically, emotionally, and spiritually, over the daily horrors of his life during these years. As he stated it (p. 39): "Had I known then that my wife was dead, I think that I still would have given myself, undisturbed by that knowledge, to the contemplation of her image, and that my mental conversation with her would have been just as vivid and just as satisfying. 'Set me as a seal upon thy heart, love is as strong as death.'"

As he also wrote, many other types of life missions have the ability to change the entire context of one's existence. This was just his.

The truth is that one can be happy, and life can be full and meaningful, without a romantic relationship, as we will explore in Part II. Nonetheless, it

Love's promises and disappointments

remains a unique and life-changing gift. Furthermore, while there are many ways to love, no loving experience on earth offers the exact effect of having a loving partner. While family relationships are deeply intimate, the job of a parent is to give to the child. *In romantic love, the difference between giving and taking blends into a swirl of mutually shared joy.* It supplies a unique chemistry to life, both literally and poetically, such that it seems to fill the heart with endless blessings. That is why there are so many love songs. Love can be forever, at least in the heart of the lover, as Viktor Frankl so movingly displayed.

Unfortunately, love often resides in one's core more as a longing ache than the realization of its splendid potential. This returns us to the second fact mentioned in the preface: *It's hardest to be yourself with the people who matter the most.*

Try to digest that fact. Doesn't it seem unfair? I find it a tormenting observation, like being encased suddenly in a plastic bubble every time you most want to touch someone. The profession of psychotherapy originally appealed to me mostly because of this. I wanted people, including me, to have the choice, the *freedom*, to have a romantically loving relationship that endures.

An important step to creating that freedom consists of knowing how to "shop for the right ingredients," so to speak, to be right for you. Now, some people love to shop, but many of us hate it. It can be so discouraging! Think about it: If this chapter applies to you, it means that no relationship you have ever had has worked out permanently, even if it seemed to hold promise at first. That is a startling and daunting thought. It is so depressing that you might wonder why I am even mentioning it.

Shop-phobia

Then, it gets worse. You probably feel old, whatever your age. I have noticed that almost all my adult clients feel old, no matter how old they are. This may be the case because you are now the oldest you have ever been. Of course, several years ago, you felt this same way about your age at that time — yet you now know you were wrong about that! Today, it seems too late for you.

So, here you are, feeling old and never having had a relationship that worked out. You probably are ready for some good news, so here it is: *Everyone who has ever found a terrific and abiding relationship was in the same exact state before they found the right person.* Nothing had worked out before, and then it did. That is our plan for you too. So, let's prepare to go shopping.

CHAPTER 2

How to Avoid Desperation While Shopping for Inspiration

"You'll find it when you stop looking for it." Have you ever heard that? Some clichés are completely true, but this one is off base. You really can find the right person while looking for her or him, just in a particular way. The most surefooted path is not one of desperation, but one of *inspiration*.

When people have not yet made this distinction, they tend to swing like a pendulum between two states: *desperate yearning* and *cynical reserve*. In the cynical state, after getting fed up once again, they aim to be towers of independent strength. This could be called the jaded phase, except that some of us never leave this state of bitterness. In this state of mind, it seems that potential partners are *all* just:

Evil

Crazy

Stupid

Useless

Amusing

Troublesome

Dangerous

You can fill in your own adjectives, and maybe you have. In her song "Both Sides Now," Joni Mitchell poetically contrasts the blind-eyed optimism stage of youthful hopefulness with the later blind-eyed pessimism stage of guarded cynicism. In the rest of the song, Mitchell expands her images of such a jaded view, applying it to all of life. For a closer look at the temptation to ingest such a "bitter pill," see the sidebar.

Have you ever taken the bitter pill?

There is a big difference between the inevitable pain in life and optional bitterness about life.

Emotional pain is specific and localized to particular events, while bitterness generalizes pain, changing our overall opinion about life.

We can take as big a bitter pill as we want.

We can dislike men, or women, or ethnic groups, or bosses, or police, or people in suits, or rich people, or poor people.

If we decide to make it even bigger, we can dislike life, the entire world, or God.

Such bitterness weaves pain throughout one's world.

As a result, the course of many people's lives travels from blind-eyed optimism to blind-eyed pessimism.

Why would someone decide to broadcast wide the expectation of pain?

It makes some sense as a (futile) attempt to protect us from further hurt.

Yet, it is a big mistake, because it becomes self-fulfilling, bringing us more hurt.

When we begin to expect only pain, our guarded attitudes bring pain to others.

In AA, they express this phenomenon as "Hurt people hurt people."

We hurt others, prompting their own defenses.

They hurt us back, proving our worries to be true. The other way that bitterness is self-fulfilling is that we miss the opportunity to be loved and healed, thinking such redemptive experiences to be nonexistent.

Fortunately, we have better alternatives.

One solution is to keep our eyes open for the diversity among people, as well as the mix of selfish and loving urges in most everyone.

You can prove the first part of this (the variety) to yourself, gradually, by focusing careful attention on the world around you.

You can prove the second part of this (the duality) immediately.

Just look at yourself.

Notice the mix of giving and taking in yourself, and how elusive the balance be can be.

For example, have you ever failed in your attempt to rise above a selfish concern?

On the other hand, you know that your effort to be less selfish shows your wish to rise higher.

If you did not have love to give and potential to express, then you would not be disappointed when unable to express it.

Like everyone else, there are two sides to you.

Of course, after being hurt, you become cautious.

So does everyone else.

That means other people are also afraid of you.

In this reciprocal fear lies a hint at your own power to begin making the world safer for love.

Healing the world, one loving moment at a time, is much better than being bitter.

Like an alcoholic on the wagon, the jaded individual swears off love, thinking, "If it's supposed to happen, it will happen" — perhaps followed by the admission, "but I don't think so." Whether or not the person is celibate during this period, the heart is stowed in a lockbox, emotionally celibate. Any alcoholic in recovery can also tell you what usually follows periodic abstinence: the next binge. Starving for affection, when love-hungry souls stumble upon a chance to relieve the loneliness, they "fall in love," madly and deeply, as Cupid's arrow sends them reeling.

Is bitter better?

After a few rides — or one awful ride — on such a roller coaster, some choose to get off. They hide away out of Cupid's reach, thinking bitterness is better.

A more effective choice is to take a different route altogether, to move away from desperation to inspiration. An inspired search is neither bitter nor anxious. Inspiration (meaning, "having spirit within") is the emotional result of commitment to an important goal. Commitment requires both focusing

Inspired commitment

one's resources toward that goal and staying the course when one feels like quitting. *In this way, commitment is the source of the feeling of inspiration.*

Commitment leads to the kind of success that matters to us. Accordingly, Frankl's teachings on the power of having a devoted mission not only can save one's life, but also make life worth living. Maybe this is why we have so many words for varieties of commitment: *aim, vocation, mission, charge, dedication, aspiration, calling, purpose, goal, work, profession, devotion, venture, direction, pursuit, passion.* We even have names for the condition of lacking such dedication: *aimless, purposeless, directionless, goalless, passionless.*

If freedom from both sides of the desperation/cynicism pendulum arises through committed action, it would be good to know how to achieve it. Where

Locating commitment

are you usefully committed in your life? To locate it, you can ask some other questions: What parts of your life work best? Where in your life do you usually do what you say you will do? When are

you most able to follow an intentional path of action, despite fluctuations in your mood? Is it as a friend, a pet owner, a professional? Is it in cleaning your home, caring for others, exercising? Perhaps you have this type of commitment just for brief periods — a few days, or even a few hours. Wherever you find this, it is where you already understand a sense of living *on purpose.*

If, even after reflection, you do not believe that any portion of your life reflects committed action, you might want to review the final chapter of this book. There, we talk about when and how to access a therapist. The rest of Part I may ask too much of you if you cannot yet locate any committed courses of action, even in short moments. On the other hand, if you recognize the power of a sense of mission anywhere in your life, then this is how you will want to operate for our purposes in this part.

All of this talk of commitment to a goal is valuable, yet it also begs a question: How do we commit to a goal not entirely in our hands? Clearly, we find a difference between getting up when the alarm goes off on a workday and finding a soul mate. We cannot just make the latter happen, can we?

Goals like this are what I call *desirable side effects.* They cannot be achieved directly, but they are consequences of certain other actions we can choose. These by-product goals also happen to include the most sought-after experiences in life. People are often miserable when they cannot achieve one of these states, yet aiming to produce them intentionally doesn't work. On the contrary, trying to produce the experience actually interferes with achieving it. It is quite a list, including: a sense of meaning, happiness, self-esteem, religious or spiritual experience, sleep, sexual response, deep friendship, closeness with one's children, getting in better physical shape, and certainly romantic love.

Love as a by-product

Fortunately, every one of these goals is attainable, but aiming directly for them actually prevents them! In each case, the desirable experience will be a side effect of committed performance to other actions. In our specific case, you do not have to go out tonight and find the right person. The task is much simpler. Finding a person with the right qualities is a by-product of the rest of the activities in this part: two secret ingredients, three spices, predicting your likelihood of success, and improving your evaluation strategies.

CHAPTER 3

Two Secret Ingredients and Three Spices to Include

The perspective of the previous chapter — that the right activities eventually and even indirectly produce a cherished goal — brings us to the two ingredients of success. They are really two sides of the same coin of commitment. Each side balances the other, creating the result you want. These two consist of passion for the goal and trust that it is possible. *Passion without trust brings us back to desperation; trust without passion brings complacency.* So, how do they work, and how do we develop them?

Our bodies actually supply us with an amazing resource to build our desire for a relationship. We call it *pain*, and we usually avoid thinking about it.

The purpose of pain

To understand the value of emotional pain, first consider the value of physical pain, which makes us move out of trouble in order to avoid it. Children born with the rare disorder called congenital insensitivity to pain usually end up crippled without the physical feedback that signals the rest of us to move away from sources of pain. Could emotional pains have a similar purpose? We know that emotional anguish can even be deadly, if you consider the phenomenon of suicide. Yet, it is universal. Perhaps emotional pain has a similar purpose to physical pain — it makes us move, or tries to. In other words, if you felt no distress over any aspect of your love life, would you even be reading this?

There is a terrific saying that goes: When the pain of where I am exceeds the fear of where I am going, then I will move. Another way to state this is: Comfortable equals stuck. As a result, once I understand the purpose of my feeling of loneliness, I can leverage it toward moving ahead.

Naturally, relief from suffering is not the whole source of passion for a relationship. We began Part I considering love's radiance, and I will expand on that considerably when we focus on the gold-standard recipe in Part V. If you have never been loved like that and never loved like that, it is a place you will definitely want to live, once you find your way there. So, this focus on the pain of longing for such a bond is not meant to be a negative outlook. Rather, as the marketing people know, *fear of loss is more motivating than expectation of gain.* Fear of never having a rewarding relationship provides an even greater push than the quest for its many splendors.

As a therapist, I leverage such motivation every day. Most people arrive at my office seeking to lessen pain in some part of their lives. As we discover the path toward freedom, I look for that motivating pain to push the process. If the person is not hurting, I may not know how to help. That is how important an ally distress becomes in guiding life progress overall, not just in one's passion to find the right person.

Of course, the process only works if there is some belief that the efforts might pay off. This leads us to the other side of the coin, the second secret ingredient, which is trust that you can succeed.

For pain to provide a productive motivation for moving our lives in a happy direction, we need to believe we can get there. Without any trust in your prospects, pain is just pain. I once heard a good illustration of this, which I often retell in counseling sessions.

Have a little faith in you.

Imagine I told you, and you believed, that I had inherited several billion dollars, so the multimillion-dollar lottery ticket I also have is just not important to me. I am offering it to you, and telling you exactly where I left it, in a closet in a house at the address I am giving you. If I could verify all this to your satisfaction, you would be happy with me. But you would become unhappy with me if I added another detail. Suppose I warn you that there is a grizzly bear in that same closet, and those who attempted to claim the ticket previously have not returned. Why, you now wonder, am I teasing you? Naturally, you still desire that ticket, but no longer expect you can retrieve it. On the other hand, if you are a hunter with a rifle that can effectively remove the threat of the grizzly, you still like me. You might let me know there will be some bullet damage to the house, but your lottery winnings will easily take care of the repair.

Clearly, trust is as important an ingredient as passion to keep you on track. You already come equipped with the innate feelings that will provide the passion. This leaves the trust element, which is the subject of the rest of this part. We will begin with three spices that you can use to speed up your search.

I often call these *three maximizations,* as they supercharge the process of shopping around. They are the three activities that, as a side effect, speed up the process of finding someone with high potential for you. If you do not like the pace things are going, you can just step up any of these three elements rather than worry about when you will find that person. They are:

Spicing up your search three ways

❖ increasing appeal

❖ increasing receptivity

❖ increasing exposure

As we describe these elements, some will feel an objection rising from the Fateful Voice within. Somehow, it seems to violate some natural or even divine law to willfully speed up your search for the right partner. We learn this at the movies more than anywhere else: There is one right person for us in the universe. If and when the universe wants us to find this person, he or she will appear. Before then, it can't be helped, so the Fateful Voice tells us.

To answer that voice within you, I suggest the following rationale: If you are naturalistic in your understanding of the world, then how could there be any intention on the part of nature that you wait? Why not speed up the process? If you have a religious sensibility, spiritual leaders would agree that we are not supposed to go through life passively and depend on miracles. We are supposed to apply ourselves fully to the miracle involved in living each day. Only when we are really, really out of all the options at our disposal are we supposed to turn the rest over to God. What is in your hands? You can spice up your search as follows.

The three spicy factors are *appeal, receptivity,* and *exposure to others.* Augmenting any or all of these tends to speed up your search. Like looking for any opportunity, it is often about numbers.

The first item listed above, increasing appeal, is one of the most awkward aspects of the recipe to discuss. It has to do with how you present to others, or how you look. If we are looking for a deep and abiding love, why should superficial appearances matter? In a way, they don't.

Appeal is on the surface.

Long-term loving couples can weather each other's weathering over time without losing either love or attraction. We will even explore the way this works in later chapters. Yet, appearances matter, nevertheless, because most people are not going to love you deeply before they know you. If they did, you would have cause to worry! *Instead, when people first meet, we are commodities of sorts to each other.* Later in Part I, we will fine tune your initial assessment of others as part of an evaluation phase.

In short, people start in the evaluation phase when they are shopping, and have to move beyond that into an unconditional love when they make a full commitment to each other. The better you present to others, the more people will be interested in finding out more.

So, what features of appeal are partially in our hands? There are three:

health, style, and expression. People are attracted to the appearance of health in others, which is the reason that becoming stronger and sleeker will improve the numbers for you. Similarly, even people who are not fashion conscious will be somewhat influenced by cultural style elements, because they affect what looks right to us. As well, clothing, hairstyle, and men's facial hair do more than shape and frame our faces — they change the superficial appearance of personality. In the next part, we will address directly how improving your relationship with yourself does even more to affect how you come across to others. In terms of style, ample books, magazines, and experts are available to those who want advice on any of these subjects.

Just as you are shopping for the right ingredients in someone else, the person you are looking for is also seeking such a match, perhaps right now. You can simply tune up or turn down your efforts in the dimension of increasing appeal, depending on your comfort with the pace of your search. If you are feeling bored or impatient, just dial it up; if you are feeling pressured by the process, you can even dial it down.

While increasing appeal presents a challenge to the self-image of many people, receptivity can be just as daunting. In the arena of receptivity, as in

Eyes: open versus shut

so many others, *our mistakes usually consist of living in one extreme to avoid the opposite extreme. I call this pendulemia.* It is not a mental illness, just the normal judgment errors of everyday life. We have already looked at the pendulemia of living like a solitary island in order to avoid a desperate dependency in searching for someone. A related type of pendulemia that limits our receptivity to meeting people is the fear of looking too aggressively interested. This avoidance of receptivity usually shows up differently in men and in women.

Women have two versions of avoiding receptivity, though they are not mutually exclusive. In the first, a woman studiously avoids giving any visible sign of interest even when it is there. Do you know what happens if a woman gives men no signals? Most of the time, *the only men who approach her with interest are the men who don't read signals.* If she looks good to him, this kind of bloke just clomps right over to meet her. It does not much matter to him what she wants or does not want. That is not a question he is asking himself. After fending off one insensitive man after another — or worse, getting involved with one or two — she is on her way to the jaded state we noted in Chapter 2!

The second way that women commonly avoid looking overly interested in relationships is by presenting themselves as too independent for emotional intimacy. Probably because they think that men do not want clingy women, they act very cool. They look a bit distant, maybe even aloof. Eventually, if they begin to like someone, they want to get closer. *The problem is that anyone who wanted to get close would have left already, thinking this woman is too independent for the cuddly relationship he has in mind.* Who stays around? Only the sort of fellow who wants it just the way it has been, so he moves away when she begins to change. Thus, she is in effect filtering out the kind of man she really wants and attracting those who will hurt her.

Lest we suppose that only women avoid receptivity, let us consider the most common male version. One could term this *selective shyness.* If a man is shy overall, it could certainly cramp his social life. On the other hand, sometimes he will be viewed as the strong, silent type, and some women will want to draw him out. A quiet man can seem intriguing to women who suppose all sorts of profound thoughts are hiding behind the silence. Of course, it is more likely that he is thinking thoughts like, "Hmm ... Hungry .... Pizza?" Yet, a man who isn't generally shy but specifically avoids a woman who actually interests him will be sending the wrong signals — and, most women *do* read signals. Why would he do this? Because he wants to avoid seeming overly aggressive, and to avoid intruding on her.

In my late 20s, I thought the same way. I did not want to be the "clomping over" kind, and through the miracle of pendulemia I went far in the opposite direction. If I had been at a social event and a particular woman caught my attention, she would have had no way of knowing. In fact, at the end of the evening, if you asked her which man had been the least interested in her, she would have picked me. I had perfected hiding any evidence that I even knew she was there. Such an approach is painfully polite, with the emphasis on *painful.*

Although different from each other, all three of these are ways that men and women avoid letting the potentially right people know they may be the right people too. Fortunately, all three respond to the same correction. Instead of focusing on our shyness about taking anyone's time or attention, we can focus on giving them a break. It is natural to be afraid of the unknown in other people. Yet, we forget that, to other people, *we ourselves are among the other people.* The three versions of inhibited receptivity all show up in kind and gentle people. This same kindness can offer the solution.

For the women who do not give signals, I recommend realizing that nice men, one of whom you would really enjoy meeting, need reassurance too.

The gentle-man will look to see if you return his interest. Sometimes all it takes is a look, one that lasts just long enough to seem on purpose, and maybe another similar look a few seconds later. If you glance at him discreetly in this manner, he can tell himself, "OK, I might not be bothering her. She looks a bit curious too." It is not desperation to give him this little bit of encouragement; *it is making his life easier.*

Similarly, women who act aloof are discouraging the right kind of men. Instead, showing a bit of the warmth and good-heartedness lets the caring type of fellow know you might be a kindred spirit, while ridding yourself of those who are not really your type.

Finally, if you are one of the overly polite men, your showing interest is not a burden, especially because you are so very easy to get rid of. Granted, you are probably not every woman's favorite type, but you are not so bad either. In other words, it is at least somewhat flattering when you, as a single man, find a single woman appealing. The successful marketing of clothing and cosmetics shows that women generally wish to be attractive, and your interest validates that she is appealing to you. The bottom line is that you are giving her a gift of interest, and if she does not return yours, you are still leaving her a little better off.

We are now ready to access the third maximization, increased exposure. With the added confidence of improving your appeal and new openness from heightening your receptivity, you are ready for

Getting around the need to get around

the most important of the three. Like so much of life, meeting a prospective mate can be more about numbers than anything else. Whenever one is shopping, whether for employment, clothes, or any situation, *higher numbers naturally nurture success.* In fact, the first two spicy maximizations are useful mostly because of the third. Increased appeal and increased receptivity both add to the numbers of people who will pass before you for consideration.

Aiming to meet more people, as the steps above accomplish, does not have to be a reflection of desperation and insecurity. Actually, it can be the opposite. The more literally average a person is, the more other people will be similar to him or her. One of the reasons many people have difficulty finding a match is that they are extraordinary in some way. People with a lot to offer often need more exposure to find someone because of these positive qualities. For example, the more intelligence, balance, versatility, courage, and loyalty one person has, the more potential for an interpersonal imbalance that leads to dissatisfaction in *both* partners. Yes, both — in psychology, this phenomenon has the name *equity theory* (Adams, 1965). *In this way, needing higher exposure reflects higher rather than lower self-esteem.* As a result, numbers become even more important.

Fortunately, this instrumental third factor of exposure is easier to achieve than ever. The best tried-and-true method of increasing the numbers of people one meets is still networking, otherwise known as being friendly. Even an introvert can step up into *friendly mode* during the process of shopping for the right person. For more on how to do this, see the sidebar on shyness.

A word to the mildly shy: The biggest tactical mistake that shy people make is to pressure themselves to be interesting. Actually, the job is a lot easier than that. Instead of being interesting, just be interested! Before you meet anyone, you already know their favorite subject, which consists of their own lives. Further, you can ask questions about three areas without being intrusive. Think of the acronym FOR, as in For Opening Relationships. The F-O-R subjects are: Family, Occupation, Recreation. People usually respond to questions about who and where their relatives are, how their current job/schooling is going, and what they do for fun.

Also, keep in mind that most areas of anxiety are more easily tackled in small steps. Joining a conversation silently, nodding in agreement and smiling, saying a sentence of comment, and asking a FOR question are all small steps. Doing one step until it is comfortable prepares the path for the next step to become less anxiety provoking.

It can also reduce feelings of shyness to be prepared with some content: a story, event, or scientific discovery. Perhaps due to market pressures, today's publications are masterful at providing fascinating content. Depending on the crowd, you can find such in Scientific American, National Geographic, or People magazine. Finally, it is useful to distinguish between the physical sensations of mild anxiety and the negative thoughts of futility, as in, "I can't do this. I'll make a fool of myself." (If the social anxiety is more severe, it can be best treated professionally.)

Friendly mode means maintaining a social openness around people. It is hard to change gears suddenly when you meet someone you might want to get to know. Being generally friendly aids the cause.

Unless the person you seek comes knocking on your door, you may want to go out more. And do what? Anything you do increases your exposure, especially in friendly mode. Accordingly, of all the group activities you could choose, pick the one you like most or dislike least. Keep in mind that *people like you might do similar activities as you, whether volunteer, aesthetic, intellectual, or professional activities.* Bars may be too random a source of meeting people, but can be useful for social practice (see the sidebar on shyness, above). If you choose activities that you find meaningful, then you will likely enjoy participating even when, most of the time, you do not meet someone new.

The oldest form of networking is probably the best: meeting the friends and family of friends. In the sales world the term for existing acquaintances is your *warm market,* and the people they know are called your lukewarm market. This is indeed a warmer way to shop for the right ingredients. *Right now you may know people who know someone worth meeting.* This makes all increased socialization useful, because every new friend you meet also becomes a warm market contact. The problem is that those people, if they have thought of making an introduction, are probably hesitant to suggest it. They are afraid of two reactions. The first is, "What, do you think I can't get a date for myself?" That is the milder reaction they fear. The other is, "You thought I would have something in common with him/her?" If you want to open the possibility of an introduction, try bringing up the subject with something like, "You know, I'm feeling ready to find the right person for me. So, if you know anyone you think I should meet, even if I decide the person's not for me, I'd be grateful for the effort."

Having touched on friendly mode and on networking, if you think we are going to talk next about the Internet, you are right. Online options have changed the landscape of increased exposure immensely. In addition to a variety of sites specifically devoted to dating, social networking sites have enhanced the ability to gain exposure. As of this writing, Facebook affords the opportunity to find old friends and meet the friends of friends easily, and meetup.com allows people to find others with similar interests in ways not easily conceivable before. The most popular sites may change in the future, but social media is probably here to stay. Dating sites offer lots of choices, such as how involved the site is in selecting matches and how much and how long it guards the privacy of users.

Such sites are popular today, which is what makes them so useful. Once upon a time, there were (non-Internet) video dating services. Some people used them, but often they had a reputation as a hard-up option. I would sometimes hear about it during couples sessions, but the admission would be followed by, "We're not telling anyone that." If the dating services had a better public perception, they would have become a better option, but elements such as reputation can become self-fulfilling. Too few people used them because they thought that too few people used them. In contrast, online dating sites now enjoy the image of being efficient and fun, so most people use them without embarrassment.

Of course, the major advantage and disadvantage of online sites is the same: They bring you far out of your own network. As a result, they present both a strong requirement and an opportunity to practice the evaluation strategies presented in Chapter Five. Like the rest of the maximization methods, the point of these options is to speed up your search. So, let's turn next to the question of how to predict your results.

CHAPTER 4

How Much Shopping Will You Need to Do?

The future is dark to our vision until it slips quietly into the past. It's impossible to ascertain how long it will take you to find somebody with whom you can cook up a beautiful relationship. As a result, *the fear of never finding that individual is one of the largest barriers to fully engaging in the search itself.* The best way I know to break through the paralyzing effects of this uncertainty is through the thought exercise that follows.

Imagine that you have heard, from a reliable source, about an amazing oracle. Someone has developed the uncanny ability to tell you exactly how many people you have to meet to find the right one. This does not mean how many people you have to have a relationship with, or even how many people you have to date. Rather, you can discover how many people you have to meet just long enough to see if they fit the evaluation strategies (to come) enough to even have a date. You become convinced that this is unbelievable but true. Perhaps you have a list of people, hundreds of them, whom you can call to verify it. Sure enough, you hear from each reference that the oracle nailed it to the precise number. Now, you are ready to receive your prediction.

Suppose you find out that it is seven. "Only seven?" you respond. "That's great!" Chances are you would meet that person by tonight. You might find yourself shaking the hands of strangers on the street, saying odd things like, "Three … four …"

On the other hand, suppose the number is 77. "OK," you say, "77." This is more of a challenge, but with the confidence that it is really 77, you would set about working the maximizations we discussed previously. You would meet that person within the year, probably within a few months.

What if the number were 777? "That's a lot of people," you might say. "Is that certain?" If, in fact, you had complete conviction that the oracle knew what was going to happen, you would still probably set about finding that person. Daunting though that number might seem, if you were certain your search ultimately would be successful, and if you wanted the results strongly, wouldn't you do it?

Actually, *chances are the real number is somewhere between 7 and 777.* We do not in fact know the actual number, but we do know the pace of getting to that real number is in your hands.

This thought experiment occurred to me after an experience I had when

I was young and single. It happened after an apparently wasted night. Well, I did not intend it to be a wasted night, but that is how it began to look. During this period, I did anything I thought of doing to increase my exposure to others. Doing nothing was not an option, so I would just pick the most enjoyable or least unpleasant activity available. In this way, I was following the advice I gave others in counseling sessions. I had noticed that people similar to me, who normally avoided bars, might go to newly opened places. On this Saturday night, I showed up at the barroom of a new Mexican restaurant. Sure enough, the place was packed, and I was efficient. I took a good look at every young woman in the place and spoke with several. No one was for me. In fact, the setting was not for me, and I would not be returning. I went home.

None of this was surprising. Certainly, I had had similar nights before. My surprise came when I noticed how good I felt. As I removed my shoes, I began to wonder why I was in a good mood about the evening. After all, something ventured, nothing gained. Why, then, did I have a sense of accomplishment?

At that moment, I realized I was on track with my commitment. I intended to do anything that occurred to me, and to meet person after person until I succeeded. *I did not know how many places I had to go, but I had just crossed one more off my list.* I was one place closer, one evening closer, and several people closer! Of course I did not know the real number, but whatever it was, I was now closer to it. (See the sidebar on rejecting others.)

Almost as painful as being rejected — even more painful, at times — is the need to reject those who may have interest in you but are just not right for you. Some people even avoid dating because of a difficulty saying no. In fact, it is psychologically impossible to ruin someone else's life by not dating that person. If someone acts as if you are destroying him or her emotionally, all this means is that the other person is already laden with problems that have nothing to do with you — and you certainly made the right choice not pursing the relationship.

Having said that, as a kind person, you would prefer to be as face-saving as possible for others, so I suggest two possible steps. First, there is nothing wrong with beginning with a subtle hint, which usually takes the form of not pursuing or following through with interest. For many people, that is enough. There is a big difference between "I'm sorry, I can't make that" and "I can't make that time, but how about another?" Those of us who take such hints notice the difference and usually do not want or need more than that.

(If you are on the receiving side of such apparent hints and you particularly like the person, you still have an option. You can leave a message such as, "I'm getting the sense you don't want to follow up on this, so just leave me a message back if I'm getting the wrong impression.")

On the other side of it, what if the person doesn't leave such a message, but keeps persisting? The kindest letdown would be something like, "I don't see us dating each other, but it was nice to meet you, and I wish you all the best in your own search."

One supreme factor, because it strongly affects the pace of your search, is your capability of discerning whether to spend more time with any particular person. Indeed, the most typical barrier to meeting the right person is spending too much time with the wrong ones. A counselor I knew called this *serial monogamy.* People often pick their current dating partners through a single dimension of attraction. The major criterion is if they notice in-love sensations when they see or think about these new prospects. They give it a try, and see it through to the often bitter end. After the break-up and going through the aforementioned jaded state (which takes up more time), they set about finding another person who inspires some passion and any prospect of becoming Mr. or Ms. Right. The cycle continues accordingly. While a healthy spark of attraction is an important gauge for whether to get to know someone better, it is just one of the guidelines. As we are about to see, having a set of explicit evaluation strategies fills out the rest of the picture, so you can more quickly rule another person in or out.

CHAPTER 5

Checking the Ingredients:
Evaluation Strategies

Perhaps the best way to introduce the important topic of this chapter is through an intriguing personal example. Many years ago, I found myself in what can only be described as a truly perfect relationship. It was astonishingly good. As I stared into the eyes of my beloved, I knew I was finally home. She had every virtue I could want — she was highly intelligent, loving, wise, playful, and focused. Moreover, her focus was on me, and, incredibly, she felt the same about me as I did for her. Just looking at her made me the happiest I had ever been or could imagine being.

Then, something strange happened. I heard an annoying but familiar electronic sound. No mistaking it — it was my alarm clock going off. As it dragged me into awareness, I realized I was dreaming and was losing my lover. I watched her fade from view as I awoke. I had the distinct thought that I would rather stay dreaming indefinitely. It was no use. Once fully awake, I felt unusually depressed. Why, I wondered, had my subconscious mind so tormented me? Not only was I not in a relationship with this woman, but I did not even know her. It was not as if I could go up to her and say, "You know, I had this interesting dream, and we have to talk!"

I remained in my disconsolate state for about a half hour. Then, while shaving, I looked in the mirror and realized all my relationships had been kind of like that. In a way, I had dreamed them all up. Most of the time, I found someone appealing and tried to convince myself to feel the way I had in my dream, only to be slowly dragged into awareness as I faced the more nightmarish fact that the person I was dating was somehow not right for me. It took a lot more time than my dream and caused a lot more pain, to myself and to the other person.

Perhaps you have had relationships like this too. The good news is that we can highly increase your chances of not making this mistake repeatedly. In actuality, there is one case worse than making this mistake repeatedly, and that is making it *permanently*. This mistake, rightly termed *settling*, can even become a conscious intention. For instance, I have heard of women who say they dated "ice cream" and now they were looking to marry "spinach." *Most of the time, people will not get more than they are willing to settle for.* This occurs because, when they find it, they stop looking

Wishing away the nightmare of settling

further. Clearly, whether settling is time-wasting or life-wasting, it would be better to know what we are looking for. It is hard to hit a target you cannot see.

To address this we are going to violate the convention that views wish lists as unromantic. Certainly, being in love with someone ought to be one of the criteria in selecting a mate. Yet, if that were sufficient, you probably would not be reading this chapter. You would still be happy with the first person you fell in love with. The point of a wish list is to be reasonable but effective, so the next relationship you have is more likely to last.

Actually, I even recommend two different types wish lists. The first is idiosyncratic; it is just for you and assessed privately by you. The second is more generic; it consists of criteria that I recommend to everyone — and even can be shared with a prospective mate.

For the first, make a list of every single quality you could possibly enjoy about someone, including ones that you definitely do not need. Make that person ideal in every way. She or he can be friends with your favorite musician, or *be* your favorite musician! If you like to ski, this person can have a Swiss chalet. You might get a kick out of doing this part with a friend. If your friend is single, he or she will also probably be asking you for the rest of the methods below.

The private wish list

The next method is one of discernment. *What are the deal-breakers?* Signify with an asterisk those features on your long list that are absolute requirements for you. For example, most people would include integrity. This means that even if somebody has every single other quality on the list, even the Swiss chalet, you would pass if she or he showed signs of dishonesty.

As a general rule, fixer-uppers are fine for houses, because they let you change them to your specifications, but people do not reliably change for us. Putting it differently, the expression that "charity begins at home" does not advise us to engage in charity-dating. Further, if there is one state more frustrating than marrying your project, it's living as someone else's project.

This gives you a working list, but two refinements can help. The first is to go through your list asking the following question: Do I have each of the must-have qualities I am seeking?

You will probably have most of them, which will reassure you that it is a reasonable wish list. *This set of qualities is not too much to ask for, if you in fact embody them.* Indeed, if your own contributions to others are not sufficient evidence that you deserve to receive in like measure, what possible criteria could there ever be?

The listed characteristics that you do not possess still might be fair for you to seek, but it is good to consider each one. For example, an extrovert might look for an introvert, or vice versa. Opposite personality traits can complement each other. On the other hand, if you are asking for an athletic person but you have never exercised a day in your life, this could be more problematic. *Personality traits can be contrasting and attractive, but values need to be consistent.*

The second test of the list is historical. I can compare my list to actual people I have known, especially those I would have or should have avoided. *Would my list have filtered out mistakes I have made or have seen others make?* If I had used this list in the past, would it have saved me from wrong choices? If not, what else should be on the must-have list for it to accomplish that end?

The next question is how to work this list once you have it. Essentially, anyone you are seeing either possesses these must-have characteristics, or you don't have sufficient information yet. Anyone who lacks some characteristic you require is hopefully out of the picture.

Living with your list

Maintaining motivation for lucid evaluation can be challenging. Many of us like falling in love and resist being dissuaded by the facts. It can be fun to have love-smoke in our eyes. When based upon illusions about the other person, the beginning is usually appealing, but the endings burn. Our memories of such past painful break-ups can fuel our resolve.

Speaking of facts, an even bigger challenge is the likelihood that the other person, if into the relationship, will be *on good behavior.* Most people give a lot to a relationship during the beginning. They are feeling high on romance, and generosity comes naturally. Of course, if someone acts like a big taker right way, that is a simpler matter. Yet, how about an apparent giver? The genuine article would naturally be a feature of great value in a future mate. *One hint is whether they give to you on your terms or theirs.* Someone who works to understand specifically how to be good *to you* is more likely to be a bona fide giver than someone who acts sweet but mostly without much attention toward learning how best to do that.

Another clue to an authentic giver consists of noticing how a person responds to his or her world. If a person seems to have a "screw them before they can screw me" perspective, do not believe that you will long remain an exception to that. A giving person will usually show it in generous personal choices. On the other hand, beware if this personal generosity extends to the detriment of his or her own life. In other words, a person who sacrifices excessively for others, having almost no time left for himself, will eventually include you in that condition of almost no time. For some additional discernment tips, see the sidebar on *The Waitress Test.*

As the guidelines above imply, several characteristics should probably be on everyone's wish lists. You would likely want to pass on a relationship with someone devoid of:

❖ integrity

❖ consideration

❖ humor

❖ good sense

❖ self-control

The Waitress Test: During graduate school, a friend insisted that no one should get married to anyone without playing a game of Monopoly with them. She reasoned that it would tell you a lot about the other person's relationship with power and even how he or she would handle marital spats. My preference is for something I call the waitress test. You can determine a lot about someone's heart when you see him or her in a position of power, especially when displeased. For this reason, you might not be able to learn much in a fancy place, where you would likely see more good behavior. Instead, go to a family restaurant, where the servers and cooks might be either young and inexperienced or middle-aged and working three jobs. Notice how your new friend treats the wait staff when he or she is hungry and may be feeling ignored. If you witness sarcastic, demanding, or contemptuous responses, it might speed up your evaluation process.

While a list of characteristics, fine-tuned with the above strategies, can be instrumental to your search, there is another feature people wonder about often. It goes by the vague term *compatibility.* Again, anyone would hope for a compatible mate. Yet, how could you know? With my clients' help, I have developed the following *Compatibility-Plus Guidelines.*

These guidelines consist of overall compatibility, friendship, and a segment I call *paradoxes of relationship.* One of the most enjoyable parts of applying this second list is that it does not have to be a private endeavor. Actually, it is a delightful activity to share with the right person at the right time. Working through it together can both confirm your mutual compatibility and serve as a potent tool for setting the relationship in the right direction to thrive into the future.

A list for all of us

To begin, consider the elements of overall compatibility: *Common values, affinity during stress,* and *rapport in behavior patterns* all make a long-term relationship more viable.

While we have mentioned that contrasts in personality can round a couple out, incompatible values can be a pain that never goes away. Values usually will not, and need not, be identical. Yet, *it is best if one's top five were not more than two or three off from those in the other person.*

Values compatibility: matching priorities

If you look at a generic list of personal values, you will probably agree that each one is a worthy pursuit. However, you will not hold them all at the same level of importance. Psychologist Milton Rokeach (1989), a prominent researcher of values, showed that much of our behavior and beliefs could be predicted with a relatively short (18) list of what he called *terminal values.* We can benefit from his work.

While they are all desirable, you will notice that you prioritize the following goals in your own way:

- ❖ taking care of the members of your family

- ❖ the world at peace

- ❖ your own independent freedom of choice

- ❖ the feeling of happiness

- ❖ the achievement of self-esteem

- ❖ the attainment of wisdom

- ❖ the establishment of equality for all

- ❖ finding eternal salvation

❖ a prosperous life

❖ accomplishing a lasting legacy of contribution

❖ discovering close friendship

❖ protecting national security

❖ promoting inner harmony

❖ building a loving and intimate relationship

❖ contributing to aesthetic beauty in the world, whether natural or artistic

❖ earning high social esteem and respect from those you respect

❖ being surrounded by opportunities for leisurely pleasure

❖ having a vibrantly stimulating life

Suppose that you value world peace and equal human opportunity at about level nine in your list. This ranks above half of your other values, using Rokeach's list. Now, you meet someone for whom it is number two. He or she devotes most weekends to promoting these valuable goals. With such a disparity, you will not quite want to go on all these trips, though a few might work out for you. You can see why I am suggesting it would be better that the top five are not more than two or three off.

A related aspect of common values has to do with lifestyle. This is straightforward. *You have to both be able to live in the same place comfortably.* While

Values compatibility: matching lifestyles

lifestyle reflects values, they are not the same. It is possible to be compatible in values and, for that exact reason, incompatible in lifestyle. You might both highly value professional accomplishments, yet, if one of you is an oceanographer and the other a professional skier, it could be insurmountable. I once met someone who, like me, valued family highly, but she lived in California and I lived in Connecticut. The relationship clearly had to end shortly after it began.

Another aspect of compatible values is also straightforward, but often

Values compatibility: matching life timing

overlooked. The timing of both of your lives must work. One can carry this too far, of course. Sometimes people marry whoever they are dating when they feel ready to get married! Our evaluation strategies are aiming to correct for this, but if you are looking to marry and another person is looking to recuperate from a former marriage, it would probably bode trouble both ways. The worst case of bad timing is when you are both married, of course, but that is a subject for a future chapter (15).

No conversation about values is foolproof. Still, talking together about your values compatibility can be a helpful step, as can the next aspect of compatibility, which I call the *three stress conditions.*

Everyone has heard about couples who get along wonderfully, only to run aground a few months after marriage. A typical reason is that they do not know

Compatibility in three levels of stress

how to work together in the lows and highs of life stress. Their experience with each other so far has been in the moderate middle. Most couples enjoy each other during the moderate stress of dating. If you define stress as the level of demand on people relative to their belief in their own abilities, moderate stress is the happiest place to be. It is the Goldilocks level of stress, neither too low nor too high. The situation matters to them, but they are up to the challenge. Another name for moderate stress is *motivation. Accordingly, most couples get along well in enjoyably moderate stress.* If they did not enjoy that, they would hopefully stop going out.

Sooner or later, each of you will see the other stressed out. We'll discuss conflict resolution in Chapter 27; however, *if you just cannot stand how the other person acts during high stress, be prepared to see a lot of that if you spend the rest of your lives together.*

Sometimes you meet a person who is a work-in-progress, and behavior in high stress may change if the person works on it effectively. But, keep in mind that you cannot be his or her sole motivation to change, because that is much too ephemeral. Don't talk someone into changing, just notice if he or she is working on it. If you meet someone who is already growing, whether in therapy or in a 12-step group, it can make sense to stick around for a while and see how things turn out.

In contrast, if someone often overreacts (anger) or under-reacts (withdrawal) in stress, do not argue with him or her about it. This observation on your part is much too important to fight about. *Arguments create the illusion of progress, because you think you are supplying motivation for change.* Instead, mention any concern that is important to you, then watch whether the other person is changing, and in which direction.

Similarly, in low stress, sometimes couples are like a battery that drains without recharging. We will learn some effective ways to jump-start that recharge, but it is better if more than one partner is supplying the energy. I have known some people who were the only party doing so, and it got lonely. Therefore, a discussion of the three stress conditions can supply a good direction for a budding relationship.

A final element of compatibility is finding a good fit between each of your typical behavior patterns. Let us explore what that means.

Every couple has two relationships: One consists of who they both are in the present and the other is what happens when their childhoods collide. Fortunately, we have an entire chapter, the 17th, devoted to handling that, but handle it you must.

Compatibility in behavior patterns

A good relationship is a peer relationship. This may seem too obvious to mention, but that is because you are reading it post the 20th century. Marriages were institutionalized to be parent-child for most of our history, and sometimes couples will still not notice that one of them is mostly in charge and the other is mostly childish. In other cases, couples will think they have a peer relationship because each has different areas of dominance, yet they share few periods during which both partners simultaneously feel and act like grown-ups.

Having said that, there is an important exception. It is actually possible for couples to be too peer! I call this requirement *pattern flexibility. Vulnerability is a crucial aspect of emotional intimacy.* It works best if we can lean on each other sometimes. If both parties are too grown-up too much of the time, it usually means they are not showing their deeper feelings. After all, life is not always easy, and all of us are shaken up by it at times. So, a close relationship usually has pattern flexibility — sometimes I comfort you and sometimes you comfort me.

The Finger Thing: A therapist I met described this pattern flexibility as the finger thing. Holding up her index fingers, she leaned one on the other, saying, "Sometimes one person leans on the other." Reversing the fingers, she added, "And sometimes the other one leans." Then, she touched the fingertips together, smiling and saying, "Sometimes they lean on each other, but it's not like this." At this point, she raised one finger higher than the other one.

As you explore these compatibility factors together, you can advance your evaluation and set the right tone for growing together as a couple. Another way to do that is to check out the following *friendship elements*. I identified these elements when speaking to a couple and hearing that the wife loved her husband, but did not think of him as her friend. We next explored how she would know if he were her friend. Once we noted these components of friendship, it allowed us to chart what happily became their rapid progress.

One friendship element is essential reliability. A friend does not want to make a friend worry, feel disappointed, or have their time wasted. Everyone

Best friends first and foremost

flakes out occasionally, but a true friend is quite concerned about not letting you down and takes steps, without prompting, to make it not happen again. Another friendship element is a factor we will return to a lot. A friend enjoys making you happy and looks for opportunities to be good to you. This sounds so simple, but we will see that it is the basis for so much. Related to this is enjoying making you laugh.

The final elements will become main subjects in later chapters, but are important to include here. *A close friend is both vulnerable in self-disclosure and encouraging of self-disclosure in you.* I often think of the flow of emotions as a single conduit — you cannot selectively block the feelings that flow through, at least not for long. Loving someone deeply means taking on more feelings of all sorts, not just pleasant ones. What affects your close friend now affects you. You learn about each other's victories and defeats, the agonies and the ecstasies. In this way, these features of showing vulnerability and encouraging vulnerability in you complete the friendship dimensions of a relationship, whether an old one, a new one, or the love of a lifetime. This brings us to the last part of the evaluation process that you can share with someone else, which is really a set of beliefs. I call these the *three paradoxes of relationships*.

Paradoxes are statements that seem contradictory but are nonetheless true. The attitudes most conducive to a thriving relationship include three of

Love thrives on three paradoxes

them. Throughout most of my life, I would have failed all three. I customarily told people, as my own training had prepared me to do, that you do not need anyone, that making someone else happy is impossible, and that promising forever is a lie.

Like most of us, I could have proven each of them. After all, you do not need any person. If you need something and you do not have it, then you are unable to survive. Healthy people can and do survive the loss of anyone, no matter how devastating. Regarding making other people happy, that is their own job, and if they are neglecting this job, no one can compensate for it. As for promising forever, with half the marriages ending in divorce, such a promise seems empty indeed.

Yet, my training was off base about these attitudes toward relationships, as my clients gradually taught me. In fact: Most parents can tell you it is possible to love someone so much that, for all intents and purposes, you feel as if you absolutely need that person. Spouses also can, and need to, allow this level of vulnerability to each other.

And while it is actually impossible to make someone else happy, when two people endeavor at the same time to do exactly that, it becomes the formula for a terrific relationship.

Finally, while promising forever is literally impossible, those who earnestly mean it are much more likely to achieve it.

As a result, a relationship kicks off from a much better footing with two partners who allow themselves to be vulnerable to needing each other, aim to make each other happy, and promise to stay together no matter what. Because it is culturally common for people nowadays not to understand these paradoxes, questioning these attitudes are not deal-breaking, relationship-killing tests. On the contrary, they are points of departure to explore together. Looking at these paradoxical truths together can help the relationship grow with vigor.

As we finish our shopping trip together, there are several final points to keep in mind. All of these are pitfalls that frequently trip people up during their searches. Sorting through them can save you a lot of time. We have already included some tips in sidebars above, and we will conclude with a few more.

Hint number one: Do not feel guilty about requiring sexual attraction as a necessary criterion in your search. People vary widely in terms of what appeals to them. The physical part of a relationship

Attraction matters

is as important as the other dimensions, and it has to work for you on that level too. Biology determines many of the elements of sexual attraction, and it will not be ignored. It informs the element of the romantic feelings that we call *chemistry*.

Biologically (and reductionistically), women are baby-makers and men are baby-raising resources. As a result, no matter how egalitarian our politics and no matter how disinterested we may be in making a baby at a particular time, heterosexual attraction will be infused through that filter. Every feature that is usually considered attractive in women unconsciously signals maternal fertility to men, and every attractive male feature somehow signals useful power to women.

The good news is that no one need be ruled by the arbitrary whims of the physical dimension alone. We are more than complex enough that our other dimensions — for example, the intellectual, emotional, and spiritual dimensions — interact heavily with the physical. So, if there is at least a healthy spark of attraction, the totality of the right relationship will fan it into a warming furnace. Conversely, without the other dimensions working, even the strongest sexual connection will tire and fade. The topic of sexual connections brings us to the next hint.

Hint number two: If your goal is to *find* a mate rather than just to mate, then delaying early sexual involvement is often a good idea. Keep in mind that I am speaking as a psychologist, and this has nothing to do with prescribing cultural or religious mores. The issue is that men will often advance the physical relationship without awareness of the effects it has. Those effects frequently include deepening the feelings for the woman and freezing them in place for the man. This can happen even when the man is not consciously predatory at all in terms of his intentions. Often he sincerely feels extremes of ardor, only to dash her hopes after sharing a bed together. He may not know that he is fooling her, because he may be fooling himself. The only way to find out is to wait.

When and why to wait

The central point is that a woman will never lose a man over delaying sex, especially if she shows interest in him. If he leaves because she delays, he was going to leave anyway, just afterward. If his interest is reliable, waiting will only deepen it. This has to do with the psychology of wanting to be *exceptionally important* to the other person, a phenomenon we will explore in depth in the 16th chapter (about men and women). As you will see, this is not game playing, it actually helps the man feel the way he wants to, but he will probably have to rely on her leadership. (Of course, some men have figured this out and will participate fully in setting a gradual pace. This tip is for the more common circumstance where the fellow is in a hurry.) Another psychological advantage is that people have to talk a lot more to each other if they delay sexual involvement. How long should she wait? If she were not looking for a permanent relationship, it could be until she would still be glad if this were the last night they were together. But if she is aiming for something more substantial, I would recommend deciding in advance (not in a moment of passion!) on a level of commitment to which she would not mind the relationship adhering. In other words, because sex tends to fix a relationship at a certain place for a man, is she happy fixing it there for a while?

> While on the subject of providing tips for women in dating men, we must include an important and related guideline, having to do with believing what men may say during early dating. Putting it bluntly and in a manner that may seem harsh: If you like what he says, go by what he actually does; if you don't like what he says, believe him. The first part is true because most men are affected by mood in ways they often do not recognize. The second part is equally important, because men often rely upon the parameters of their previous statements. In other words, if a man says he is not looking for a commitment and he acts loving and affectionate, this does not mean he changed his mind. Like the boundaries of a football field, he believes he has set up the field and the ground rules, and now he can do whatever he wants within those parameters. Believe him unless he starts to speak differently — then go by what he actually does!

Another way to delay early sexual involvement has to do with sharing war stories. For women, conversation is a primary way to get closer to someone, including a new man in her life. It is natural to want to connect by talking about past hurts. It may seem to her to be complimentary to him, because she is comparing him favorably to her past lovers, after all!

In fact, representing oneself as having been hurt by many past men and eager to be saved by this one will almost always create a barrier, not a bridge. This is not the kind of exception that a man usually wants to be, as we will see in Chapter 16 on gender dynamics.

Hint number three: Avoid incremental improvements! This pitfall is one of the most common reasons people resist really applying the evaluation strategies. People have a natural and understandable sense of accomplishment and satisfaction whenever their lives move ahead.

New and improved

As an example, imagine you really like cars,

specifically sporty models, but you do not own one. One day you learn that a distant relative has died and named you in her will, and you are receiving one of your favorite sports cars, but with one detail: The car has been in a small parking lot mishap. The owner of the other car has taken full responsibility, and all you have to do is schedule the minor repair. The shop work is paid for, and the car will then be yours. In such a case, this is a good day.

On the other hand, suppose you already own the vehicle. You return to a parking lot to find a note from the driver who bumped your car with the same offer to pay for the repair. This is not such a good day. This is human nature. Pleasure and pain have a lot to do with the direction of changing events, whether they add to or subtract from what we already have. In relationships, it is the same. Many of us settle for relationships that are at least better than the last one, but will not work either. I recommend that you employ the evaluation strategies instead.

Hint number four: What can you do about feelings? This question comes up a lot in counseling sessions. All these plans and techniques make a lot of

Be still
my heart

sense logically, but evaluation strategies do not automatically govern your emotions. You can tell your feet where to go, but you cannot tell your heart what to feel. The good news is that you do not have to numb yourself to romantic feelings in order to keep your head. Surprisingly, they can go hand in hand. *You can have whatever feelings you want, as long as they are really about the person in front of you.* One might call this a *head in the clouds and feet on the ground* approach. In this way, you allow yourself to enjoy the other person fully, while keeping in mind how she or he fits your list — both what you know and what you do not yet know. The sobriety of keeping this in mind will temper the feelings appropriately. Usually, people get most hurt when they dream up the person rather than enjoying themselves with open eyes.

Hint number five: Anticipate childrearing. If the relationship might produce children, or if you will be blending existing families, you may not see

The triangle
corral

clashes in parenting styles until later. This is a classic cause for faltering relationships. Psychotherapists even have a name for the form it usually takes. It is called *triangulation*, because the child is one apex and the parents become the other two, with one playing the authoritarian role and the other playing the role of permissive rescuer. Instead of working together, the parents push each other to further extremes, and the child cannot resist the power. Divorced parents are often tempted to be permissive because of their guilt over what the children have been through. Instead, talk about this pitfall in advance, including real or imagined scenarios and how you could handle them together as parenting partners to avoid being stretched across such a painful triangle. For a good resource on a middle road that works well for both parents, check out loveandlogic.com or access the books and recordings of Jim Fay.

Final tip: Avoid project relationships! This is such an important point that we will discuss it at length when we look at the question of whether to stay in a troubled relationship (in Part III). Naturally, the best choice is to avoid getting into a troublesome relationship in the first place. As I mentioned above, *charity begins at home, but that doesn't mean to marry a fixer-upper.* Do not think that you can make someone improve to fit your wish lists. If they are already improving, it is OK to watch for a while, but it has to be based upon his or her own will to change, not your wishful thinking. As a result, please avoid charity dating, let alone charity marriages. The better path is to seek WYSIWYG relationships — What You See Is What You Get.

No charity dating!

We will finish this chapter where we began Part I, with encouragement for a motivated search. Like many objectives worth winning, this one seldom succeeds without wanting to quit along the way. Most important missions include some painful costs that stretch one's perseverance to the breaking point.

Ending at the beginning point

Searching for the right person involves embarking on an ocean of hope, with deep waves thrusting up to impossible and soaring flights and intermittently tumbling down to painful and dizzying crashes before once again ascending. *It is an easy matter to become discouraged, before you eventually learn to surf.*

Most of the people you meet will have weathered failed relationships that left them single, some by surprising circumstances, some by mistakes since corrected, and some for a very good reason. The last group can daunt your spirits, especially because they will not announce themselves as such. A friend joked that, during many years of finding himself single, he met hundreds of other single people, all of whom had break-up stories. During this time, he underwent a personal miracle. Somehow, he never met the mean or crazy member of the break-up, but only the good and stable party. Funny as this story is, it is also accurate in terms of what to expect to hear.

Dating is like any of the other numbers games of life, such as looking for the right job. It is like looking for the pearl in an oyster. I once heard an

Diving for the right pearl

instructive story having to do with two pearl divers, one quite successful and the other equally impoverished. They were friends, and the successful one offered to go out diving together. Perhaps he could be helpful. They dove together, each with their buckets. The first one loaded up his bucket with every oyster he found and headed up, while the second looked and looked, and finally selected an oyster that struck him as having potential. By the time he reached the boat, his friend was shucking oyster after oyster, found a medium-sized pearl, and readied himself to dive again. The poor fisherman slowly and hopefully opened the shell of his oyster and, seeing no pearl, closed it back up. As the successful diver bent to dive, he looked at his friend. "Are you coming down?" he asked. "No, I have a really good feeling about this one," his friend responded. "I'm going to hold it and wait."

The successful diver knew that if you keep light and keep moving, every dive can be successful. In our case, *every contact and every date can be a win-win*. Success means finding out whether both people want to know more about each other. One possible win is that this person may be appropriate for your future; the alternative win is that you become more ready than before, by applying what you learn and practice, to meet and be with the right person once you find each other.

In this way, it is a very good idea to get your hopes up. Your wisest inner self will know whether you are giving yourself a chance. Surprisingly, people tend not to get depressed over that which is truly out of their hands. Yet, when change is possible but we do not seek it, even when we do not acknowledge this consciously, it saddens our spirits.

With the evaluation strategies stashed in tow, you can now have confidence in your ability to assess people more quickly, which will allow you to explore your options freely. Meanwhile, your next step is the same, whether you are looking for someone special, deciding whether to engage in that journey, or wanting to improve the relationship you are already in: learning how to be happy when the only company you have is yourself.

PART II

Preparation

CHAPTER 6

Why Are We Starting with You?

If you want to find yourself as part of a terrific and enduring couple, Part II will show you steps to discovering the first member of that couple: *you*. (If you are satisfied with your self-esteem and not particularly lonely, this part is optional, though you still will benefit from

The first step in finding whom you want

it.) The goal is to fill your heart with gratitude for the gift of your life and to experience a sense of being a complete person with or without a romantic partner. Feeling fulfilled inside, you will have more of you to give to others. As you may recall from our exploration of evaluation strategies, the person you want to find already has a good life that he or she will want to share with you. *That person is looking for the same thing in you.*

Because the central focus of this book is relationships rather than self-esteem, we will sketch the strategies in this section briefly. They are the most useful ones I have yet encountered. If you are working on similar goals with a therapist, these strategies also could become jumping off points for your direction and expectations.

So, how are you? Typically, this question is automatically asked and automatically answered, which seems fine because we assume no one is listening

How are you today?

to the answer anyway. But, really — how are you right now? Surprisingly, it is possible to always and accurately answer that question, "I'm good." It all depends on what you are assessing.

The goodness of your life can reflect not the varying hues of enjoyment versus struggle, but rather a clear light seen through the lens of your purpose and your mission.

The latter is a much more reliable standard and an endlessly renewable source of a rich life. *If I am good* today, it does not have to mean I am in a state of pleasure, but can mean *I am on track with my most important purposes.* In other words, I am living *on purpose.*

The good news is that this source is entirely in our hands and decided anew each day. The challenge is that any purpose worth having is not one easily achieved. Just the task of determining our next missions in life can itself be daunting. Conversely — and fortunately! — even searching for a life mission is a type of purpose in itself. Three sets of clues help us find our mission.

One source of clues comes from noticing what matters to us. People have a sense of meaning and a feeling of happiness when they are pursuing ends that make a difference to them. These objectives do not have to be important to the rest of the world. To pick what probably seems like a trivial endeavor, imagine that someone collects beer cans from around the world. If you have any doubt whether anyone actually does so, search the Web for the Brewery Collectibles Club of America (at least as of this writing). To such a collector, the day he locates a can of Bintang, a beer from Indonesia, is a happy day. It does not have to matter to you, but it matters to him.

What's the matter?

Similarly, if you walk into a fitness club and see someone just finishing a set of exercises at a higher weight than she ever before achieved, she may look agonized. Yet, if you ask her how she is, she may sincerely tell you she is thrilled. *Our activities prove they matter to us by captivating us.* (We will differentiate this kind of captivation from addiction in Chapter 11.)

A second source of hints to life-purpose consists of one's talents. *Our abilities are usefully burdensome in that it would bother us not to use them.* Most of us will never lose a night's sleep because of not developing ourselves as artists, but some of us will do exactly that. Others will feel pulled toward music, or writing, or website creation, or politics, or charitable endeavors. If it bugs you not to do it, that is a good clue. (We will soon focus more extensively on finding such personal gifts.)

Gifts and burdens

The most surprising source of clues into our life's purpose stems directly from our problems. Suffering and pain, never welcome guests at the feast of life, nevertheless find their way onto the menu. They often demand the best of us in order to resolve them. Many people have had their lives turned upside down, finding themselves tossed unexpectedly by misfortune, only to right themselves upon a new path not before considered. (See Csikszentmihalyi's book *Flow* in the reference section for more on this.) In fact, we seem to have an innate need to find some such resolution to the difficult barriers of life. This is sometimes described as turning a *breakdown* into a *breakthrough*.

One of life's most amazing surprises is how *events that we stumble into with eyes closed, only to wince in pain as they overtake us, can then startle our eyes open into transformational directions.*

Before going any further with the subject of self-fulfillment, we must speak about the challenge of balancing personal development with the importance of caring about others. All this focus

Is it all about me?

upon ourselves in the cause of assessing our inner wholeness, typically called *self-esteem*, can seem like (and in fact lead to) narcissistic self-absorption. For this reason, personal growth fads tend to fade away. People who aim to improve their self-esteem often end up either self-conscious or self-absorbed. Similarly, people who seek to fulfill themselves spiritually often struggle with the egotistical pride of becoming more spiritual than others. You can see why balance in the area of self-development can be a challenge.

Part of the AA wisdom heard in 12-step meetings includes a useful question: Are you living inside out or outside in? That is, where is the focus of your attention — on your own program of development, or on the reactions of others to you?

When I first heard this question, it hit me that there is *a certain sense in which it is better to live inside out and another sense in which it is better to live outside in.* The difference relates to *locus of evaluation versus focus of attention.*

When it comes to locus of evaluation — who decides what you think — it would be best for that to be you. While open-minded, you must ultimately trust your own conclusions. In this sense, you would be looking at the world from the inside out, trusting your own judgment. Having such an internal locus is sometimes called *being centered.*

Yet, there is a big difference between being centered and being *self-centered.* When it comes to the focus of your attention — what's mostly on

When outside in is actually better

your mind — it is better to live outside in. People are happiest when their gaze is focused in front of them, when they have the free and available attention to take in the world with crystalline vision, unclouded by the *narcissistic mirrored box.*

To understand this analogy, think about an office that has one-way glass to see out on the floor of the business. These are actually thinly silvered mirrors. Made with a thin reflective coating, they allow half of the light to pass through. As a result, if one of the rooms is dark and the other lit, it becomes a window for those on the dark side and a mirror for those on the brightly lit side. What happens when there is full lighting in both the office and the business floor? Everyone sees a double image. You see yourself as strongly as you see through to the other side. This results in a double-exposure experience, both distracting and annoying if it lasts too long. *Narcissistic self-absorption is like living imprisoned in a one-way mirrored box, lit both inside and out.* Wherever you look, you can only see through the distracting filter of your self-image.

This brings us back to the need to balance the inside locus with the outside focus. If out of balance, self-image becomes fragile, and most social interactions become trials. For example, a person with a *superiority complex* (read: narcissism) will think excessively of himself or herself most of the time. However, a person with an *inferiority complex* (read: reverse narcissism) will be just as self-absorbed. (We will return to narcissistic patterns in Chapter 8, when we look at ways to grow self-esteem.) The rest of Part II is devoted to making you able to live inside out enough and outside in enough to find love in your life. *It will ready you for a great relationship, but also leave you happy with yourself, with or without a romantic relationship.*

CHAPTER 7

The Anti-Lonely List:
Finding a Full Life While Single

As we have seen, if you care about the cooking, you have to take care of the cook. One way to do that is to learn the difference between *aloneness* and *loneliness*. Single people have use for some degree of loneliness, as we saw in Chapter 3, in order to motivate change, but in the right measure. The *anti-lonely list is a method to dial loneliness to the right level,* so it is possible to live a full life today while still experiencing enough emotional impetus to grow the future.

The anti-lonely list is both an exercise in expressing such a balance and a strategy to achieve it. In fact, its essential structure augments self-appreciation while helping a person discern how and when to reach out to others. The basic premise of the anti-lonely list consists of a theory of loneliness: *Loneliness is a state in which a person has cherished qualities or important personal characteristics that are not sufficiently shared with others.* What does *sufficient* mean here? It is subjective: It means sharing important parts of oneself enough to bring emotional self-satisfaction. In this way, the needs of an extrovert will be higher, but even an introvert will have a minimal threshold to avoid loneliness.

If this understanding of loneliness is accurate, it means it is not necessary to share all of you with others, only the parts you value most. It also means you ought to be able to diagnose the specific cause of your loneliness at any particular time and, more important, to know how to address it.

Here's how it works: Make a list of every positive quality that comes to mind when you think about yourself. (For some, this can be an ordeal in itself. If so, you may decide to make or revise your list after reading the next chapter on enhanced self-esteem.)

The steps to making an anti-lonely list

Your list of virtues aims to include any useful characteristic you have ever displayed. To illustrate this search for positive qualities, imagine hiking up a mountain and discovering the ore of some valuable mineral, such as gold. Sometime later, the exact location of that gold may have been forgotten, but if it had been found once, then it must be there. *Similarly, one cannot exhibit a quality that one does not possess.* If you have previously found the precious resource of any talent or virtue, it must still exist within. At the same time, not every gift we have, even those well appreciated by others, necessarily matters to us. This leads us to the next step.

Take a look at your list and put an asterisk next to the attributes that matter to you. One way of identifying them is to ask yourself: Which qualities are you most grateful for? Which qualities do you cherish? Which qualities would you most miss if you imagine not having them? *These are the qualities that, if not shared, make you most miss the company of others* with whom to share them. Again, this is our working definition of loneliness.

Equipped with this list of asterisked qualities, you are ready to start diagnosing the feeling of loneliness. Begin with a sheet of paper with four columns. The first column lists the *qualities* we just identified, and the second column asks *with whom you share* each of these. In other words, who do you imagine is with you when you want to express that aspect of yourself? The third column asks the inevitable question of whether you think you have *enough people* available to you relative to your need to express that particular quality. Finally, the fourth column is the most important in a practical sense because it asks *where else you might find* people with whom to share each of the cherished qualities. Over time, you may want to revise your list as the answers change, such as when your self-esteem grows, or your network of friends grows, or you discover other venues in which to express important qualities.

The final step is to start to apply it. When you feel lonely, you can scan your list and notice which qualities thrust themselves out to you as most in need of sharing at that moment. This experiential selection is like picking out a particular song to listen to because *you feel drawn to it at that time.* Similarly, you may feel drawn toward expressing specific facets of your personality with other people at different times.

Working with your list

Next, let's consider a few situations. Imagine, and perhaps it is not difficult to do so, a period during which there is no sexual activity. Suppose further that this person does not want to seek sex just for the sake of sex, and is therefore likely to remain celibate for a while. In such a case, it would be advantageous to be able to be celibate without being lonely.

Applying our handy list, a behavior as complex as sexual sharing can be broken down into anti-lonely-list traits. Perhaps a person appreciates being tender, or likes being affectionate, or sensual, or even vulnerable. As you can see, each of these personal qualities can have a prominent place on an anti-lonely list. Most important, these particular forms of loneliness can be addressed without having a sexual partner available. *The specificity of the list allows for remarkable precision.* For instance, missing one's own sensuality may suggest getting a massage. Further, if one is not at the moment missing the quality of being affectionate, the massage may completely fulfill the requirements of self-expression at that time.

During my single years, I found the anti-lonely list very useful. On one particular evening during those years, feeling a surge of loneliness, I scanned my list. The quality that popped out surprised me. It was about being musically inclined. It had been a long time since I had shared music with a friend, let alone danced with anyone. On this particular evening I was not in need of affection, or intellectual stimulation, or even the prospect of romance. I simply wanted to dance.

In my case ...

Realizing this, I researched where I could find people listening to the kind of band I would also enjoy. That was simple. I like blues. So, I picked a club to go to, not based upon whom I might meet there, or even if I would particularly fit in there, but where I would find the music I wanted. The place I went to, in fact, was a bit too young for me, but the music was fine. Having diagnosed my loneliness accurately, I did not look around for anyone to date. Instead, I looked for women who seemed to be dancing in their chairs to the music. This was my only criterion. At one point, I noticed two quite young ladies who looked like they wanted a dance. I walked up to them and said, "You know, the rules are that I have to ask one of you to dance and then the other person has to keep sitting here. But, it seems to me that the three of us really want to dance. So let's dance." They laughed and joined me, and the three of us danced throughout the set. Afterward, I thanked them genuinely, and we went our separate ways. Decades later, I recall how astounded I felt about the reliable effectiveness of this little list for me. I hope it is the same for you.

The intended outcome of all this is that you enjoy the company even when you are completely alone. At first, it may seem paradoxical to realize that quality time alone is the foundation for readiness to find a high-quality relationship. Nevertheless, it is essential. This is why it is important to take this seeming detour from the subject of relationships to provide guidelines for a sufficiently strong relationship with oneself. Otherwise, people may find it hard to stay single long enough to really select the person who is right for them, rather than just settling.

The paradox of unlonely

It can be useful to ask yourself the following question: If I believe that I am looking for a relationship, am I really living like that, or am just trying to avoid loneliness? If it is the latter, then I have to be willing to be lonelier at first in order to achieve my real goal. I must be able to be alone without feeling overcome by loneliness.

As we have just seen, the process of managing loneliness and converting it into a healthy, if hungry, aloneness requires workable self-esteem. Turning in the next chapter to the process of discovering how to like oneself, we will see that self-esteem is largely a process of getting past domination by very old and outdated messages, usually forgotten but persuasive nonetheless.

CHAPTER 8

What Gets in the Way
of a Full Single Life —
Turning Off the Old Recordings
and Building New Ones

Most babies are born with good self-esteem, wouldn't you agree? On one hand, according to psychologists, babies do not have much of a sense of self, as distinct from their world. Yet, they have much to teach us about being fully oneself. When they get hurt, they cry out for help. When the pain is over, they let go of the suffering. They reach out with enthusiasm for whatever life has to offer. Infants are not born feeling unworthy of whatever joys are available to them. People become that way because they learn from others that they are undeserving.

What did you learn? It is fairly easy to know the sum total of the self-esteem messages you received growing up. You memorized them. They result in a sound recording of sorts, which psychologists call *self-talk*. Consequently, some people have what you could term an *inner cheerleader*. This self-referential voice encourages you along, very much as a supportive parent would. When you hit snags in life, it reminds you of those virtues that could avail you, and when clouds darken, it urges hopefulness. It is a very useful personal asset to have such an automatically reinforcing source of confidence.

Identifying the recording

On the other hand, many of us have a much different inner voice. *We could call this an inner jeer-leader!* It is the opposite of the cheerleading voice in every way. It discourages us along our way, very much as a harsh parent (or older sibling) would. During the snags of life, it reminds us of all the deficiencies that hinder us, and when we suffer, it urges despair.

Another term for the snags of life is *high stress*. For good biological reasons (Blum, 2011), people regress to old, familiar responses during stressful times. It provides an instant reaction, whether the stress consists of physical danger or interpersonal relations. These emergency responses are rapid and automatic, which also makes them rigid and unaware. *Stress-regress* is a central challenge to having a full and satisfying life. For this reason, we mentioned high stress during our evaluation strategies (Chapter 5), and we will revisit it in several chapters to come. Regarding the current subject of self-talk, the stress-regress guarantees that the negative messages from our childhoods will become even more inflexible and unyielding when circumstances demand the most of us.

Incidentally, this is not about blaming your parents, or even nasty siblings. After all, parents and other caregivers also had parents or caregivers, who in turn had parents or caregivers, and so on. In other words, excepting situations in which our family members actually did monstrous things to us, we can blame either Adam and Eve, or nobody! Finally, having an inner jeer-leader does not always mean your family members berated you excessively; it can mean you berated yourself as a means to gain their reassurance or otherwise fit your role in the family. *Our point is not how to find blaming opportunities, but how to make change happen.*

Message on a T-shirt: "It's never too late to have a happy childhood!" Is that true? If the major effect of our childhoods — which affect us every day — can be differentiated by self-talk that either cheers or jeers, the big question is whether that inner voice is malleable. The bad news, of course, is that we have no delete button. We cannot simply erase unwanted learning. In fact, some psychologists suggest that people do not forget much of anything, and the false impression of forgetting only occurs because of what might be called *crossed wires*. Especially with disuse, old neural pathways get a bit tangled, so you might look at Mike and keep thinking *Mark*, knowing that is not his name. It is a little like a corrupted software file.

"It's never too late to have a happy childhood!"

The good news, extending the computer analogy, is that we can create go-to functions, as in *when you get here, go to there*. Putting it differently, *you cannot subtract*, as in removing the old, *but you can add*, as in chaining new learning onto the old. How does this work in practice? Whether intentionally or fortuitously, positive change occurs through three steps: awareness, pattern-interruption, and alternatives.

Awareness means a matter-of-fact recognition of where I came from and what I learned there. It is a variety of what some therapists call *mindfulness* (which is a translation of the Buddhist term *vipassana*). In this case, we are becoming mindful of the similarity of present patterns of thinking to past patterns of thinking. Few people spend much time aware in this sense. More often than not, the opportunity for awareness is lost while our attention swings between guilt and blame. When we are blaming ourselves or others, it is all we get to do.

The first step: awareness

Consciousness is like a magical gem that shines a light. That light can be diffuse or focused, but it is a very limited, single beam. It seems big to us, because it is all we know. Whatever is out of the focus of our attention is nonexistent to our consciousness. If you want to see how limited your attention is, just experiment with it: Maintain consciousness of one part of you, perhaps your left hand. Now add your right knee. Next, include your right elbow. So far so good — your left hand, right knee, and right elbow. Now add your left foot. What just happened? You probably started to shift your attention among parts of your body, rather than be able to keep all in consciousness. If somehow you did not start to scan from location to location, try adding another part of you to this awareness task. You can see how limited a resource attention really is.

Experimenting with the limitations of attention answers two important questions: why we do not have the luxury of spending much attention on guilt and blame if we want to develop awareness; and why we have so many automatic patterns of behavior. We rely on automatic patterns to literally move us through life. If you were to stand up right now, which muscle would you move first? You do not know, and you probably do not care to know. It works fine automatically.

Despite the fact that they can later become outdated, the interpersonal patterns picked up in childhood were usually the best application of our in-

Instant analysis

dividual resources to whatever was going on around us at the time. All of this leads to something I call *instant analysis*, which proceeds like this: Why do I continue to act the way I don't want to act now? I do it now because I did it before, a long time ago, and many times. Why did I do it? I did it because I learned it. Why did I learn it? *I learned it because it worked, either for me or for someone else who I often watched.*

As a result of such instant analysis, it occurs to people that *if some of their old skills have become outdated, this fact is actually to their credit.* In other words, for those old, outdated patterns not to have become anachronistic, it would mean they had not succeeded in changing the circumstances of their childhoods. The old patterns would still fit perfectly, because they had gotten themselves into the same conditions. "Congratulations," I often say. "You have improved your situation, and your old coping mechanisms have become outdated. That's the worst thing you can accurately say about yourself, and it's not bad at all!"

Such awareness is a great gift to the quality of life. People often want to skip this step along the way to changing their lives, because accessing such awareness necessitates revisiting painful times in their lives. Nonetheless, *awareness comprises about 90 percent of the process of change.* Without awareness, we are stuck inside the old recordings without knowing about it.

A metaphor for this: Imagine someone is locked in a prison cell, imprisoned by a warden who broadcasts abusive messages through a loudspeaker frequently and loudly. The messages are painful, so one tries not to listen. Yet, if a person pays close attention to the voice, it becomes clear that the message is very repetitive. In fact, it is just a recording, and there is no actual warden! So the person tries the prison door and discovers with amazement that it is unlocked, perhaps for years. The messages were just recordings, and they had no power in the present to confine anyone.

Putting it differently, think of a time you were engrossed in a book. Perhaps the characters in the plot are in a boat during a storm, plentiful water above them, under them, surrounding them. Just then, the phone rings, and you look up from the book. In fact, it is a sunny and warm day, and you feel surprised as you are jolted out of the plot. In this situation you know that you are actually reading. How much more so can we be fooled when the recorded words are already in our heads and play automatically!

Now that we have had a taste of how awareness feels, as distinct from either guilt or blame, we can look at strategies to interrupt these old patterns and shut off the old jeer-leader tape. This sounds like a formidable task. How does one interrupt the playback of an indelible recording? My original mentor in counseling, Tom Sargent (see sidebar), explained this with the analogy of an old LP music recording. I especially enjoy this example because the technology itself is considered outdated. Before MP4s, before CDs, before tapes, there were mostly vinyl records. They were played by a turntable and read by a diamond needle. Not surprisingly, a track could easily develop what was called a *skip*, causing the record to play the same phrase repeatedly. Imagine if the phrase was, "You're really a jerk, and no one will like you." Even worse, what if the electrical cord attaches to your own emotions, so the more upsetting the message, the more loudly it plays. "YOU'RE REALLY A JERK, AND NO ONE WILL LIKE YOU!" The recording is rigid, indelible, and unchangeable. As Sargent explained, however, the solution is contained in the rigidity itself. Even a little clump of dust on that track of the record will interrupt the playback.

Pattern interruption

Some acknowledgments are too extensive for an "Acknowledgments" section. Much of the material in this chapter originated in training I received at an organization called the Designed Change Institute. It was headed by an ingenious therapist named Tom Sargent, who had an uncanny ability to maintain contradictions inside a single therapeutic style. Beginning by applying 12-step principles to other areas of life, he later incorporated an improbable mixture of Human Potential Movement perspectives, including Transactional Analysis, Reciprocal Counseling, and Gestalt Therapy. When I met him, I soon sensed he had somehow and unknowingly synthesized Humanism and Behaviorism. This was as impossible as an electron being both a wave and a particle. Yet, electrons do indeed act as waves and as particles, due to quantum effects. Similarly, Sargent's synthesis conveyed a quantum power for personal development. Synthesizing his work became the foundation of much of my style of practice and most of this chapter.

This is the logic of pattern interruption. Attach something, almost anything, onto the pattern itself to interrupt it. That is the magic of the clump of dust. It can be small, simple, and insubstantial — but it works because it is incompatible with the phonograph record. The best pattern interrupters are just like that. They attach incompatible thoughts and feelings through repetition or practice. My favorite combination links new information and humor. An AA example of this is labeling excessive resentments (a dangerous emotional state for someone in recovery) as stinkin' thinkin'.

For this strategy to work, the information must seem to the person both different from today's reality and funny. For example, I knew a fellow who went to sleep and woke up in an anxious state. It turned out that his older brothers had tormented him growing up, especially at night when the parents were not around, leaving him nervous about bedtime. He laughed at the strategy of checking under the bed to make certain none of his brother's had stowed away. Had he still lived with any of them, or if he was otherwise afraid about his environment, this method would not have worked. Similarly, suppose the critical inner voice resembles that of one's father. Saying, "Shut up, Dad!" can be a much more effective interrupter if one does not still live with that parent!

Such a strategy begins with insights about where the tape originated, along with the humorous enhancement of pretending it never changed. *The overall effect is that of an absurd superposition of the past onto the present.* The result of intentionally pretending the situation has never changed effects a ridiculous satire that breaks the rigidity.

Now what? As miraculous as it is to turn off the static that has dictated our behavior and self-image for decades, the silence can become a deafening void without something to replace it. For many people the negative self-talk, because it replicates childhood relationships, feels like a sort of company. *As many times as we turn them off, they will continually turn themselves back on unless we replace them.* Thus, the third aspect of change — after awareness and pattern interruption — is development of an alternative.

Somewhere better to go

When a person succeeds in becoming conscious that the tape is indeed only a recording, and that it has a figurative switch — which can be as simple as laughing about it — the room suddenly brightens. *The darkness of decades can suddenly dissipate with the illumination of a freed sense of self.* Immediately and without effort, he or she appears unchained and clothed with what novelist Don Robertson calls "the sum and total of your personal now." This filled sense of self becomes the alternative that comprises the third step to change. Next, we will see how to develop and grow who you are in your personal now.

Besides the old, recorded messages we have been discussing and interrupting, another barrier to robust and realistic self-esteem is a healthy fear of egotism. Just as we referred to narcissistic features as a counterpoint to the benefits of an outside-in focus of attention, we will now see that these tendencies are truly the opposite of self-esteem. Narcissistic people present themselves as fabulous, a good term for them, as we will see. Their lives are also fabulous — except when they are not, in which case the situation is horrific and never their fault. Their emotions are intense and sensitive, yet their sensitivity, when sincere, is mostly about themselves.

Self-esteem is not narcissistic

Their public may love them, because they appear to be truly magnanimous and emotionally warm. Those who have to live or work with them often have a much different impression — they are self-absorbed and self-promotional, and whatever occurs is all about them.

So, if we are not talking about an excess of self-esteem, what is this? These fabulous (from the Latin *fabulosus*, or "fabled") folks are living in the fable of Narcissus, who fell in love with his own reflection in a pool of water and could never again see anything else. He spent his eternity in front of that reflection.

We have named the Narcissistic Personality Disorder in his honor. Unlike Narcissus, however, people with narcissistic features are not really suffering from excessive self-love. They are suffering instead from extremes of self-assessment. It is a problem of always being, in one's own eyes, either a 1 or a 10. AA talks a lot about this problem, because drinking (*active*) alcoholics temporarily appear to have personality disorders such as narcissism. For this reason, in 12-step meetings, the grandiosity of the active alcoholic is described as "an egomaniac with an inferiority complex." With typical AA wisdom, they nail the cause right on the head. To themselves, narcissists are either heroes or zeros, either top or a flop.

Hero or zero, top or flop

Recall our metaphor of living inside a box constructed of one-way mirrors, with the lights on in both directions. A person would continually be distracted by his or her own reflection. That is the prison of narcissism, only mitigated by the fact that these individuals know nothing else.

How does a person get wedged into such a box? It is not caused by excessive self-esteem, but usually the influence of narcissistic relatives or other environmental messages. There are societies where everyone seems to be and feels pressure to be amazing, in which narcissism is practically breathed in from the atmosphere. Parents can help insulate their children from hero-or-zero values, if they themselves have escaped it, by encouraging the kind of self-esteem below.

After understanding this phenomenon, it should be clear that we are aiming in a much different direction when we develop realistic self-esteem. Indeed, it is the opposite of narcissistic folly, because we recognize there are very few 10s. Further, we see that if any person achieves the very top, he or she becomes bored, because the middle is the place of growth. As an example of this phenomenon, basketball legend Michael Jordan played baseball for a while, where he had room for growth, then he returned to basketball when he was older. Self-esteem is a by-product of a life that is growing, fertilized by a sober assessment of one's own gifts. In contrast to the self-aggrandizing embellishments of narcissism, healthy self-esteem incorporates ongoing questioning and challenging of oneself. For more on this, see the sidebar.

Good-hearted people usually think they're not good enough. This is not necessarily a sign of poor self-esteem, but instead reflects a hunger to reach their potentials. Life will contain struggles; the question is whether people struggle for the right objectives.

Givers and takers each think they do not have enough of what they want. People who are more selfish focus on what they think they need and do not yet possess. People who are more loving reflect that they might have given better of themselves in the past and fault themselves for it. This is not a problem of shame: It is not about what others think. It is about what Carl Jung referred to as the healthy variety of guilt. Healthy guilt compares one's capacity to one's performance.

If I could have done better, I have the uneasy feeling that I should have done better. Accordingly, response-ability yields responsibility. The key to life progress is to harness the uneasiness into aiming higher. I can move from noticing myself falling short, to comparing my greater potential, and finally to corrective action. Of course, such progress increases both my potential and my future expectations of myself.

Too much dissatisfaction with your failings takes you away from the task of contributing your efforts to others. Too much satisfaction with your personal gifts leads to complacency and laziness. Accurate self-esteem includes the right balance of challenging yourself, as you need to do, but then getting back in the game.

Having distinguished self-appreciation from narcissism, we can see more clearly what it is and how to achieve it. A positive self-image reflects a state of gratitude for the particular constellation of gifts you were born with. Notice the word *gifts*. Whatever your metaphor for the source of your abilities, one source we can certainly rule out is you. While it is up to you to develop your talents and virtues, they are what you were born with. *You didn't make yourself. It is just up to you to make something of yourself by developing those gifts.*

Humble and grateful self-appreciation

This brings us to the subject of discovering what they are. As we have mentioned, it takes awareness of your positive characteristics to build your anti-lonely list. It also helps you stay single long enough to select the best relationship for you. In other words, *when no one is around, it helps if you like the company.*

Approaching this in a different way, if you were not alone, but were with the best friend you could imagine, what would that person's characteristics be? Delineate these virtues as specifically as you can. If you decide to do this, please stop reading now, so we can use your results next.

Perhaps you have already surmised why I wanted you to stop reading. I have never seen a person produce a series of best-friend characteristics that do not in fact describe themselves, whether or not they know it yet. (If you did not create the friend-based list, you can still do it now.)

Keep in mind that, if you have ever exhibited a trait, then you possess it, as we previously noted with the metaphor of finding gold ore while hiking. *You cannot show a quality that you do not already possess.* (See sidebar: *Which me is the real me?*) You may not yet access it often, especially if you have not credited yourself with possessing it, but if it were not there, it would never have revealed itself. In addition, you do not have to achieve superlative status to appreciate your personal characteristics. For example, only one person in the world can have the most perfect eyes, whatever they would be, but there are millions of delightful configurations of facial features, all of them unique. Personal qualities are the same, but even better, because once we put our inner qualities together with our physical features, all of us can be beautiful and each as different as a snowflake. This unique configuration of characteristics is what makes you who you are.

> *Which me is the real me? There are certain moments when I am at my best and other times that make these better moments seem like flukes. The question is which is most real. If I spend less time enjoying that best-me zone, how could it be the real me? A different and better question is: When am I the most effective? When are my perceptions and assessments most accurate? Which state of mind am I going to trust to tell me who I am?*

The *Which is the real me?* self-reflection is one of the shortcuts you can take to learn about your innate gifts, which become available to you when you shut off the aforementioned recordings. Another helpful activity could be called a *self-appreciation journal*. It takes about five minutes a day and becomes a reliable resource for learning who you are and for remembering it when you forget. To start, pick any recent event in which you think you (1) did well or (2) simply enjoyed. If you are not coming up with any situation in which you liked your performance, then just pick any time you enjoyed yourself.

The self-appreciation journal

If your mood has been deflated recently, then even the second option can be a challenge. Here is a way to find it: Suppose everything has been unpleasant for you recently, unfortunately. Some events were more unpleasant than others, right? In that case, ask yourself what the least unpleasant event was in the past few days. Inevitably, the least unpleasant event was also the most pleasant event. The efficacy of this method teaches a lot about how our filters affect what we see in life.

Now that you have an enjoyable or well-performed event, think of a positive feeling associated with it — excitement, confidence, love, peacefulness, relief, fulfillment, etc.

If you liked your performance (1), ask what that accomplishment says about you. For example, if you wrote a poem, perhaps it shows that you are creative, or talented in writing, or committed to the effort. If you have difficulty attributing a positive quality to yourself, ask yourself what you would say about someone else who did what you did.

If you simply enjoyed the event (2), look at the associated feeling. What does that feeling say about you? For instance, suppose you did not write the poem, but felt excited as you listened to it. Perhaps that says you are empathetic, or spiritually oriented, or a deep thinker. Again, you can reference another person as an aid. What would you say about someone else who enjoyed the poem to the extent that you did?

As we can see, activities that fill out the details of our self-appreciation can be straightforward. A simple journal like this, written in several days each week, eventually becomes full of evidence of who you are. The power of written exercises is that *you write it when you can, and you read it when you need it!*

The list of qualities you discover becomes the starting point for the anti-lonely list we described in Chapter 7. Applying that list helps you overcome desperation, *so you can be at home with yourself when you are in your home with yourself.* In turn, this allows you to apply more patiently the evaluation strategies in Chapter 5. It also allows you to find three kinds of love before you even leave your kitchen, which is the subject of the next chapter.

CHAPTER 9

Building a Warm Kitchen: Love Begins at Home, Three Ways

You do not need a romantic relationship to have a full life. Although I have described many advantages of just such a relationship, love of many sorts can be found without dating anyone. For example, friend relationships can be remarkably fulfilling, as many readers already know.

Interestingly, there are many similarities between dating relationships and other friendships. For example, people often flirt during the initial process of making friends, both people expressing interest in getting to know each other better but privately wondering if the other person really meant it or was just being polite! Evaluating a potential friend is similar to evaluating a potential mate. After all, it would be cumbersome to the extreme to love deeply and equally every person one met.

Friends with different benefits

In addition, friendship relationships pass through stages of deepening commitment, just as dating relationships do. In a book of remarkable wisdom called *Simple Words*, Adin Steinsaltz describes the typical progression of a successful friendship. Paraphrasing his analysis, one could say that people can have many acquaintances, and many of these can become friendly acquaintances. These are people we are happy to see, but they are not yet friends. We do not expect them to be there for us, and vice versa. If they do become friends, then we start keeping track of each other and looking after each other. We try to be good to each other and to nurture the friendship. When our friends are happy, we want to make them even happier. If our friends are struggling, we offer ourselves as life preservers.

Friendships can end; "family" is forever.

However sweet, friendships are conditional. If a friend betrays our trust profoundly enough or often enough, the friendship will likely end. Conversely, sometimes friends become elevated to family status. The difference is that almost nothing can break such a connection. If the family/friend profoundly disappoints us, there may be some hell to pay, but we do not throw away the relationship. (Looking at it this way, we can see that some biological families do not really operate psychologically as families, according to this description.) Like a romantic relationship that blossoms into a marital relationship, *friends can become the best kind of family, the kind that stays no matter what.*

Indeed, a useful way to imagine a terrific romantic or marital relationship is like a *sexual best friend* — a soul mate relationship elevated to family status, accompanied by a strong physical attraction. This comparison simultaneously shows why to search for such a heart-mate.

Another connection between friendships and dating is the role of friendships as a route to relationships, in terms of both networking and building a full single life, which is linked to readiness for a good relationship. An additional similarity, however, is that finding deep friendships and loving spouses requires venturing forth from home.

So, the question remains whether any additional forms of love are inherent to our potential, available to us before we leave home, and enabling us to explore the outside world from a position of inner strength. This innate form of love would be ideal, but its actual existence might surprise many readers. What is *inner love*, after all? We have no word for it. The word *selfless* exists, and its antonym *selfish*. Yet, there is no single term designating a state of self-caring, for having a full sense of self so there is plenty to contribute to others. As I heard this put when I was a counseling student: If I am a caring person, the first object I encounter as I enter the world happens to be me. If I try to jump over myself to get to you, I am likely to have a lot less to give.

Back to the kitchen

Fortunately, being loving yet self-caring can become a natural state. Indeed, *three different sources of innate love are available to bathe one's being with devoted confidence and passionate strength.* That sounds inviting, but it begs the question whether we are contradicting ourselves. Love is about relationships of various sorts. How can we have relationships inside ourselves without multiple selves? Further, would multiple selves not constitute a form of insanity?

Truly, we do all have multiple selves. Pathological states, such as Dissociative Identity Disorder (which used to be called Multiple Personality Disorder), are now classified as *dissociative* because one or more of the selves literally does not know about the others. The rest of us are free of amnesia about our activities, but we still can have different personas. If you meet someone at a work event, or at a party, or at a religious event, your demeanor with that person might be very different. If you later run into that person in a supermarket, the conversation may vary

How many of me are there, anyway?

widely depending on where you first met. If we thus allow for the possibility of multiple selves in normal people (which we could also call *various forms of consciousness*), we are ready to identify three ways that your relationship with yourself can progress.

To begin, most of us have heard references to an *inner child*, although our chances of finding one anywhere inside are unlikely. We retain old memories, but shouldn't that result in a continuum of experiences that we recall, rather than the experience of an inner child? We should have whatever memories we preserve from being four years old, whatever memories remain from being 11 years old, and so on. Nonetheless, we do have a psychological inner child. It is the result of a healthy and necessary psychological defense during childhood, which we all know as *denial.*

The kid

Denial (which, as people in AA sometimes say, is not just a river in Egypt) keeps the intolerable unknowable for a while. It is the way people get through hard times that would otherwise overwhelm them. Such times are quite common during childhood.

Most children feel inadequate to some degree, and indeed they *are* inadequate. Certainly, they may be more than adequate versions of children, but in terms of most of the kinds of things adults have to do, they are of course woefully unprepared. This is why they need so many years of care. Part of this is their inability to manage events that adults might easily handle.

For example, children tend to blame themselves for their parents' faults. Often this results from being told they are the cause, yet they usually take responsibility even when they hear no such thing. Do you know why? Actually, it is probably for three reasons. First, they can. Children think in magic not logic, so it does not have to make sense.

Why it was all your fault

Second, they want to. If it is my fault, then I can try to be better so maybe it will change. In contrast, if it is not my fault, then there is nothing I can do. Finally, they feel like they have to. Childhood seems like forever when it is happening. Therefore, if there is nothing I can do, that also seems eternal.

It is easy to see why the healthy defense of denial comes in so handy. As a result of many episodes of appropriate cognitive exile, *all the experiences we had that were too painful to manage at the time become congealed into a separate identity.* Often there are two childhood identities in a person. The first consists of all the wounding experiences we blocked out of awareness.

The second, somewhat older, childhood self consists of the manner in which we applied whatever strengths we had as children to protect ourselves. These were "never again!" moments in which we drew on our resources so as not to feel such weakness, such abandonment, or such embarrassment.

This is the rationale for accepting that you may have a kid inside, psychologically. It leaves open the question of what to do about it. Ordinarily, we assiduously avoid that part of consciousness. We want nothing to do with it. We refuse to be in the same psychological room with it. Even people who take inner child workshops often aim to absorb the separate identity, bring it lovingly inside, then be done with it. In short, most of us do not treat that inner child any better than anyone else did. On the contrary, *we may in fact treat these much younger versions of us as painfully as other people did in those early experiences, which is how we formed as separate identities to begin with!*

The need to adopt yourself

We are not being intentionally cruel to ourselves, we just misunderstand the experience. When the child-memory cries out, we think he or she is pain, but in fact he or she is just *in* pain. *We think the child is hurting us, but the child is just hurting.*

In this way, the first love I suggest people claim before they leave their own kitchens is to bring the child home to live with you. The inner child will speak to you, will make deals with you, and will keep them. One way to experience this is through an exercise called *split page* writing. With a line down the middle of the page, write with your nondominant hand as the child on one side, and respond to the child's voice on the other. Writing with the nondominant hand comes out looking like a child's scrawl.

The goal is to begin an ongoing relationship in which we will take care of the child — sort of like buckling a child into a car seat — and the child agrees we will do the driving. With practice, you develop an easily available dialogue with the child you were. He or she becomes increasingly healed through access to the love and wisdom of the caring adult you have become. If you want to do some extra homework, watch Disney's *The Kid* (released in 2000). Though miscast as a comedy, the film is insightful and cathartic. The healing possible from returning the inner child from exile, transforming the relationship into a loving and playful collaboration, can be astonishing. By the way, the kid remembers how to play!

As well as being psychologically appropriate to recognize a childlike identity, you can also gain 24/7 access to an inner voice of guidance. This aspect of consciousness is harder to explain than the inner child, because the way you will frame it has to do with the symbolism by which you understand your world. For example, people with a spiritual out-

Finding your inner guru

look might view this as an experience of their souls. Those who believe they are capable of a form of prophecy may even report that they are speaking to the voice of God inside them, but this is harder to accept. This experience can also easily be rendered in naturalistic, psychological terms, as a form of self-nurturing.

Here is a thought exercise to locate this inner voice. Going back to our understanding of the inadequate little children we were, think about all the forms of caring you received. Whether your caregivers were loving, reserved, or cruel, you had to receive a certain amount of nurturing in order to survive. Someone had to feed you, groom you, keep you warm, dress you, and suffi-ciently keep you away from danger. So, here you are, all grown up. Who does these things for you now? Naturally, you do, and you probably do not expe-rience it as nurturing — but you could. To take this further, think about a time when you were nurturing, when you took care of someone else in a car-ing fashion. Notice the aspect of you that did this, the way it felt, the innate capacity for support that you expressed. *Now imagine taking that same aspect of you and giving it to yourself.* Mostly, this also does not occur to us.

The best part is next. Just as the child, with encouragement, will have an ongoing dialogue with us anytime we want, so will the inner voice of guid-ance. With practice, you can ask questions and wait for responses. I usually suggest that people begin this with a type of meditation. Sitting still, perhaps after going through the thought exercise in the previous paragraph, say hello to that nurturing inner voice and ask for a dialogue. The answer may appear in any representational form — an image, words, or even a feeling. You have now begun contact. Eventually, you will find that you can take a walk, estab-lish a link to this part of you, and talk/think through anything you want.

This brings us directly to the third form of innate love. Many people un-derstand the inner voice of guidance as the contact point through which they

"Within you, without you"

access spiritual experiences. These experiences are available to everyone, and I like to render them in psychological terms that do not require any theological assumptions whatsoever. *If the first form of love I can find inside is between the child I once was and me, and the second form of love is between my inner voice of guidance and me, the third variety is between Everything and me.* This experience of a loving connection to a reality much greater than oneself is what I call *spirituality.*

When it comes to spirituality, some people seem to be naturals. If you are, it is probably easy to tell. You look around and are sometimes astounded that all of this exists, beginning with yourself. You are

Some people are more naturally awake to the moment

fascinated that, of all the things in the world, you somehow managed to appear in a material form that gets to wonder about stuff like this. You are grateful for the opportunity to be conscious, alive, and subtle. Further, you are deeply appre-

ciative of possessing some delightful talents, which can easily take a lifetime to explore. You probably take very little credit for the existence of these talents, but you experience an inner mandate to develop them as gifts. Most important, despite the temporary nature of all that you see, you feel an intrinsic passion to deliver the fruits of these talents to everyone who might make use of them. It is just your nature.

Some people who fit this description participate in some kind of spiritual practice that expresses similar sentiments. Others do not, but find that their nature tends in this direction even without the structure of a religious or philosophical system. Still others report they have never felt even an ounce of this sense of wonder. Most of us occasionally experience feelings of awe, but only in the form of infrequent lightning bolts. If so, you have an opportunity to expand and extend this capacity. Like all abilities, the tendency to experience grateful amazement is a gift you can enhance.

Why should we develop the spiritual dimension? Defined as a grateful connection to realities much greater than ourselves, there is an intuitive psy-

Why should it matter to us?

chological meaning to hitching our temporary wagons to an eternal train. It sounds enjoyable, and it is. When spirituality is the connection to all humanity, we commonly call it *universal love.*

Further, like a continuum, people can experience a spiritual connection as specific as a reverence for Mother Earth or as abstract as feeling connected to the vast something-nothing of the Cosmos. Defining it as "self-transcendence," some psychologists (Cloninger, *et.al*, 1993) have established a strong statistical association between spirituality and satisfaction once people exceed 40 years of age. Given a hopefully long life, this is helpful to know.

Because it is a sure form of love that one can never lose, it is indispensable. *While we do not always have somebody to love, all of us have the "Everything" available to love if only we know how.* When we actually do have close family or friends available to love, the ability to transcend ourselves helps us achieve the kind of intimacy that deepens love to spiritual dimensions. And don't forget those lightning bolts! How sweet it would be to spend more time amazed at being alive and filled with a sense of purpose.

One ready source of information about these levels of meaning is the Internet. Sometimes, the easiest way to learn how to connect to the essential web of your existence may be by connecting your computer to the Web of cyberspace. A few minutes of searching will reveal both sources and seekers, which will lead to a more symbolic dimension within any tradition you wish to explore. A search for "Christian spirituality" on ask.com yielded 3.4 million hits in half a second. Meanwhile, the "related topics" frame offered to take me to Christian mysticism, Jewish mysticism, and others.

You might prefer the traditional browsing domains, such as bookstores and libraries. Local clergy may be helpful or disappointing. Nonetheless, many of the guides to spiritual development, including Carl Jung, suggest that we find our teachers within the tradition of our youth, the tradition that planted its symbols in our developing bones.

Each tradition has produced brilliant guides who wrote or whose teachings were transcribed. Catholics can begin with Meister Eckhart and Thomas Merton. Protestants can read Paul Tillich and Reinhold Niebuhr. Jews can learn from Tzvi Freeman, Simon Jacobson, Arthur Kurzweil, or Adin Steinsaltz. First, you can engage your mind in study, then you can engage your awareness in an experience of what you have learned, and finally you can engage your heart in love with the source of that study.

This brings us back to the point of Part II: *A loving relationship with yourself is the best emotional place to prepare for whatever comes next.* Some of the time, we just do not yet know what we want. None of the time, can we know with certainty what is going to happen to us. Yet, all of the time, we can figure out our next step.

I call this a *lighthouse concept.* It refers to having heuristic goals. Imagine you are in a small boat in a big sea, which is appropriate because, metaphorically, you are. The boat is rocking and you are

It's all about the lighthouse

seasick. We know the good advice is to fix our eyes at a distant point, perhaps a far-off lighthouse. We probably will pick a different destination when we get closer, but the lighthouse offers a consistent direction and just enough light to navigate.

In the same way, even if you are in a recuperative period, or in circumstances not conducive to meeting someone, or if you just do not know when or if the right person will appear (see Chapter 4 for more on this), the best next step is to become fulfilled as a person, to become the member you already know of the couple you want to be part of.

At one point, while single, I had a disquieting thought. I did not know any couples whose relationship I found personally appealing. I would not have wanted to be in any of the relationships I knew. This unsettling feeling left as I realized it was OK. After all, there was no other person I wanted to be, so it was likely that the relationship I would be in would reflect who I was and not be the same as anyone else's relationship.

In the spirit of first things first, it is important to find that first member of the team first. Then, not only are you ready for whatever you are seeking, but you do not have to wait to start sharing. There is a whole world that needs you. Opportunities for contribution are numerous and increased fulfillment awaits those who make giving to others their lifestyle. Fulfilled in this manner, you can approach the prospects of finding a mate with a feeling of confidence. Actually, every part of the recipe to come will be more accessible if you do not wait for a romantic partner to start loving, and if that love extends to yourself.

The next chapter presents a formidable challenge, if it applies to you. Sometimes, the next step after strengthening ourselves is to decide whether we will be able to thrive in a relationship that we chose beforehand.

PART III

(Dis)Qualifications —
Are You in the Wrong Kitchen?

CHAPTER 10

Does this Chapter Apply to You?

Whenever you are wondering whether to change your current direction, first ask yourself: *Where is the road I am traveling really heading?* If you stay on your current course, where do you see yourself five years from now? In terms of the relationship you are in, if nothing changes, do you see yourselves apart, or physically together but miserable? Do you think you have no other option? The point of Part III is to provide better choices for those struggling in relationships that might not have held up to the assessment we recommended in Chapter 5. If you both see yourselves together as the years progress, then you can "pass go" and skip this reevaluation.

We will begin by assessing a struggling relationship to determine the route you are on. Then, we will look at whether your relationship is more like love or more like an addiction, and we will learn how love addiction recovery works. Next, we will see how to experiment with the potential of your relationship, so that you know whether it can improve or not. That section will begin with strategies to deal with distant and/or angry partners, and then move into a particular method to be certain you are not bringing out the worst in each other. If you must take another road, we will learn how to heal a broken heart. *In these ways, you can start new one way or another — by either renewing a relationship that was off course, or changing course yourself.* We will conclude with a section on how to deal successfully with betrayal, though that may require additional resources beyond this book.

The first step in this process consists of asking yourself two questions: Do you want to know where your relationship is heading? Do you want to know whether or not it can improve? Yes, knowledge is power, but it can also add pressure. A lucid view of your situation can challenge you to do something about it — hence, the pressure.

If the first part of this book included an evaluation mode, perhaps this part can serve as a *reevaluation mode.* Yet, this begs a question: Didn't we say the point of the evaluation strategies was moving past them to the point of an enduring commitment? In fact, in our discussion of the shared wish list, wasn't *promising forever* one of the criteria?

As a psychologist, I do not get to prescribe values for my clients or my readers. So, I will respond with my personal take on the matter. Once in a committed bond, especially a marriage, unless I were in danger, I would commit my efforts to improve even a failing relationship, and do so for a long time. I do not believe that five years of various attempts is an excessive expectation, especially if children are involved.

Yet, I have noticed that people vary widely on their endurance to withstand the pain of a fractured relationship, and I tell people that only they can decide when they have learned enough to make a decision. The essential point is that, whether undertaking one or three or seven years of concerted effort, these strategies will clarify whether it is possible to improve the situation. As I often put this in sessions: *I can't tell you whether to go or stay, but I can show you how to find out.*

If you have been in a rut for a while, the key is to get your life moving again, which the steps below will accomplish. Although we will be effective in this process, or perhaps because we will be effective, the rest of Part III tells a painful story. Yet, pain is not the problem in life — stagnation is. *Living things are always either growing or dying.* When winter ends and the season of growth begins, some plantings will have died over the winter, even though they are still green. If they are not sending forth shoots, their greenery may have only been preserved by the cold, and they will soon turn brown and brittle.

I have heard it said that life is a slowly downward escalator. Those not moving against the machinery are just riding down. This is true for any of the dimensions of our lives, whether physical, intellectual, spiritual, or social.

Perhaps you agree with me about the growth versus stagnation part, but what about the pain part? Sometimes, I think people understand this part of life more clearly at the movies, where we know that pain must be part of the process of growth. At the beginning of Chapter 3, I suggested that pain is so essential to achieving your dreams that *comfortable equals stuck.* For more on this, see the sidebar on becoming a psychological self-healer. Assessing your situation will likely be an uncomfortable process, because finding out whether something painful can improve is also quite frightening. But if this chapter applies to you, staying stuck and imagining no change is no less scary.

How to become a psychological self-healer: The ability to deal with emotional pain is essential to courage, and courage is essential to having a full, free, and fantastic life. If we do not learn how to heal, we are done trying after the first time we fall.

By the way, everybody falls. Yet, some people never fall in love again, after the first heartbreak. Other people settle for a relationship that is wrong for them in order to avoid the heartbreak.

Almost any adventure can fail, or else it was probably not a worthy adventure. Indeed, the most important goals we could have are those that we will sometimes feel like quitting. In this way, the expression "no pain — no gain" applies to more than sports. No dream becomes birthed without labor pains along the way.

Bottom line: If you want the freedom to seek your ambitions, whatever they are, learn to become a psychological self-healer. It is simpler than it seems.

As babies, we are born with three varieties of emotional pain, each with its own distinctive cry: loss (grief), anger, and fear. Painful events trigger one or more of these. Our innate emotional equipment allows us to feel the particular response, and then we are done with it.

Pain is the worst that life can give us psychologically, but life also supplies us with a brain with the psychological ability to heal.

What goes wrong? While still children, we start to learn the social rules around us, which is when the situation becomes more complicated. Often, we learn which feelings we should suppress. Otherwise, we may court negative judgments from the people around us.

Sometimes, certain feelings become dangerous to have, for example, anger in a child experiencing abuse. Boys (and sometimes girls) learn that tears function as "blood to the sharks" in the schoolyard. Girls (and sometimes boys) learn that anger results in rejection, especially by adults. Other times, we may decide not of have one or more of these feelings ourselves, for example, in order to not be similar to a particular person or to not give someone else the power to hurt us.

The result of all this is that we cover one feeling with another. We may become angrier instead of feeling hurt, or we may become sadder to avoid the experience of anger. This is costly. It takes a lot of rage to express a few tears and a lot of tears to express "liquid anger."

Other times we imitate or construct complicated emotions, like anxiety and depression, in order to accomplish the same goal of hiding from feelings we do not accept.

Remember our first point: Accepting the actual emotion allows us to heal and get past it.

So, how do you know which is the actual emotion? Now, it gets simple. The healing is a good clue. Expressing the right feeling at the right time brings relief.

As a result, we have the phrase "a good cry" for a healing experience of loss or "getting that off my chest" for a healing experience of anger.

If you are experiencing/expressing a feeling and you do not experience relief, this is a hint that you may be covering up the true emotion.

Which one? It is not difficult to find it — there are only three.

Move away from the one that just increases and choose the one that diminishes when you allow it.

Knowing how to heal, you become free to seek your cherished aspirations.

As we proceed, here is your second "pass go" card: If your partner is already expressing willingness to work on the state of your union together, then you can hold this part in reserve, in case he or she has a change of mind. *The strategies in Part III are only necessary if you are solo in your endeavor to improve your bond.* The good news is that some of these methods may result in your no longer being alone in your efforts to grow the relationship. The win-win is that, no matter how your reevaluation turns out, you will start growing again. Enlivened, you will be moving again on the road toward your future. So, you have now taken the first step: You have decided that you want to know. The next step is differentiating between love and love-addiction, the subject of the next chapter.

CHAPTER 11

Getting Fed Up
with Love Addiction

B efore we can reevaluate any relationship and its potential, we have to screen for *love addiction*. All addictions perpetuate themselves by hiding the truth of our situations, masking them from the light. To correct this, we can unmask the mask itself.

Unmasking the mask

Addictive versions of love do not have to offer much satisfaction in order keep someone imprisoned. In fact, excruciating attachments only strengthen feelings of love in the addicted partner. Putting it metaphorically, *love as an addiction is a dish best served dangerous*. At the same time, no one who really wanted to live that way would be reading a book on "relationships made simple." Indeed, to simplify psychological addictions is to start to recover from them. Below is a short primer on the nature of addictions, including how they both fool and capture us.

First, here is what they are not: Addictions are not habits, though sometimes people use the terms interchangeably. One of the best ways to understand addictions is to compare them to positive habits.

A positive activity, if it has the potential to become a good habit for you, will grow on you. Doing it for a while induces you to want to do it more. Nu-

A habit is a habit is a habit

tritionists and exercise advocates encourage people to cultivate good habits. Addictions also grow on you, in which case it is called developing tolerance. As a good habit, exercise is healthy, yet eating disorders sometimes include addiction to excessive exercise.

One of the difficult effects of addictions is *withdrawal*. Not only does the dose of the activity increase, but it is sorely missed if it becomes unavailable. This, also, is a similarity to positive habits, not a difference. If you enjoy frequent exercise and cannot do so, you miss it. You can also long for friends who become unavailable, for a savored fruit that is out of season, or for a periodical that gets lost in the mail. These are usually positive habits, not addictions.

Both the desire for more and the longing during absence result from the biggest similarity. Healthy habits and unhealthy addictions have a strongly pleasant aspect, at least for those people drawn to them.

So, with those features in common, how can we tell them apart? The difference is simple. There are three psychological stages in the development of an addiction. *The first stage necessary for an addictive behavior is that it hurts a lot more than it helps.* If they hurt us more than they benefit us, how do they fool us? It has to do with the sequence of the pleasure and the pain.

Habits that help you versus habits that hurt you

At least most of the time, healthy habits start out as less pleasant, maybe even distasteful, only to prove more and more enjoyable. They are mood incongruent; that is, we do not feel like doing them initially. Later, we are able to tolerate them, then to enjoy them, and finally to crave them in a nonaddictive fashion. In contrast, addictive habits usually start out as highly pleasing, hiding their punishment in reserve. They are *mood altering* immediately, and *mood destroying* soon after. With their torment delayed long enough not to be consciously linked to the addictive habit, *these charming enemies roll into our lives like a veritable Trojan Horse.*

The proof that addictive behavior has to cost a lot more than it benefits is revealed by the second stage. Addictive habits are the result of an insidious feedback loop: People handle the pain caused by the addiction with more of the addiction. Any activity that benefits people more than it costs them cannot fall into that addictive cycle.

Sometimes people catch on quickly to this bad deal and halt the cycle before it gets going. They stop or do less of whatever hurt them, and this is the end of the story. *Others miss the connection and handle the pain (termed abuse) with more of the additive pleasure that caused it.* This move launches the addictive train from the station, turning *abuse* into *dependence.* Around and around the track goes the pain-train, with agony ascending on each round and prompting ever more cravings for release. As this horrible loop accelerates into disaster, it leads to the next psychological stage in addiction.

This third stage consists of the terror of losing the addiction. What's to fear? Indeed, anyone not addicted will echo former First Lady Nancy Reagan's famous "Just say no!" An addiction we do not have will look foolish to us, whether it is smoking, drinking, medication, the use of some kind of "dope" (substance), or the love of a certain dope (person). Yet, we are now in a position to understand it. *Without the stimulus, the addicted person imagines all the agony without relief, but does not yet know that the addiction itself in fact causes the pain.*

The development of addictive habits produces some recognizable features.

The first — *denial* — helps people protect themselves from the terrible thought of losing what they erroneously believe they need. In Chapter 9 we understood denial as a healthy and indispensable tool for rendering the intolerable unknowable for a while. Just so here: *The addict marshals the power of denial as a distraction from anything that would prompt rejecting the addiction.* As a result, this feature of denial, so visible from the outside, will remain unknown to the individual imprisoned by the addiction — until recovery.

Blinding disrtractions along the addictive road

Another feature so readily identifies addiction that it sometimes can be visible even from inside the syndrome. Addicted people are so owned by their addictions that *their plans become irrelevant.* This yields the feature of unpredictability. It becomes simple to recognize when we really do not know what we are going to do.

Instead of asking yourself, "How much am I going to drink?" or "How much am I going to spend?" a better question is: Is the planned behavior, which I am trying to predict, part of a plan that I would recommend to my own child, if I had one?

When we are addicted, we feel highly motivated to maintain the behavior. Denial provides an opaque curtain, but the unpredictability and unmanageability of our lives threatens to throw the curtain back, so the addicted habit needs an assist. It gets this help through the this poignant psychological feature of addiction: *the illusion of control.* Every addiction needs such an illusion to strengthen the power of denial.

For instance, addicted gamblers always think they have a way to set the odds in their favor, while the rest of us know the casino is guaranteed to win. Even active substance abusers have endless plans to manage their habits. These may include periodic abstinence, just enough to prove only to oneself that the problem is under control. As my counseling mentor would state it, "Imagine if part of having a broken arm was not believing that you had one, and that every six months it was painless and usable for a few weeks. No one would get it set!"

The illusion of control provides a clue to the miracle of recovery.

Unlike unnecessary behavior like smoking or substance-abuse, some addictions — to food or to people — cannot simply be avoided. Fortunately, avoidance is not necessary. *Instead, one can give up the illusion of control.*

Surrendering this illusion is the first of three elements of recovery. For people with eating disorders, the illusion of control is spontaneous eating, the belief that there is a way to choose food by whim and still have manageable health. With addictive love, the illusion of control is that we can change other people. This fantasy is the lynchpin. *Without the misapprehension that we can succeed in remaking someone into our image of his or her potential, we begin to exit our captivity.*

Perhaps you wonder how this initial element of recovery — surrendering the illusion of control — can truly help unleash us. The psychological power of this first element is that it empowers the second. *Without the illusion of control, one can begin to avoid the small steps, previously unnoticed, into addictive behavior.* As AA has long said, "It's the first drink that does it." People beginning alcoholic recovery will avoid even the settings in which they drank, as will new nonsmokers with their own triggers. The previously unnoticed "first drink" for love addicts is pretending they can change others. It may consist of futile arguments, or reasoning one more time, or endless varieties of wishful thinking. The alternative is WYSIWYG relationships — What You See Is What You Get.

Loosening the grip of addiction by challenging the illusion of control and avoiding the first steps of addictive behavior are powerful steps toward securing reliable recovery. For solid and reliable freedom, one needs the third element: to embrace and replace. *Embrace a new way of life that replaces addictive prisons with positive habits.* For recovering alcoholics, AA describes sobriety, not just as abstinence, as going AWOL — A Whole new way Of Living.

For love addiction, part of that new way of living includes the ability to assess people and situations as they are, rather than as we wish they would be. This ability is a potent resource for recovery. To provide exactly such a resource, let us look at specific reevaluation criteria. *What are the signs that you may be in love with an illusion?*

Reevaluation criteria

❖ Sign number one: the *high potential* fantasy. This refers to the trap of being in a relationship with what you think is someone's potential. *Unless you are with someone who is actually making progress in his or her life, you must recognize that the new-and-improved person is not someone you have actually met.* It is impossible to be in a relationship with someone you have never met, unless the relationship is addictive.

❖ Sign number two: You cannot be yourself. Have you ever put on clothes that do not fit you? It is tempting to adjust your body so it is less noticeable, but the better solution is to change your clothes. *If you are walking on eggshells around the person who is supposed to be close to you, it could be that your relationship is addictive.*

❖ Sign number three: You seek love as another drug. Is your overall focus on making your partner happy, or do you spend more time evaluating how satisfying your infatuation is? Other signs to this pitfall are possessiveness, jealousy over past relationships, and demands for reassurance that you won't believe. Or, do you find yourself looking over your lover's shoulder to see who else is out there? While these are all reliable signs of addiction, it does not have to mean there is any particular fault in the other person. Instead, it can result from your attempt to use the relationship for more than it can be. *The right person can bring a lot of joy to your life, but cannot rescue you from yourself.* Going back to the challenge of Part II, are you happy with yourself alone and hoping to share yourself with another, or is a relationship meant to fill a deep emptiness you brought with you? If the latter is true, your task is probably to reevaluate yourself first, before the other person.

❖ Sign number four: You were not ready for this relationship because of timing. After a break-up, people often find someone who is as different as possible from the former mate. I call this a *sorbet relationship*, because it may just be a refreshing change but not a satisfying main course. Other examples of bad timing are inexperience (a first love) or rebirth (such as recovery from substance addiction). *You may have thought you were discovering the other person, but in fact you were discovering yourself — that is, your capacity for love and joy.* Now you are trying to make the other person become someone you would have chosen at a more ready time.

❖ Sign number five: You are trying to motivate a taker into becoming a giver by giving a lot. *You cannot.*

❖ Sign number six: You do not really want it. Here is a thought experiment: You enter a store, let us call it The Free Choice Store. Consider all the pleasure and all the pain of this relationship. Imagine separating it from the actual person supplying it. Just put it all in one package. Here is the box; this is how much it hurts and how much it helps. *Would you buy it?*

❖ Sign number seven: The two of you are not in the same relationship. Imagine a continuum of commitment. Every person is at some level in every relationship. Specifically, you can be committed to spending some time together, to getting to know each other, to getting closer to each other, to getting close to only each other (exclusivity), to getting as close as possible, to staying close no matter what, to becoming family, to making family (children). How closely are you matched? If your level does not match the other person's level, is the person who is less involved moving? The pace is less important than the direction. *If the levels of commitment neither match nor move, the relationship is probably addictive.*

❖ Sign number eight: You are in love but not alike. *There is an important difference between being* in-love *(infatuated), and* love *(caring deeply).*

It goes like this:

In-love is a feeling, a place to enjoy;

Love is both state and verb, a place to live.

In-love is only for one person at a time;

Love is for anyone you choose to love.

In-love is Nature's reward for obedience to mating;

Love is a reflection of the Love by which we were created.

In-love is the euphoria of a beginning, but allows for an end;

Love is placing someone's well-being as nearly equal to your own forever.

In-love is capricious and masquerades as being selfless;

Love is quiet, unassuming, and has no artificial bounds.

In-love is agony and ecstasy, heaven and hell, but high all the while;

Love brings a full range of feelings of all sorts, deeper and fuller.

In-love is a lovely fog, the more dangerous the more beautiful;

Love is a clear lens, but spares us nothing.

In-love can take an instant to boil the blood;

Love grows like an oak tree, at first just a twig.

In-love is the fantasy of lovers, it comes and goes;

Love is what you feel for your best friend, it is eternal.

Now that we have differentiated love from addiction, we will review straightforward alternatives that provide a chance to improve a struggling relationship while moving away from its addictive elements. This will show us whether or not the relationship has potential to be a happy one. When we are in such a reevaluation mode, how can we discover the difference between what is possible to achieve and what is not? This seemingly mystifying question has a simple if odd answer: *You cannot make someone better, but you can make him or her worse.* This sounds counterintuitive, but it is true.

Now what?

You cannot make people better because you cannot make them grow — that is their job and not within your arena of choice. Actually, you can help them if they are attempting to change on their own, *but it must be their initiative*, not yours. Lacking such power to improve other people, how can you make them worse?

If you stress people out, you do not usually see their *true colors* but their *old colors*. As noted in Chapter 8, you witness old, rigid patterns of response that were formed well before you two met. When you diminish and regress other people, you temporarily but assuredly make them worse.

This sounds like bad news, I know. Surprisingly, it supplies us with a potent option. If we are stressed out too, then we are not in our best shape either, and we probably are indeed making the other person worse. We can do better than that. *When we stop making other people worse, it often looks like we really did make them better!* In the next chapter, we will find out how.

CHAPTER 12

How to Stop Making
Someone Else a Worse Partner

In this chapter, we will explore a kind of relationship experiment that will reveal some options to improve our situations. To frame our goal during this experiment in scientific terms: We are aiming to remove ourselves as *extraneous variables.*

During an experiment, a central goal is to discover the answer to a scientific hypothesis, *a specific guess that could be proven wrong with observation.* If you fail to prove it wrong (to an acceptable level of probability), you accept it, pending future experiments.

This act of observation can affect whatever you are studying. To correct this, researchers may aim for what they call *unobtrusive observation,* making

The point of the experiment

observations without the knowledge of those being observed. Our experimental goal is similar. We must remove ourselves as negative variables, because we are very likely making the situation worse. Because we cannot hide like a researcher, our best option is to make ourselves into positive effects on the situation. As we have learned, this effort will not make the other person change in a positive direction, as that is not in our power. It means that the positive behavior will not become another extraneous variable. Instead, our improvements will allow us to see what we have to observe. *We hope to see that we are wrong about our hypothesis that the relationship is irrevocably flawed.*

Before beginning the actual experiment, let's review a few pre-experimental strategies. Although it is possible to perform the experiment we have in mind

Before the experiment

with someone who is distant, angry, or wounded, *it would obviously be easier to begin with a partner who is engaged, calm, and comfortable.* The pre-experimental prep helps that happen. These powerful steps help restore readiness in other people to reengage in a happy relationship. That is a smart move, even if you are angry with the other person. A motivational point: You may find that your own anger hinders your resolve to perform a good experiment, let alone these extra steps. Keep in mind that you are in large part doing the experiment prep for yourself, because you later will want to find out what the experiment can reveal.

One caveat though: The rationale above does not require that you work this hard forever. *Do the experiment once, if you need it; do it well, but do not take up permanent residence in Part III.* It will not nourish you; it just prepares you for whatever comes next. On the other hand, if you never do these strategies at all in a faltering partnership, it guarantees much harder work and much worse results.

Indeed, if you do not learn this now and break up instead, *the unwanted opportunity will reappear in your next relationship.* After your recovery from the split, the next person you seriously date will be as happy as you and will tell you what a fool your ex was to let you get away. But, sooner or later, he or she will do something that reminds you of your ex, and you will be off to the races again. It is better to learn this now, even if it becomes just for yourself.

We will begin with the problem of an emotionally remote mate. Living with an emotionally distant partner is desperately painful. You find yourself

When you seem to be in it alone

trying to guess what the other person may be thinking, imagining the absent conversation, and trying to convince him or her to want to speak to you. When someone is generally ignoring you, pestering seems to be the most natural response, though far from the most useful. If you wonder whether you are making the situation worse, just ask a friend to tug at your sleeve and sadly repeat, "Please stay." Even when performed as a game, it produces a creepy, clinging effect. If the distant partner comes closer for any purpose, you immediately doubt their motives and may not respond well. *The bottom line is that we unconsciously train distant people to distance even more.*

The best pre-experimental step with a disengaged partner would reverse that effect. Ideally, it is better to reward a loved one for approaching than for distancing. My favorite analogy for the way to accomplish this is fishing.

Imagine you are deep-sea fishing. Think marlin, think *The Old Man and the Sea.* You are equipped with a special rod and reel, complete with heavy

Lesson taught by a fish

line. Now, how do you know if the fish is on your line? You feel a pull, in this case a strong one. Is it pulling toward you or away? Of course, the direction is away, and this is how you know the creature is hooked. A fish not on your line does not bother to swim away. It is not worried. Your fish is big and powerful and unhappy. If you reel in as hard as you can, you will either end up in the water, your line will break, or the hook will rip out.

What should you do instead? Flip the reel into drag mode so it gives line to the fish, but with resistance, which tires it. When the fish loses momentum, reel it in slowly and steadily, until it takes off again, whereupon the process repeats. Eventually, you land it.

Just the same with people — if someone is pulling away, it is because they feel *hooked*, which produces the urge to run. Similarly, your "reel drag mode" includes every positive experience you have ever had together. By learning not to pursue a distant partner, *you are allowing the positive history of the relationship to have an impact.* Next is what it looks like in action.

When trying to figure out remote partners, people strain their brains wondering what every nuance of word or gesture means. Instead, just ask yourself one question: *At this very moment, is the other person coming forward or pulling back?* Pulling back is more obvious, but coming forward can be more complicated. Any form of engagement, even anger, is a form of coming forward.

Only one question really matters

Your responses can be simple to understand and to plan. Whenever the other person is pulling back, give even more room than was asked. In this way, you are *outdistancing the distancer.* Whenever the other person comes forward, gently welcome him or her. Act happy and receptive, but do not throw a party.

Example of outdistancing:

"I recognize you're right that we may not end up together — and, in fact, the direction of things looks kind of negative at the moment, doesn't it?"

Or, "Yes, I can see you have a lot to do, so you can't tell me what time you will be coming over. Maybe it would help if you just took the time to get that stuff done, and we can assume you won't be visiting today."

Conversely, when the person begins to return, whether in anger or affection, act suitably receptive, just not thrilled (even if you are). *The point is to warmly reinforce the other person's slow approach, and give nothing for distance.* This does not *change* the other person. If he or she truly does not care or has another lover, nothing will help, but it is best to know. This strategy simply removes oneself as a negative variable and allows the other person to experience caring, if it is there. This technique is remarkably effective, because the distant person is usually operating automatically, whereas you are not. (See the sidebar for exceptions to the fishing strategy.)

Fishing Exceptions: Does pursuit ever work — or is that only in the movies? Mostly it does not, but there are exceptions. Although it requires a lot of endurance, relentless chasing can actually work with a person who is reticent about dating and/or shy about relationships. But pursuit tends to backfire with someone who has more options.

Another exception pertains to temporary distance. People who are not by nature emotionally remote may show short-term distance based on situations or timing. Specifically, distant responses can arise quickly in women if they expect pressure regarding sexual involvement. In contrast, for men, it commonly comes up right after sexual involvement. In a long-term relationship, short-term distancing can be the result of a personal crisis or after a specific conflict.

The final exception to our presentation is the opposite, when the distance is permanent and irrevocable. Your partner might have a personality issue that prevents empathy, might have an untreated addiction that you do not see, including to another person, or just does not want to be in a committed relationship. Sometimes either a husband or a wife discovers that the spouse wanted children but not really a mate. Keep in mind that these fishing strategies are worth doing once, but you do not have to live on a fishing boat!

Simple though the fishing strategies are, they take practice to be available during stress. The stress-regress described in Chapter 8 causes us to forget new strategies when we most need them. This

Remembering new learning during stress

will be equally true for all the strategies to come, so we ought to consider how to correct for this phenomenon. As we have noted, the thing about high stress is that we become much more automatic, and the same old patterns come up every time. This happens to everyone. The cause is an instant change in brain function that enables immediate responses during physical danger (see Blum, 2011). We have to expect, anticipate, and prepare for this change. Accordingly, the best way to access any new skill when you need it is to leave it where you will be able to find it. *We have to attach it to the old pattern.*

To achieve that, practice it until it gets more familiar. In this case, write down the kind of statements you have been hearing and practice identifying them as statements of either approach or distance. Next, practice responses of either receptivity or distance, again writing down descriptions. Then, actually think about past times you would have needed to do this. Imagining the past instances brings back the experience of stress. Act out your prepared solutions until you become practiced in responding this new way even when distressed. If you do this a bunch of times, you will start to connect the experience of distance in your partner with the way out of it. You can then imagine future situations that have not happened yet, again practicing your response.

If an emotionally remote partner presents a daunting challenge, how much more does an explosive one! I am referring here only to verbal aggres-

Dealing with intimidation

sion. If your partner's rage is expressed physically in violence toward you or others, stop reading now and leave. You can continue reading once you are in a truly safe location, where the other person cannot find you. The only exception is if you and/or your partner are in treatment with licensed professionals who you trust, and who have advised you that you are not in imminent danger.

As with distant partners, our natural reactions to verbal explosions tend to make the other person worse. When the situation is quiet, we keep our heads down and stay out of the line of fire. When our partner becomes angry, we avoid him or her as long as possible, until we run out of tolerance. At that point, we either start justifying ourselves or yell back briefly. As a result, *they get little benefit from any calmness they display and a far more vigorous response from their anger.*

Arguing is one of the most intense activities a couple can do together. Setting aside the obvious pain of a verbal fight, you can see that it clearly com-

I love to hate you

prises a very robust form of interaction. During an argument, agony aside, you become each other's entire world. Nothing else matters, and you are riveted to each other, because the angry person is trying to have such an intense experience with you. You do not even need to argue back for such intensity. One person blaming and the other placating is just as fervent an experience, apart from the suffering. Do you notice how I keep setting aside the aspect of pain in order to describe the appeal of argument? This is the point: People starting arguments are not comparing fighting to loving. To them, loving does not seem an option. Negative attention is better than no attention. This is how we train people to do what we don't want them to do. *If someone is doing something you don't like, and they keep doing it, chances are it is working.*

How is it possible to reverse this? Again, the goal is not to try to change anyone else — but we can stop making him or her worse. With the following strategy, we can turn around our influence. Try these steps:

❖ First, start nice and friendly. If anger comes up, say what you would prefer — for example, "Let's talk about this together as friends."

❖ When that is refused (as it will be at first), say what you cannot do together. Perhaps phrase it like this, "I'm not able to treat you the way you deserve if I experience the names you're calling." If you cannot bring yourself to say it that way, an easier version is, "I will talk with you, but not if you are yelling and calling me names."

❖ When that is no help (which it will not be until you have run through several cycles of this), take a *timed break*. Do not storm out, but rather say something like, "As I said, I cannot do this like this, so I will be back in xx minutes, and we can try again." If you leave soon enough, you will not feel abused and will be able to begin again with step one. This simple sequence is usually remarkably effective, though progress is gradual. (A notable exception to this efficacy is in dealing with substance abusers, who will use their drink or drug of choice in order never to experience the loneliness. In this case, consider moving right to the experiment and also consider a 12-step program like Alanon.)

Not only rage-prone people blow their tops. Many of us have moments or subjects that inspire a passable imitation. For this reason, we will return to this three-step strategy when we consider communication techniques in Part VI. However, when this approach is necessary as a pre-experimental step, it usually means that our partner is addicted to his or her anger, with the same addictive dynamics discussed earlier in Chapter 11. We helped provide the emotional strength to deal with a distant partner with the therapeutic metaphor of fishing. We need another metaphor now, and it is available in the form of an initially scary, then lovable character from *The Wizard of Oz*.

Do you remember the terrifying wizard? Everyone is afraid of the giant face on the screen, until little Toto pulls back the curtain. The booming face commands, "Pay no attention to that man behind the curtain!" Fortunately, Dorothy ignores the admonition and pays all her attention to him, and

Who is the wizard really?

he ends up being quite sweet — as well as everyone's salvation.

Chronically angry people are often such wizards. Over the years, they learn to cover their softer feelings with anger, usually for good reasons. I call the result *the Wizard Syndrome*. Your choice is whether you want to squint through the screen and uncover the sweet person — or more likely the little boy or girl — behind the scary persona. It is not your responsibility to do this, but the strategy can change your demeanor.

The last pre-experimental step is the most difficult to discuss because it applies to our own mistakes. In truth, we may have been the intimidating wizards or the elusive fish. Some of us have been both. I have met many women who perceive their husbands as overly controlling. As long as he is not aggressive, they want to improve the situation. They may say, "He's crazy, but he's also crazy about me." Other women see their husbands as distant but agreeable. They report, "He has little to do with me, but I can do whatever I want." Sometimes I meet wives who essentially want to dump their husbands on my doorstep, as if saying, "Here, take care of him." They see their husbands as both distant and controlling, and they have usually given up. I call it the *double whammy*.

Sorry situations

Nonetheless, I have worked with wizards, fish, even combinations of the two, and seen spouses surprised to have their interests revive. *This turnaround has to do with the previously hurtful person knowing how to apologize.* People have a great capacity for forgiveness if they see some sign that things could improve, but it has to be convincing. Nothing is more convincing than sincerity.

Marketers recognize that fear of loss is more motivating than expectation of gain. If you have hurt your spouse into distance, instead inspire him or her with both potential gain and possible loss.

I have heard many spouses worry out loud that their partner is finally going to change, but for someone else! This is especially so when I speak to disenchanted wives, because women often do not expect men to grow.

As a result, *a husband who is authentically changing is an intriguing sight to his turned-off wife.* Of course wives may also be in the position of needing to effectively offer commitment to change. The following three statements, if heartfelt, begin to subvert your mate's view of you. If you mean them sincerely and follow through, you would then be able to proceed according to the fishing instructions above, assuming your partner is still emotionally distant from you. I suggest writing this and following up verbally.

❖ You agree that you need to change, including in the ways that your partner has urged in the past. In fact, you now realize (if you do) that this is necessary for you to have a good life and to be the best person you can. *You are fully committed to achieving this, whether the relationship continues or ends.*

❖ Regardless of whether or not the other person decides to continue in this relationship, you are *forever grateful for the gifts* of knowing him or her and for everything that he or she gave you while you were together.

❖ You are especially *grateful for the wakeup call.* Because you recognize that you would not have learned all this about yourself without this blowup in our life, you thank the other person for finally getting through to you. Finally, you apologize for all he or she went through in order to get to this point.

CHAPTER 13

Working It Out on Your Own — The Experiment

If any of the pre-experimental steps in the previous chapter are necessary, some follow-through time is required before attempting the experiment described in this chapter. For the fishing and wizard strategies, between two and four weeks of successfully staying on course would be the minimum. If you are in need of making the above apology, the most convincing follow-through is to seek a qualified counselor. Otherwise, it will seem to lack credibility. (For guidance on how to select a therapist, see the conclusion of this book.)

Having concluded any pre-experimental work, you are ready to find out what the relationship would look like if you were not a negative variable. The

The experiment concept

information you will learn from this experiment is valuable, even necessary, but also frightening. *If you perform it well, you will really know the best that your partner has to offer, and that best may or may not suffice you.* For that reason, the experimental method includes options that could move to an *end game.* You are in charge of the pace and whether you take it through to that end, but it is good to be cognizant of this possible outcome. You will discover how this relationship fits or does not fit with the kind of life you would like to live, but that answer could make you even more disenchanted than you already are.

First, we will consider the beginning to such an experiment, and then we will review some insights that help people stay motivated. The reason motivation becomes a challenge is that you are temporarily doing all the work, and it will feel that way. Finally, we will look at options if the experiment confirms the feared hypothesis that no change is possible in the relationship.

The beginning of the experiment is getting feedback, if possible. I usually suggest approaching your partner in this way: "I have decided to work on my

May I be of service?

part of making things between us the best they can be, and I could use your help. *Can you let me know everything you can think of that I am doing that I should stop and everything I am not doing that you would like me to start?"* The answers will probably be vague, so you will want to pin them down into see-hear terms. You might say, "I want to understand exactly what you mean. So, how would it look if I did that?" or

"How can you tell when I am being that way?" If the list only consists of negatives, a good question is, "What would you like instead of that?"

If the person refuses to provide this information, you could say, "I really would like to do this with your feedback. I'll make my own list and give it to you, and then you can feel free to make any changes to it if you want." You can probably guess most of the items anyway, based on past conflicts.

Once you have the list, go through it privately. Your next question is for yourself. Anything on the list that is just not you, that you would not be like even in the best possible relationship, you cannot wisely do. Further, anything that is too emotionally difficult right now, such as the sexual part of the relationship, you also cannot do, but you can let the person know you want that too, and expect it to return as things improve. This advice sometimes applies to men as much as to women.

The rest of both the do and not-do lists are what you would be like if things were going well. *Your goal is to act your best, without any preceding change in your mate.* In order to achieve this, your initial expectation has to be that, not only will your partner not change, but he or she will not even notice any change in you at first.

An optimal experiment will take at least two months just for the initial phase. Most of us need at least a month to practice and become skilled at this unilateral effort, after which we require a second month just to collect data. The question is not whether each day is any better than the day before, but whether each week is. Mark a mental or actual calendar when you are ready to start counting that month. Keep in mind that, any time you divert from your plan, you have to start counting again.

Following are several insights into relationships in general and these experiments in particular. Reread them as necessary to help stay the course.

❖ Eyes go outward, so it is easy to miss my effect on others. The experiment corrects for this by only focusing on my own impact for a while.

❖ The experiment presents a clear screen upon which the other person's issues can be projected in crisp relief, giving both of us a better chance to see them.

❖ Some subjects are too important for arguments. Discovering whether the relationship can improve is certainly one of these.

❖ Arguments are a distraction from seeing who this other person really is.

❖ The best way to increase my endurance is to make an absolute commitment to myself that I will seek a fully loving relationship. This is the next step in that process, so I can see if that is possible in my current situation.

❖ *The best options offer options.* I can do this experiment, assess the results, and make appropriate decisions. Without such a step, I will never know what it would have revealed.

❖ Whatever time I fear wasting on this experiment is much shorter than the time I have already been losing without learning anything.

❖ If I do not have children but want them, my commitment to them can exist before they are even born. I will follow through on this so I can eventually be in the situation in which they become possible.

❖ Doing this experiment is a win-win option because I will come out of it either in a wonderful relationship or in a much more ready state to have one in the future.

❖ While I have always heard that relationships are a 50-50 proposition, this process is allowing me to take 100 percent responsibility for my relationship with the other person. His or her 100 percent relationship with me is out of my hands and not the place to start.

❖ Perhaps only I have changed, and the other person has not, and I am no longer satisfied in the relationship. However, if I have changed, then perhaps the other person actually has also, but I cannot see it because of our negative interaction. I know I have not been able to offer my best to the relationship recently. This may be true of the other person too.

Once you see why it appears that you are doing all the work and that it also benefits your life, you can stay motivated to continue. Meanwhile, watch.

Keeping score, but slowly

The four weeks pass, and the question becomes whether there was movement or not. Did your changes stimulate changes in the other person? If so, then you might decide to extend the experiment, because you like the results.

If you do not appreciate the results, it usually means the other person is not changing or is even getting worse. The latter raises a different question: Is the behavior the same as past behavior, or is it different? Worse behavior could surprisingly be a good sign. People sometimes have trouble moving from one extreme to the middle, but first have to swing like a pendulum. For example, people seldom move from compliant to independent without first passing through oppositional. As Thomas Jefferson said in a much different context, a little rebellion now and then can be a good thing. Similarly, people seldom move from cold and indifferent to warm and loving without passing through hot and angry. A pendulum swing can signal it is worth extending the experiment, perhaps with a follow-up, to update the other person's request lists.

If there is no movement at all, you can take other measures. Each presents a new option for you to experiment and a new opportunity for the other person to wake up. *Only you can decide how far to take these and at what pace.* We will present the scenario as if you have decided to resolve this situation as soon as possible. So, please keep in mind that the pace below may not be yours.

Multiple wake-up calls

After four weeks of successfully following through, suppose I notice that nothing has changed. My next option is to approach the other person, saying, "Recall how I have been working on my list of self-improvements to help our relationship. I think I have been doing them. Is that how it seems to you?" If the answer is no, then ask the other person to detail specifically how you have fallen short. If you see it, you can continue with those corrections.

Once you have confirmed for yourself that you have in fact followed through, you are ready for the next step. This confirmation may result from your partner's agreement that you have reached the mark, or it may result from your own decision that you are as good as you are capable of getting, even if the feedback is mixed. Either way, *just confirming your efforts and changes is an alert to the other person to notice what you are doing and possibly to follow your lead.*

Suppose two more weeks have passed since you confirmed your follow-through, but still no positive change has arisen in the other person. This prompts your next message, which might be phrased, "Remember how I have been making the changes on my list and how I confirmed them with you? I want to let you know that I have some things I could ask of you, if you'd be willing to consider them. But, my changes are not dependent on whether you do." *This friendly request is yet another chance for the other person to join your efforts.* If he or she agrees, you can help with a list of very specific items.

Whether or not you receive any receptivity to your requests, mentioning that they exist is another opportunity for the relationship to improve. If two more weeks pass without any movement, you could decide to ramp up the urgency. "You know how I've made those changes, which I've confirmed, and how I asked you to make some too? Well, this is not an ultimatum, but I should tell you that the things I want are very important to me." Although you have distinguished this statement from a direct challenge to the relationship, *just mentioning the importance in the context of a possible future ultimatum should be suitably alarming to the other person.* By this point, you want somewhat of an alarmed reaction in the hope that you do not have to proceed to the next phase.

Perhaps you now sadly see that you are in this alone; you are no longer part of the problems, yet you notice no significant improvement. After even as short as another couple of weeks from this point, you may have arrived at that ultimatum

What an end-game looks like

point. Announcing this, you could say, "By now you know about the efforts I have been making and my requests of you. It seems to me that you are turning me down, despite my telling you how important they are to me. *I find myself at the point where I cannot go on without some cause for hope.* Can you give me that? If you don't think you are able to make those changes on your own, would you seek help to get things moving?"

As dramatic as this seems, I have still seen situations in which even this step did not foment any changes. Some people need to be hit (figuratively) by a two-by-four to gain their attention. This can take the form of a one-month break. It has more impact if it is a literal separation, although an alternative could be a two-part break — a first month in-house and a second month physically apart. Because of possible legal ramifications, I am not suggesting that anyone move out without gaining legal counsel. If agreed upon, this could be a short-term disengagement, after which one could move back.

This strategy is sometimes the impetus for the situation to change, but the break is not and cannot be a threat or manipulation. *One really has to be ready to end the relationship if nothing changes.*

Hands off the machine

The ground rules include a safety contract: Both parties promise to have no spontaneous social time together, other than to discuss logistics as needed. If the couple agrees to see each other, keep it light and do not discuss the relationship. Each promises not to date another person and neither will serve the other with divorce papers during this break. Note that this follows the stated preference for options that offer further options. When the month is over, the experimenting partner can again suggest working hard to improve the relationship. If the offer is still turned down, you sadly have the information you sought but had hoped would not be the case.

You may find yourself inside a painful ending in two ways. First, as above, the experimental outcome is bleak and you have decided not to live with it any more. As the tailor in *Fiddler on the Roof* said, "Even a poor tailor is entitled to a little happiness." Second, perhaps your partner has denied you the chance for any such experiment by breaking up with you before you had the opportunity to try to improve your relationship. Both cases benefit from a rapid and healing path for recovery from the pain of a break-up, which we will turn to next.

CHAPTER 14

When It Has to Be Over

Managing the pain of a break-up involves classic grief or an accelerated version. The biggest difference is the time frame. The first is typically a two-year process, and the second takes less than six months. Although most people choose the shorter course, some feel an obligation to mourn the loss of a cherished relationship, especially a marriage, for a more extensive period.

If so, no specific healing technique is necessary. Rather, one grieves the psychological amputation of the relationship as if it were a kind of death, and gradually absorbs it. *The mourning process proceeds naturally as long as one figuratively "closes the book" on the relationship.* To extend this metaphor, if one instead keeps reopening the book to read the good parts, or continues to reread the end in the hope that it ends better this time, that would delay the healing.

Few of us opt for this extended version, however. Unlike actual bereavement, break-ups have a legitimate component of blame. If we are making the choice, it is after many efforts, so in some ways we have already *pre-grieved the relationship.* When the other person decides to break up, there is a good chance that we were not given the opportunity of the experiment of the previous chapter. As a result, we have reason to be disenchanted. This disappointment both prompts us to seek a more rapid recovery and provides the fuel to achieve it.

Choosing a shorter path to recovery

Break-up strategies include a sequence of methods that will turn you off to the relationship and help you to move on. While they have cognitive (thought-related) components, they are mostly behavioral, that is, working with our automatic programming. To understand the reason for this, imagine that you have many *pleasure connections* wired to this person. It was not always that way. Before you met, you could have met someone else. The psychological term for this is *generalization.* After you fell in love, you focused completely on this one person, the term for which is *discrimination.* At the beginning of the break-up process, discrimination is still in place, so whenever you think about someone to love, someone with whom to make love, someone to hold, someone to make plans with, even someone with whom to discuss all this pain, you think of him or her. *The goal is to short-circuit these pleasure connections, so you become again generalized in your interest in the other gender.*

We will achieve this by harnessing every emotion you are having and using it to help you get over the loss of this love. Every feeling, even the sense of deeply missing the other person, will be enlisted in the cause of helping you move on.

Everything you're feeling becomes an ally.

These are can't-miss strategies, and you will only use them if you are ready to have them work. Imagine there is a secret break-up button hidden under your chair, and it is highly effective. If you press it, you will no longer have any significant pain at the thought of the other person. At the same time, you will no longer have any significant pleasure at the thought of him or her. You will feel indifference. *If you fully believed this button was going to work, would you press it today?* Faced with that prospect, many people demur the first time, but are ready to press it the second time I ask. What gets them ready to press it? Actually, the strongest motivation is the pain you are in right now. The anguish over the break-up eventually will cause you to *hit bottom* and desire to end the attachment.

The heartache is most of what remains of the previous bond. Yet, there is more. You also have fond memories, all of them now painfully fond. If you add up all the pain and all the pleasure, you will see that all that pain is not worth whatever pleasure remains. Now, you will want to press that button. This bottoming-out process comprises the first strategy in the break-up list. Making the decision to press that figurative button, to be free of both the pleasure and the pain, is the second strategy.

After bottoming out and making the decision to press the button, you are ready to utilize all of your current feelings toward turning you off fully. For

Finding and using your anger

example, part of this painful experience is inevitable frustration. After all, you have to go through all this because, one way or another, the other person dropped the ball. Whatever mistakes you made, you were willing to correct them according to the steps outlined in Chapters 12 and 13. Although the fault may have been divided during previous time periods, the other person has just unintentionally claimed the blame. *The person who will not join you as an agent of repair has put you in this position.* This realization is sad, and it will also make you angry — which fuels the third strategy.

Write an angry letter that you will not send. Because your goal is both to relieve yourself of some of that anger and harness it toward breaking your emotional connection, do not make it a fair and balanced account. Make it as scathing as you can stand. Any letter you would consider sending, even on your angriest day, is not angry enough. Start by calling him or her something you would not want to see printed here, and go downhill from there! Reread this letter anytime you want to express your anger, perhaps editing it to add further insults.

The second part of this anger strategy is to write another letter, one you might actually send. It can even be a toned-down edit of the first, which is how the two letters are coordinated into one strategy. In this second letter, include anything you want to be sure you have communicated. This may consist of your point of view on what happened and what, if any, conditions exist under which you would currently consider a new start. Otherwise, you might find yourself ruminating about not having been clear about your point of view. This sent letter can remove the risk of that regret by including *anything unsaid that you might wish were said.* This allows you to let go of any such worries. A common example of this occurs when someone wants to leave some future possibility of reengaging together.

From anger to resolve

This is one of the benefits of these break-up strategies. You are ending the relationship with the person as they are. You may decide to rule out any future, but you are not required to do this in order to recover. Your next relationship will be with someone who would pass the evaluation criteria of Chapter 5, even if it were with some future iteration of the same person. Such a turn of events would be long in the future, and you have no indication this will ever occur.

Now that we have harnessed your resolve and harnessed your anger, we need to exploit even your pain, which is usually plentiful. This is the *goodbye room.* With the help of this strategy, even your anguish will help you move on. Imagine a small room, inside which are you, a door, and the other person — but this is not really the other person you know. The other person you know was proven not to be someone you actually want. The person you once thought you were involved with would not have put you in the position you now are in. In that sense, *the person you miss is not your actual ex, but your previously idealized version.* That fantasy is what we miss and what we have to mourn.

Entering and leaving the goodbye room

Accordingly, say goodbye in that room as often as you feel the need. The strategy is structured carefully to help you absorb the loss. Your words might be something like this:

Goodbye forever. I will never again see you as this person, the person I hoped you were. I miss you. I wish you were real so I wouldn't have to send you away, but you're not. Thank you for the good times we had when I could believe in you. I hope for your sake that the real you becomes more like the person I am saying goodbye to. Goodbye forever.

The special torque of this strategy to get your life rolling again is powered by what happens next. You open the imagined door and repeat the kinds of statements above. You have the idealized person move out the door — and do it again. As he or she moves down the walk and gets smaller in your view, repeat it. Finally, the person disappears from view. You say the goodbyes one last time.

Whenever you want to think well of this person and feel the subsequent heartache, only do it in the form of this goodbye room. Any other time, move to the next strategy — maintaining a negative focus. This is a powerful behavioral technique (Phillips, 1985) that applies *classical conditioning* to pair unpleasant associations with your attachment to this person in order to short-circuit the connection.

The elements of this strategy are that you think positively about your ex only when doing the goodbye room strategy. Any other time, forcefully interrupt the drift of your mind in that direction. The

STOP! in the name of less pain and more hope

best way to do that is a *STOP! technique.* If alone, you might actually yell "Stop!" to break you away. The standard method is to wear a rubber band on your wrist and snap it on the outside of your wrist as you think or say "Stop!" Having interrupted the path back to the dangerous doorstep of the past, you can proceed to turn yourself off.

In truth, we turn ourselves on or off by the focus of our attention. If we are staring into the eyes of our beloved, we are thinking about their beautiful expression and how precious they are to us. We are not counting as many little capillaries as we can find or wondering how those eyes would look during ophthalmological surgery. *Our focus determines our feelings.* The classical conditioning approach (Phillips, 1985) would make associations between the former partner and disgusting images (for example, visualizing the person in a bathtub full of vomit). I am sure this works, but my preference has always been parody.

Once off the proverbial pedestal, everyone has some features with turn-off potential. The best parody takes any physical features you overlooked while in love and adds them to nonverbal expressions that fit the person's least desirable personal traits. Particularly, *look for the kinds of behavior that turned you off while the relationship was active*, whether sleeping on the couch, furtive conversations, stony-faced expressions, or other signs of self-absorption.

You make me laugh!

In the following conversation, I never got so far as personality traits, as we hit gold before that. I was working with a woman who had been completely blindsided. Our past conversations had not been about her relationship, which she thought was fine. Her dating partner for several years had sounded a bit vague and distant from her descriptions, but I had not anticipated what I learned on this day. He had never told her that he was beginning to date his ex-wife again, and suddenly announced he was going back with her. In the interview below, my comments are in italics.

Was there anything about him physically that turned you off — or could have, if you had focused on it?

Well, I'm really not like that. I don't care about physical attributes in a man, if I like him.

Sure, I know others who feel that way. Just the same, was there anything?

Well, he wasn't that tall. But, it didn't bother me.

So, he was short. Anything else?

He really can't see too well, but I didn't mind that.

You're saying that he has thick glasses.

They are, but that's fine.

I understand. Was there anything else?

He doesn't have a lot of hair.

So, he's bald? [She nods.] I bet that didn't bother you, though. [Nods again.] OK, was their anything ... Wait a minute! Bald, thick glasses, short — you've been dating Mr. Magoo!

Fortunately, she knew the cartoon character. When we both stopped laughing, we knew we had found her turnoff image. With this example as the pinnacle, see how close you can get to Mr. Magoo. Of course, in a pinch, there is always that disgusting bathtub as an alternative.

The next method consists of a list of *Reasons I'm Glad*. This one can be fun, especially if you write it with a supportive friend, particularly one with

You get to laugh again.

a good sense of humor. Many of the items will start with the phrase "No more ... " and list what you will not be putting up with any longer. It can include substantial items like, "No more pretending to be happy with someone" and more trivial ones like, "No more ____ music." Write it at strong moments, and read it when you need it.

The final step in this break-up method is to fill the void left when the relationship ends. Even very painful relationships can be intensely engaging

Filling the void

and will leave an empty space inside. Though it takes a while, it is best to start filling the void intentionally; otherwise, people tend to fill it unproductively. Sometimes it is replaced with intense arguments with the former partner. If you cannot resist that trap, see the discussion about love addiction. Overwhelming sympathy can be an equally addictive substitute. Other times, the relationship is replaced with obsessions over questions of why. *It is possible to obsess about these without the other person present, which renders it an inviting intensity during the initial throes.* This comes up so often that I find myself reciting the following words:

It is not about *if*;

It is not about *why*;

It is really only about *goodbye*.

As a reliable gauge, any activity other than these break-up strategies will likely hurt rather than help, and will probably comprise an addictive alternative to them. Happily, we have some better ways to fill the void, though admittedly more gradually.

Be a bit more selfish than you usually allow yourself to be. It is for good reason that AA, one of the most generous of fellowships, calls itself a *selfish program*. People need to take good care of themselves during the early stages of recovery. Keep the stress low, if you can. Carry around other people's burdens less than usual. Spend a little money on yourself (unless you have a spending addiction).

Fill your time with friends. I know you think you are rotten company right now. Maybe you are. The question is whether there are people you would allow to be such rotten company, if they were going through a break-up or other crisis. If so, it is a good time to cash in some of your chips. Let people support you. Surprisingly, you will probably find it makes them feel closer to you, and the relationship will actually grow deeper during this time.

Fantasize a better future. This aspect of filling the void is the most challenging, but also the most necessary.

If you are in mourning for a lost love, you have what I call a *relationship flu*. The thought of a new relationship sounds at least exhausting, bordering on revolting. This is temporary and just results from a *loss of appetite*. Without an appetite, even eating is repellent. Think of the last time you had some kind of stomach flu. If I tried to comfort

The ins and outs of the relationship flu

you by suggesting that, as soon as you feel better, we will go out for a big meal at your favorite restaurant, you might reply, "Stop talking about food, or I'll throw up on your shoe!" Yet, you might just call me a week later, asking if there was a rain check for that meal. Sex is similar. Spouses who attempt sex when resentment has curbed their appetites for it will also be repelled by the experience, leading to further resentment.

The prospect of dating can be like that too. Still, just as the loss of appetite passes along with the flu and sexual desire returns when a couple's conflicts become rare, interest in dating resurrects itself too — along with its own form of hunger: loneliness. This pain is a potent force, if we allow it to push us forward. Other times, rather than ride that natural journey back to healthy hunger for the future, we recycle our pain to protect ourselves. This is why we have the term *resentment*, as in *re-sentiment. Resentment consumes our future hopes in the slow fire known as bitterness.*

The jaded state seeks to protect us, but simultaneously robs our future. It is helpful to notice that the more wounded parties are often the ones whose prospects look a lot better down the road. I am not referring to people who are excessively self-pitying, blaming everyone but themselves for their mistakes. In contrast, the people I have in mind are emotionally agonized for the same reason that they come out much better in the long-term. They gave it their best, and did everything possible for it to work.

If I have a wealth of loyalty and commitment within me, I am likely to work to stay the course, no matter how bumpy the road gets. If the relationship ends anyway, I will feel devastated. Interestingly, *the amount of pain I feel as a relationship ends is not a function of how good it was, but how much effort I put into it.* The more love, sweat, and tears I invest, the more mourning I have to do when I cannot achieve the result I was working for.

The good part is what happens next. I have seen this dozens of times. That same person, who looks like a train wreck during the break-up, takes this loyalty and commitment forward and finds somebody deserving of it. For that reason, I often quote a Bob Dylan lyric from an old song titled "You Go Your Way and I'll Go Mine." The lyrics make it clear that only in time does it become clear who most lost out in the break-up and who ultimately gains from it.

One last point about this element of the break-up strategies: Envisioning a better future is not the same as being ready to start it. If you are fortunate enough to meet someone during the first six months, you

What to do about the rebound state

are probably in a rebound state. What is a rebound state? It means you cannot evaluate someone new yet. It is easy to tell: *You are comparing the new person to the old person a lot.* Guess who is coming out better?

Rebound is not the kiss of death. Notice I wrote that you cannot evaluate yet. The solution is just to recognize it, because the comparing will end. When it does, you can begin your process of evaluation. You just do not want to make any permanent decisions in the meantime.

Now that you have can't-miss methods for breaking up a relationship that needs breaking, you may still feel hesitation to do so. At the same time, you

Speeding toward the brick wall

may judge yourself for not having ended it already. Both of these are natural, even in tandem. I suggest not judging yourself for what you have done for the sake of commitment, especially in a marriage, and even more so if children are involved.

If it is time to go, it is and should be one of the saddest things you will ever do — but go. You cannot ruin someone's life by leaving. Healing exists, rebuilding exists, and the strategies to achieve both are available. You have been reading about them. If someone else does not ever accept that direction and stays stuck, it is nothing short of tragic, but not in your hands. Staying will not avail them, and will sink you both.

If you are the one who fears all that you are losing, ask yourself a question: Do you really want the other person, or the person you hope he or she will become? If it is the latter, then you have the choice to break up with the other person *emotionally*. Even if you have been blindsided by his or her break-up with you, that does not yet accomplish your own detachment. You could spend the rest of your life pining away, though I do not recommend that. *Instead, you now have the power to reciprocate the break-up.* After all, of the features you think you will miss, how many of those have you actually been getting in the relationship?

Going through a break-up, whether initiating it or absorbing it, can be like speeding in a car toward a brick wall. It seems like certain destruction. You race toward it, then panic and jam on the brakes, then repeat the same sequence. Finally, you take a deep breath, ready yourself for disaster, and accelerate rather than braking. The brick wall approaches, grows closer, even closer. Then, you find yourself astonished. Somehow, you are on the other side of it. How is this possible? You look behind yourself and see, billowing behind you, a large curtain that was painted to look like a brick wall. It was never a core threat. You can hardly believe it, but you are free, and so you drive on.

If there is one task harder than breaking up when necessary, it is staying when every cell in your body is screaming for you to leave. Yet, some people find a good reason to choose exactly that. Next, we will learn about these strong people, why they make that choice, and how they do so.

CHAPTER 15

Can You Come Back
from Betrayal?

In one sense, this chapter does not belong in this book. I do not advise couples in need of healing from betrayal to undertake this process alone, any more than I would advise someone perform surgery on him- or herself. Healing from a major breech in trust is a delicate task, certainly. Yet, there is one additional and surprising dimension to this problem that demands its inclusion here. My experience has been that couples suffering from breeches in trust are the most successful population of couples I have worked with.

While the steps for healing a broken love are ultimately simple, not all couples in counseling apply them. I can tell a couple's immediate prospects by the extent to which the partners are willing to focus on their own contributions to the difficulty, as opposed to trying to make me into judge and jury. Fortunately, even in the case of couples too angry to focus yet on repair, I schedule individual meetings that usually help get the process on track.

When working with couples facing the most trying of circumstances, such as infidelity, my vote is irrelevant. If the betrayed spouse just wanted to be justified, this would be easily attainable. Often even the straying spouse's family will side against him or her. Consequently, I think I may meet the most motivated of such couples because they have resisted the impulses to walk away from such pain.

Throughout the years, because of their commitments, these couples have taught me what works. I am giving you what they have given me: the secret alchemy of transmuting a marital explosion into a deep intimacy. If you are wrestling with a breech in fidelity in your marriage, you can ensure that your marital therapy includes the formula. Also, I have learned that the story of such transformations is remarkably inspiring to other couples. If they can do it, you can do it.

As one wife who has made this journey reports, her friends ask, "How can we get what you two have together without going through what you went through to get it?" Learning about such delicate healing has much to teach us all. Here is what it takes.

Three types of treatment afford the possibility of recovery from such a marital ordeal: facing it as a trauma, rebuilding trust, and transforming the relationship. While these factors assist any form of betrayal, such as draining the family finances with a gambling problem, we will focus on the most intimate form: infidelity.

For the purpose of this chapter, I will address the sexual affair as the act of the husband. Of course, this is not always the case. Yet, most of the time, it is the wives who evidence the strength and endurance to work on this. The most notable exceptions are found among men who see great blame in themselves, such as by having had their own affairs. Otherwise, men seem to give up a lot more quickly. Probably for the same reason, a lot more wives than husbands use Alanon, the 12-step group for family of alcoholics. It is not a matter of the preponderance of alcoholics being male; the husbands just seem to run out of endurance for the pain a lot more quickly. Let us see what the women do instead.

Upon learning that her husband has had sexual contact with someone else, the dishonored wife finds herself in the front row of a pornographic theater residing in her thoughts. She becomes the unwilling viewer of an X-rated movie starring her husband and rerunning continually. She finds this a nearly unbearable torment and simultaneously feels irresistibly compelled to ask him for all the details needed to script the film. What's going on?

The worst of reruns

She has just learned there was a trauma in her life, but she did not witness it. Part of trauma recovery is the psychological absorption of horrific events. Neurologically, we must write a version of these memories into our brains, excruciating as they are, because they happened. Just as a bereaved person may need to see the body of the deceased in order to heal fully, the betrayed wife also needs to "see the body."

Her husband will take a while to grasp this, even partially. Her questions seem to re-traumatize her over and again, and yet she insists. It will take her months to begin to absorb this and years to heal completely. He, on the other hand, is often completely done with his mistake as soon as it becomes exposed, for reasons we will see below. He may find himself wishing it could be as over for her as it is for him. When husbands voice this in sessions, my question is always the same: "So, how long could you do what she is doing?" Almost every husband's answer is the same: "I couldn't." "Right," I respond. "So, you and I can't know how long it should take."

The wife's need to experience trauma healing is one of the reasons the couple needs to work with a therapist who understands that process. Meanwhile, the husband must fundamentally understand this: She has his heart, his future, and his potential redemption in her hands; she could crush it, and everyone in their lives would agree with her. *Because she is not doing so, she is now and forevermore his hero, nothing less.* The only appropriate response is admiration and gratitude. Those will bring him more patience.

The next step in this recovery process is the rebuilding of trust. This seems a gargantuan task, if not an impossible one. Actually, psychological trust is not an arbitrary gift, but instead consists of a set of expectations, which in turn are based upon experience. At first, there is no question that she will expect him to betray her again. These are now her painful expectations. For trust to rebuild, it takes three ingredients:

Is trust even a possibility?

❖ new words; that is, new insights about how this happened and how to prevent it

❖ new actions that fit those words, so better expectations can begin to make sense

❖ new time; time can heal, but only in the context of the new words and new actions

First, the words:

In my office, I seldom meet those men who think they are entitled to sexual affairs, though such men certainly exist. In fact, part of his wife's shock is that he just violated his own values, as she knows them. He fully agrees with her. He was acting in such a manner that consistently violated his own values. What does this remind you of?

"How could he?" "How could I?"

Actually, it sounds just like our previous discussion of addiction. (For situations in which he may believe he is in love, see the sidebar.) This diagnosis of addiction fits most men I meet in these situations. They never thought themselves capable of such a mistake, and they are almost as horrified at themselves as their wives are.

They usually proceeded into this trouble gradually, rationalizing each step along the way, never believing it was going where it was going until they were hooked. Their recovery will follow along the same lines we have reviewed, including giving up the illusion of control and never again taking even a step in the addictive direction. Interestingly, recovery from sexual acting out and recovery from alcoholic addiction can use the same phrase to avoid the first deadly step. Both types of men learn: It's the first drink that does it. If he never has a drink or a cup of coffee alone with an appealing woman other than his wife, relapse is very unlikely.

If you are the straying spouse and you believe you are in-love with someone else, you probably do not yet see this as addiction. Men and women are equally likely to fall into this trap. You may be annoyed by my point of view about this, which I promise is psychological, not judgmental. I recognize that people can be blindsided by unexpected feelings. You cannot tell your heart what to feel, but you can tell your feet where to go.

If you think there is any potential value in the relationship you have started, you must understand this is not the way for any quality relationship to begin. If you continue on this path and end up with this person, future trust of each other may become a huge challenge. Further, if there are children involved, they will understandably and perhaps permanently hate the new mate. Finally, no matter how many times you tell each other you are not leaving the former marriage(s) for each other, you cannot be sure and will quite likely resent each other when the many and diverse costs of divorce accrue.

There is a solution, and it is a painful one, but any of the paths in front of you are going to be painful. The question is only what path offers the best chance of future happiness. Here it is: Talk together about the perspectives conveyed in this sidebar and agree to have no contact at all for as long as either of you is married. Divorce proceedings are civil cases and are available online. As a result, there is no need to contact each other, even if one of you becomes single. If you are both available someday, it is easy to find out.

This works best because, without any contact whatsoever, there is no chance of gaining reassurance that the other person still cares and is waiting. For all either of you knows, the other person now hates you, has worked it out with the current spouse, or has moved on with someone else. This is the only way be certain that you could not have left a marriage for each other. Neither of you knows whether the other person is even there to find out if it could work between you.

Now that you can see the logic of this, you also get to see what happens. The break will be very painful at first, but you know why you are doing it. Don't yield if you slip up and contact each other — it is a very addictive process. Keep in mind the rationales above, and finally succeed. After a while you will be able to address the current marriage. If you cannot achieve this break, then once again you have sufficient evidence that this is not intentional behavior, and we are back to the addiction hypothesis above.

Active addicts speak differently than people in recovery. Such recovery-talk is the kind of language she will need to hear. He will not blame her for his addiction, because no spouse can compete with novel erotic stimuli. She can be wonderful, but she cannot be new. Instead, he expresses his desire to make full amends, to help her heal in every way he can. *As much as it hurts, he stands strong for her and offers himself as the lightning rod for her outrage, seeing it as the least he can do.* During breaks between rages, he supports her lovingly through her tears, as tenderly as if he were not the cause of her agony. He voices his willingness, actually his eagerness, to do whatever it takes for as long as it takes to help her past the place where he put her. Such are his words, his intention, and his tone.

As for action, the second element of rebuilding trust, she sees that the smoke screen is gone, the former vagueness he surrounded his activities with.

Proof of trustworthiness: stage one

He replaces it with rigorous accountability, because he really wants her to know where he is. *Accountability is a gift of information, not permission.* He does not feel like a child asking to go to the bathroom, but like a man who has nothing to hide. He cannot make amends by erasing past mistakes, though he sorely wishes he could, but he can offer accountability as a gift that allows his wife to experience fully this faithfulness. Options for accountability abound today. Mobile phones allow frequent contact, while their apps offer fulltime GPS tracking. Skype makes people visible even while sleeping away from home.

All this may sound laborious, and it is. Fortunately, it eventually becomes less necessary, and she can tell when that is. The actions that ultimately and permanently renew trust have less to do with being accountable than being

Proof of trustworthiness: stage two and forever

consistently loving. Because his affair violated his own values, he was not able to act attentive or devoted to his wife while betraying her trust. Instead, all the men who fell into this addictive trap acted distant, which assisted them in rationalizing that they and their wives were not close anyway. In grateful recovery, he is eager to become close to her, probably closer than he ever was. This behavior becomes her permanent reassurance, and leads the next step in recovery — transforming the relationship.

If the greatest fear of these women regarding their husbands is relapse, their second greatest fear is that he will stop trying so hard after he believes

Not just better, but extraordinary

he has won her back. She knows they cannot go back to how things were, because "back there led to where it went," as I usually put it. The only direction to go is forward to a very different future.

I worked through this process with one couple who went through the most severe betrayal trauma of any couple I met before or since. Once they finally succeeded, to the point of renewing their vows, I asked the wife how she now viewed the marriage. "The way I see it," she quickly answered, "my former husband was a jerk, and I'm not sorry to see him go. But, I really like this one." Her husband, who had in fact been both husbands, beamed in recognition of the truth of her words.

It is completely unacceptable as well as practically impossible for a wife to go through the unspeakable anguish of the betrayal of her bed, and then to hang in for her marriage, only to return to what she had before. Every woman I have worked with who insists, as she should, that they settle for nothing less than transformation has achieved this. Indeed, she eventually can say with assurance that it was hell, but if it took a trip through hell to make their marriage a loving and private garden, then she was willing to make that trip. In the new light of their progress, it all looks different. *The relationship is illuminated by his admiration for her strength, their gratitude for a chance to love at a much higher level, and her trust that she will never allow herself to live again with a remote husband.*

PART IV

Dangers —
The Safe and Successful Chef

CHAPTER 16

Gender Dynamics

T he next three chapters assist you with common pitfalls to success with the recipe that follows. The most important point about all three is contained in the word *common*. As you will see, it is a mistake to blame your particular relationship for any of these pitfalls, because they are *unfortunately normal*. Though painful, they are typical. Understanding that point is more than half of the solution.

Section A: Not Blaming the Relationship for this Challenge

People do not always talk with their friends about their private relationships. Even people who are generally open about themselves may realize that their partners have not agreed to be included in that disclosure. As a result, *couples often think of difficulties that may be very common as specifically theirs and indicative of essential flaws to their union.* This chapter concerns the first of three common challenges we will explore — gender differences.

The differences between men and women can easily become a major pitfall in a relationship. Yet, with awareness, the challenges change context. Rather than wondering, "What is wrong with us?" the task becomes a simple matter of translation. Otherwise, men and women may speak different languages and hurt each other without knowing it, and without meaning to do so.

Contrasting the genders does not downgrade either men or women. Further, such contrasts certainly do not define any individuals. *No one is a stereotype.* You will probably find yourself both similar and dissimilar to some of the gender trends we survey. There are also important cultural variations that can accentuate, blunt, or even reverse these differences.

Note that our recognition of psychological gender differences also does not determine how many of these are inherent (nature) and how many learned (nurture). On one hand, we have interesting animal studies about testosterone and aggression. On the other, socialization also encourages male aggression; for example, being "king of the hill" makes a boy a social leader, but for girls, being considered "bossy" is the kiss of social death. We may never fully distinguish the proportion of gender differences based predominantly on biology versus cultural habits. Clearly the two interact heavily.

Regardless of the causes, therapists who work with heterosexual couples see communication confusions having to do with gender variations rather than personal or relational flaws. The solution is translation. *To translate is to understand; to understand is to heal; to heal is to resume life.*

Section B: Accepting Your Taste for the Opposite Gender

Sometimes I tease my clients a little about being straight. They usually think it is cute, or at least they humor me, but they also find it interesting. I tell them that they have to accept being heterosexual and the problems that go with it. Continuing, I explain that gays and lesbians, for all the other aggravations they have to deal with, at least understand each other. The rest of us practically need a handbook.

For example, men tend to be a lot more direct than women are about what they want to do, and women are much more direct about what they are experiencing or feeling. (For a thorough treatment of this difference, including the socialization that promotes it, see Deborah Tannen's excellent book on the subject, *You Just Don't Understand*.) Because of this difference in style, men will marvel at how women communicate, and women will become confused at how differently men do.

We just don't understand

For instance, two women will simultaneously defer to each other, yet somehow come to an agreement by reading subtle nonverbal cues, which might as well be happening in another dimension as far as it seems to a male observer. In another situation, it is her turn to feel stymied, as he effortlessly suggests that things go his way without considering how she or anyone might feel about it. He is not seeing himself as selfish, just logical and direct.

Because of such communication differences, if a woman does not say what she wants, a man thinks she does not want anything. Instead, she may ask questions. "Are you cold?" Substitute your own adjectives — hot, hungry, tired, bored. A man will reply "yes" or "no." If asked such a question herself, most women would respond with, "Are you?" If he does not ask about her, how will she feel? And how confused will he be when she suddenly turns quiet and distant?

This contrast in communication style also explains why women feel so hurt by male behavior that, to men, conveys rather small expressions of dissatisfaction. When she is reading subtle cues, and he is being less subtle than he thinks, she naturally thinks he is harsh. He has no idea how much she amplifies his delivery.

The result is as if he were speaking into a microphone without realizing it. In such a case, any listeners would feel blasted by small elevations in volume. It is no wonder she wants to leave the room.

Most women learn to avoid male aggression during childhood. For this reason, psychologists had thought of females as more dependent than males. The studies seemed clear: When schoolchildren were allowed to sit anywhere in a classroom, most girls sat near the teacher, and most boys practically hung out the windows. A woman psychologist suggested modifying the situation by removing the boys. Now, the girls scattered throughout the room. With the boys present, the teacher was not an object of dependence, but of protection. Many women grow up with this entrenched pattern of shying away from the first signs of possible aggressiveness in men.

Another potentially confusing gender difference stems from our biological inheritances. There is no escaping the physical (read: animal) aspects of being a person, especially when it comes to romantic

The places your body takes you

feelings. We are not intending to be only good friends when we marry someone. Although the sexual feelings we have will be mediated strongly by feelings of closeness, the spark has to be there, too.

As I mentioned in the fifth chapter, biologically speaking, women are baby-makers and men are baby-resources. Attraction patterns follow suit, so women often fear that all they represent are bodies to men, and men often fear that all they represent are wallets to women. Each has good reasons to fear this and to feel a sense of injustice from it. When resenting the pressure, most of us miss the fact that our own attractions are similarly influenced biologically. In fact, it can soothe our indignation somewhat to recognize that we are in the counterpart position.

Another probably biological input into our responses similarly stems from reproductive imperatives. The X-chromosomes historically most represented are the result of those women who managed to attract the *best* men (best in the sense of survival potential). In other words, the women who were able to be the most selective and found mates with genetic advantages are the women who had the most children who grew up. A related factor would be the ability of these women to interest the male to stick around long enough for that baby to survive. On the other hand, the Y-chromosomes most represented are of those men who managed to have the most partners, so more of their millions of sperm found nurturing homes. For the same reasons of biological impulses, women find marriage a happy event both as intelligent people and as animals. Men are more ambivalent for the same reasons.

This difference is not surprising, but what may be more interesting is that repeated research shows married men as happier and having more longevity than unmarried men. This runs against popular conceptions, leading to the joke that married men do not actually live longer — it just feels a lot longer. Research on women does not show this difference in either satisfaction or longevity. Part of the reason may be that women often work harder than their husbands to encourage intimacy in a relationship, motivated both emotionally and biologically.

Marriage is better for men

Meanwhile, their male partners want connection too, but feel it the most through sexual contact. This leads to a very common standoff: He acts more distant because he thinks he is being punished by her withholding sex, and she is amazed that he expects her to have sex when they have limited emotional intimacy between them. See why I point out that gays may have it easier?

Most of the time, men and women also have different expectations regarding what makes them worthy of love and how they feel it. Recall my earlier point about successfully reproductive women maintaining a partner's interest in primitive times. In other words, these women were more frequently cared about. Accordingly, in relationships, women are most physically excited by feeling loved, preferably cherished. Men, seeing themselves more in terms of their resource value, also known as performance, are turned on by being appreciated, preferably admired. They would not mind being considered adorable, but they seldom expect it. Instead, they expect to perform their way into earning affection.

Another standoff

To the confusion of their spouses, husbands may point out their many contributions. His point is that he is worthy of some regard and appreciation. It sounds to her like he is pointing out either how he is the better spouse or how he is doing more than she deserves. More likely, he is trying to promote the message that she is missing: This is how I show I love you. For most women, it is nice to have a washed car, but it does not translate into her feeling loved. (To help this miscommunication, I suggest he make that exact translation for her — *verbally* — and also learn to broaden the ways he sends that message.)

Another example has to do with the opposite, uncompleted tasks. Women often wonder why their husbands, who team up with men in sports or work, won't team up with them to get things done. The men wonder why she keeps raising the bar higher on her performance expectations. He thinks he is hearing about not measuring up, and all she wants is to team up. When he doesn't engage with her, she thinks he does not care and is displeased. This confirms for him that he has been judged as inadequate.

Couples who do not understand this often find themselves in a standoff in which she feels anything but cherished and he seems far from admired. Perceiving himself as unappreciated, he is not likely to express his love for her, and, feeling unloved, she is hardly going to act appreciative. For more details about the biological influences on relationships, see the sidebar on evolutionary psychology.

The perspective you are reading reflects a psychological specialty known as evolutionary psychology. *This field starts from the premise that, much as any other organ in the body, the brain developed to maximize survival potential. The evolutionary paradigm is that the biological task of organisms is to replicate their own genetic material in the form of offspring that will do the same. The biological goal could be called viable mating. It means the behaviors and urges that aid survival in tough environments are the ones that show up prevalently in the future.*

Evolutionary psychology is not a perspective that can include experiments, so all of its conclusions are speculative, but they are also fascinating and generally convincing. For example, we have noticed that gender differences have a strong linkage to viable mating. For women that would have meant joining with men who were healthy, powerful relative to that setting, and likely to stay around for a while.

For a man, because of the capacity for profuse sperm production, there were probably three paths to viable mating. As did women, a man could pick one woman who was fertile, attractive relative to that setting, and willing to stay with him for a while. Alternatively, if he did not want monogamy, he could aim for a large number of less viable matings. Finally, if he wanted monogamy but could not inspire monogamy in his partner, he would need sufficient sperm to have a better chance of her child possessing his genes.

This third option might seem surprising, but a woman would have had an evolutionary advantage to having different children with different men, *especially if the mate who was the most powerful in resources would raise all of them. Evolutionary psychologists point out that male gorillas, who are capable of keeping other males away, have small testicles relative to their size, while male chimpanzees, who have no such luck, are the opposite. Where do humans males fall? They are in between the two.*

One can see these factors seeming to play out in attraction patterns between men and women. Secondary sex characteristics in women both aid fertility and signal maternal potential to men. Even in older couples who do not want children, external signs of apparent fertility in a woman and visible signs of apparent success in a man have an appealing effect. This extends to the point of defining notions of female beauty. As youth is associated with greater fertility, facial features usually judged attractive in women will be those more similar to younger females.

The baby-maker versus baby-resource distinction also affects the gender psychology of jealousy. Sometimes I give couples the following awful choice to imagine. Imagine your mate has informed you either about a one-night stand with an unknown person or a crush without any physical contact. Which would be worse? With rare exceptions, women consider the crush worse, as it threatens loss of his interest, presence, and resources. Men consider the trivial sex worse, as men never knew (until recently) who their children were if they did not succeed in keeping other males away from the women in their lives.

The point of our giving biological nature its due is not to reduce our relationships just to biology. Fortunately, people modify a lot of what biology offers them. Our goal is neither to fight biology nor to have it push us around. Rather, our intention can be to work with it, to harness its energy to make our relationships as close and loving as possible.

The abovementioned stalemate between being cherished and appreciated also affects the conversation when women and men talk without the other gender present. Get a bunch of women together and the topic may well be what babies men are — which makes it hurt less when women feel ignored.

When men congregate, the counterpart topic can be how impossible it is to make women happy and how nothing is good enough. This makes it hurt less that they seem unable to gain their wives' approval. Men are surprised when I let them in on the secret: The one thing she wants from you is to feel cherished. If she has that, other things can slide more. Without that, nothing is enough.

Surveying such differences is intriguing, but what do we gain? I find that, once people absorb the gender differences, they can better translate the meaning of the other person's actions. Doing so makes the behavior less hurtful and promotes healing. *People begin to understand that dealing with the opposite gender requires such translation and consequently requires being gentle with each other.* These insights also inspire couples to reassure each other in gender-effective ways, some of which we will sample later in this chapter. In the same way that we just noted how misunderstandings fuel a worsening cycle, such heightened understanding inspires reciprocal benefits.

Because there is no fully escaping biology in the arena of romantic relationships, we have to manage these differences to better enable closeness between the sexes. However, this goal requires venturing into some controversial territory. I have to be a bit more controversial personally so your relationship can have less controversy (conflict) between you. First, we will look at where men are superior. And as you might expect, that's only half the story!

Section C: Who Should Be in Charge of the Kitchen?

The typical personality differences between men and women favor men in one important circumstance and one circumstance only. The male advantage in this one situation is striking, literally. This circumstance is combat.

Especially after the onset of puberty, most men have an innate ease in covering up vulnerability with anger, as well as an increase in aggressive impulses.

Guys make good soldiers. Further, they are more able than most women to ignore the emotional consequences of their choices and experiences. These features comprise key advantages on a battlefield, which may be why men have these differences. Men have fought countless battles in frequent wars, and the survivors were probably more likely to display such features.

As a result, in combat or any life circumstances that closely resemble combat, it may be better to have a man beside you than most women. This leaves an obvious problem, however. Few circumstances, whether in a family or even in a business, highly resemble combat. Therefore, women have key contributions to bring to noncombative situations. In most of life, anticipating the emotional consequences of one's choices would improve the outcome, and women are usually better at this.

Because men successfully suppress awareness of their feelings, they are actually more likely to be controlled by them. This helps regiment men, when necessary, in military units. Men believe they are just being logical, while women readily recognize the influence of emotional factors and often can correct for them.

Despite these potential female contributions, men — being generally more aggressive — are more likely to take charge and the women in their lives will often defer. *Most of the time, women are more equipped to lead, but men are more disposed to do so.* Consequently, she will suppress her will, at least until she runs out of tolerance. Then, she will become upset and act it. This just reinforces his sense that she is illogical and he had better run things.

Ready and unwilling

Recalling the metaphor (12th chapter) of the *Wizard Syndrome*, note that the frightening wizard was a man. As you recall, everyone was happier once the fictional *Wizard of Oz* was gently unmasked by Dorothy. Men can fruitfully learn to yield to women when future consequences are the subject. Often the wives are the first to sound the alert that a marriage is in trouble, for example. The husbands may just wish she would be happier with the status quo situation, hiding his feelings like the onscreen Wizard, but if she were, then neither of them would be very happy down the road.

Your relationship may reflect or depart from these typical patterns. The main point of this analysis is to provide an understanding of whichever of these gender differences apply to you and to your partner. This will help you not blame the relationship for typical gender-based issues. It also prepares you to learn to speak the other person's language better. Next, we will survey some specific applications of this.

Section D: Men and Women Speaking the Same Language

In one word, the solution to gender-based misunderstandings is translation. This translation also provides new options.

For men, understanding gender differences can turn a home into a refuge. Men usually experience everything as a job, a demand for performance. Typically, a man comes home from work, after spending a day hoping to meet the

Beginning at the end point

job's expectations, and wonders what his wife or children need from him. Nowhere in this process does he consider home as a safe place to be himself and to receive love or comfort. *Men have a reputation for selfishness at home because they often tune out to lessen the burden.* In fact, it usually does not occur to men to receive much enjoyment or nurturance from the loved ones around them.

Seeing themselves as nothing but resources, many husbands slog on, like soldiers pushing through mud and rain. The phenomenon leads to the joke: If a man does something and his wife isn't there, is he still wrong? Men have the expectation that women want perfection and they never measure up. In fact, most women ache to be in a partnership, to have their husbands open up about their struggles, which they would then share together.

She wants to feel cherished, but when does she feel it? *She feels loved most strongly when he shows vulnerability to her.* In fact, his lack of vulnerability is what causes her to distrust him emotionally. In turn, this distrust lessens her sense of being cherished. Finally, her displeasure leads him to misperceive further harsh judgments of imperfection.

The solution sounds simple: He shows vulnerability, she feels cherished and appreciates him. The sticking point is that vulnerability seems weak to him. This perception arises often in my conversations with men, and it is also when the breakthrough happens. Men can come to understand how women really feel in this area because both men and women have a similarity: *Everyone would like to be an exception in the eyes of the ones they love.*

When a man loves a woman, he believes that she is wonderful, that anyone would be lucky to have her, but for some crazy reason, she wants him. I

King Kong and Lois Lane

call this the King Kong Fantasy: I'm just a big, dumb ape, but for some reason she loves me. Research has shown that if a man imagines a woman likes everyone, this is a turnoff. If he imagines she likes no one, including him, it is also a turnoff. Instead, if he imagines she does not like anyone else except him, he is very happy.

Women want just as much to feel like exceptions, but in the arena of vulnerability (by vulnerability, I refer to *tears, fears, and tender hopes*). If she imagines he is vulnerable to everyone, that is a turnoff. If she imagines that no one, including her, sees his softer side, she also loses interest. She does not want an action figure. On the other hand, if he is vulnerable only to her: fireworks. I call this the Lois Lane Fantasy: He is Superman, but not to me.

155

Upon understanding this, vulnerability toward their wives starts to make sense to men, and their lives get better. They can come home.

For women, life can also improve with an understanding of gender differences. Understanding a man's *job orientation* will encourage women to take a more active role in leading them toward the full benefits of relationships and family life. When women think the men in their lives do not care about them, it hardly inspires increased engagement. Once they see that men are caring insufficiently for themselves, it mobilizes strong maternal wisdom that can make a big difference.

Her turn to drive

This is a splendid direction to go, but leaves the question of how blatantly to lead. On one end of the continuum, there are men who, upon understanding the point of this chapter, will say, "That makes sense. You see ahead in ways that I won't, so you're in charge. If you see something I don't, I will take your word for it and follow your lead."

On the opposite end of the scale are men who cannot knowingly relinquish control. Actually, these fellows would benefit even more strongly from increased female leadership. As they are more polarized toward the male extreme, they are more lacking in female insight. As a result, these men are unlikely to accept female leadership knowingly. In the 2002 film *My Big Fat Greek Wedding*, the mother explains why she will be able to persuade the patriarchal father to do the right thing: The man is the head of the house, she says, but the woman is the neck — and the neck can turn the head in any direction.

In such cases, he cannot realize that he is being influenced, though he sorely needs such influence. The good news is that more role-bound men do not believe they are susceptible to manipulation, so they will usually think that good ideas, even if initially rejected, are really their own, once they reintroduce them.

Most men are probably in the middle, as is typical of continuums. They may not particularly volunteer to surrender dominance, but they will stay friendly and cooperative about it if women present their case in the same way. Keep in mind that this is not about women getting their way instead of men. It is about men benefiting from female insights in an atmosphere of love, support, affection, and playfulness. Otherwise, all the personal features that draw men to female companionship are the same features they forget to benefit from. Increased leadership from women is fully a win-win.

Without changing personality or gender traits, men and women can learn to team up and complement each other's differences. Changing our *inherent nature* is both impossible and unnecessary. All we usually need to get past the gender pitfall is translation. Some examples follow:

❖ If you want your female partner to be happy with you, find out how she feels most cherished, and do more of it. If you want your male partner to be happy with you, find out how he feels most appreciated and do more of it.

❖ In keeping with gender differences, women and men understand companionship differently. For most women, female companionship comprises conversations through which women re-create their experiences for each other. In contrast, most men experience male companionship by shared activities. (This is another reason that sex makes sense to them as the best way to promote intimacy.) If you want more closeness, participate in a man's project or ask a woman what is happening to her and really listen.

❖ Speaking of listening, men and women experience questions differently. I often hear from women who think their husbands are not interested in what they have to say, because the men do not ask questions unless they dislike what they are hearing. Conversely, men complain their wives are giving them "the third degree." The translation is that women think asking questions shows interest, and men often experience questions as interrogation. This leads to men avoiding communication with their wives, confirming the wives' fears. The wives become upset, confirming the husbands' fears. With the help of gender-translation, men ask their wives more questions and learn to welcome their wives' questions as showing caring.

❖ How do men give each other attention? Most frequently, men tease each other. If a man does not tease someone, he probably does not like him. Do women do this? See the problem? If you tease a women, she probably thinks you mean it, and the outcome is just as frightening as you imagined. If a man is teasing you, he likely wants your attention. If you want his, let him know what works better for you.

❖ Almost no husband is as romantic as his wife is capable of being. If a man wants to depress himself, all he has to do is read part of a romance novel or really pay attention to a chick flick. At the risk of extending this depression to women, only two groups of men are generally capable of that level of sustained romantic charm: gay men and men having affairs. The good news is that women, sensing this, can let *some* level of romantic attention suffice them. Ask your partner what kinds of gestures touch her, and remind yourself to show her periodically. She will appreciate it and you.

Gender differences are the first of three common relationship pitfalls that do not have to signal a deep flaw in your relationship. If I had polled you about what these three could be, you probably would have guessed the battle of the sexes as one of them. The next fallacious pitfall is also not surprising. Because people are influenced by their childhoods, so are their relationships.

CHAPTER 17

Childlike Conflicts

Therapists can usually tell how a couple is doing that week from the instant they join them in the waiting room. Some weeks, it is so clear why they are together. Their enjoyment of each other and their ease together is palpable. Other weeks, you wonder if they could last another second together, had you not seen so many couples who survived that level of tension.

The contrast is so great that you might think they were not really the same couple, or at least not in the same relationship as other times. The latter is actually true. *Every couple has two relationships, and this is unavoidable.* One consists of who both people are today, which is why they got together in the first place. The other relationship consists of what happens when their childhoods collide.

Section A: Another Way Not to Blame the Relationship

The universal problem of having two relationships, consisting of one that works and one that does not, is the second of the three pitfalls that trip up couples on their journey to happiness. Gender differences were the subject of the last chapter. The challenge of personality similarities will be the subject of the next chapter. These three comprise the main obstacles facing otherwise loving couples. Each of these pitfalls can benefit from the measures I will offer. *Yet, the strategies to correct each of them, however useful, are less important than seeing them in the right context.*

None of the pitfalls indicates an essential flaw in your relationship. Once we understand them, it becomes impossible to blame each other for such inevitable phenomena. The understanding alone becomes redemptive to help couples trust each other and deepen their intimacy.

The only way to avoid having the two-relationship challenge would be if you both were born at the age of 21, which is not only impossible but would have been disastrous for your mother. In reality, the children you both once were would have been quite incapable of an adult relationship. When you are both feeling and acting more like those children, the relationship stumbles in a hurry. Yet, this phenomenon of childlike conflicts is inevitable.

Section B: Old Recipes Get in the Way of New Ones

Nothing is more beautiful than a loving relationship, and nothing is more stressful. Both of these are true for the same reason. A marriage is a unique relationship, literally. We can have several friends, and if one of them is difficult to bear at a particular time, we can come back later, while choosing a different friend in the meantime. It does not quite work that way with a spouse. Most of us have only one spouse at a time, and a break-up, if it comes, is devastating. Such a potent potential for emotional heaven or hell must naturally add stress to any marital conflict.

What do we know about stress? As you may recall, it brings us into a rapid response mode, which I term the *stress-regress*. The automatic nature of the

The stress-regress revisited

stress response is what makes the regression part happen. If we cannot invent new reactions, old and familiar ones will be automatically elicited by the stress.

The stress-regress supplies all the ingredients for the kind of recipe no one wants. Add one part high stress and two parts consisting of a husband and wife. Avoid any advance preparation, then stir it together. *What this cooks up is a stress-regress for two.* This coupled stress-regress is the *other relationship* to which we are referring.

It also means that, no matter how the details and subjects may change, every couple only has one argument. This is part of why it is so tiresome. We

Two relationships with one argument

return to this one argument with the same script, like a grade-B movie rerunning on a TV with only one channel. Not liking it the first time we saw it, we really wish something else played on the channel. When we reenter the one argument, we pick it up right where we left it. If the last argument had us threatening divorce, we begin again, even if the days between had us thinking no such thought.

As a result, it is the hardest to be at our best with the people who matter most to us. We may find ourselves out with friends and having a great time, but upon arriving home, we may check our brains at the door, and walk in totally different people. We encounter our one and only life-partner in the home we thought would be a place of love and happiness, and he or she is similarly checked-out. Accordingly, we wish we were back with the friends, and we think something must be very wrong with this relationship for it to be so hard to be together.

When I first heard this two-relationship phenomenon described, a counseling instructor elucidated it with the help of a therapeutic metaphor. Over the years, I developed it into the following narrative poem:

Imagine you are taking a walk;

Just you and your dog;

You and your dog and a friendly sun and a gentle breeze;

You, your dog, the warmth of the sun and breeze, and an intriguing vision.

Your eyes are drawn to a another walker, a stranger for the moment,

complete with dog, and with an appealing face of his or her own,

And with a style that makes you want to see more.

Closer now, you witness an expression that births fantasies of a kindred soul.

Yes, it is true, you can now see in this person's eyes,

a look that is probably just like yours:

We want to know each other. This is a special day.

Speaking now, and it is only getting better.

Thoughts arise — there is nowhere you could be right now,

that you would not like better with this person next to you.

At this exact moment, with the scene missing nothing but a music score;

at this perfect meeting, now imagine:

The dogs get in a fight.

Snarls and growls abound, with each pet projecting the kind of canine rage,

that shows they think you are behind them 100 percent.

Grabbing them off, holding them back, anticipating the lunges,

you check your dog's coat for signs of blood.

"Make sure you keep your dog off mine," you order the stranger,

    as you eye the other dog warily.

"Well, you too! I think yours started it anyway," is the retort.

Unpleasantly engaged by the dogs for a couple of minutes,

    you do not notice that you are forgetting those first five minutes,

but you each begin to have the last connection you will ever share,

    a common thought:

"If I just go away, I will not have to keep this up; the struggle will be over,"

    and so, with a helpless glance, you leave.

Within a marriage, the childhood-to-childhood relationship functions emotionally like a cancer. *It eats up more and more of the precious time available to be the people you wanted to be to each other.*

When childhoods turn malignant

The two relationships are very disparate because the mind is bimodal, which means that we literally have two different brain circuits, one for optimal conditions and another for high stress (LeDoux, 1998). *As a result, whichever of the two relationships we are experiencing in the moment will seem like the only real one.* When we feel close to each other, we think the argument was silly and we will not repeat it. This is a sweet illusion, but a naïve expectation that prevents our preparing well for the next time, as we will learn to do in this chapter. Worse, when we are at odds because our childhoods have collided, it seems our previous belief that we could be close to each other was an illusion. The dogfight seems to be the only essential reality of the relationship; anything else was a fluke.

When people feel such vulnerability, they do not always act vulnerable. Most people have two dimensions to childhood patterns of response, based upon two different stages of childhood coping.

Love can be tough

First, we discovered the emotionally painful parts of life. Later, but still in childhood, we protected ourselves with tougher behavior. This childhood defensive behavior remains with us as our adult argument style.

For example, imagine a couple with one of the gender-related impasses I described in the last chapter. Charlie is not acting as if he cherishes Meryl, and Meryl is not showing any admiration for Charlie. He is not likely to tell her that her opinion of him is very important to him and he worries she may not think highly of him. Instead, it sounds like this:

"You know, Meryl, almost everyone else I know thinks I'm a good guy."

"That's because you treat everyone else better than you treat your family, Charlie."

Notice the sequence of feeling hurt but acting defensive in both of them. She feels hurt, thinking he means it is her fault that he is not close with her. So, she defends herself by saying his priorities are off base. All he really means is that he is not as much of a disappointment as she seems to think. Each feels defensive, but the better the job of self-defense, the more likely it is to seem like an offense.

When our childhoods collide, we each think we are only reacting and the other party is making us feel bad. Both of us think the other person is in charge of the argument. Who really is? No one is. No one really feels like a "big" person in the room, as both instead feel belittled and hurt.

As another example, Sandy and Doug find themselves in the following script:

"Why can't you be available for me when something bothers me, Doug? It's not like I ask very much."

"I can't always jump to your rescue the moment you call."

"Who's asking you to? If you said there's too much going on at work, that would be fine. It's your tone of voice that puts me off."

"I don't believe you would be fine. I think you would have an attitude about it."

What they do not yet realize is that neither of their perceptions has much to do with the other person. Based on childhood experiences, Sandy fears abandonment and Doug fears being dominated by someone's dependency. Notice how self-fulfilling such fears can be. Doug's tension elicits annoyance from Sandy, which is what he fears. When he seems not to care, her panic pushes him away, which is exactly what she does not want.

We stay stuck in such trouble because it blindsides us unprepared. Yet, each couple can learn how to predict the one argument before it ever begins.

Section C: Seeing Past the One Argument

Immersed in the initial waves of rapture and gratitude that many relationships begin with, it was difficult for this new couple to face me, so much were their arms and legs magnetized toward each other. Yet, it was a couple-therapy session. Part of why they were so appreciative of each other was that each had endured much less perfect unions in the past. They wanted this one to be different. I was describing the three typical pitfalls, and I began speaking about the two-relationship phenomenon and the one argument each couple has. Suddenly, the woman's eyes widened, as she asked, "Do you know what ours will be?"

This gave me pause, as I usually speak about this with couples who are right in the middle of the other relationship. I asked her, "What are you most afraid will happen in a close relationship?" I asked her partner the same question. Next, I addressed them both, "OK, now imagine that both of these were happening at the same time."

Preempting conflict

One of them feared being seen as a burden and the other feared being pushed away. She looked at me, intrigued by her anticipation at how these might interact. One would retreat, not wanting to intrude, while the other would become angry at being ignored. Then, she remarked brightly, because it was still a point in the relationship when this prospect was a not a daunting one, "Oh, we already did that!"

In fact, this was the best time for them to uncover the one argument, when they were not having it. Accordingly, you can ask yourselves the same questions I asked them.

❖ What are each of your deepest interpersonal fears? Is it a form of abandonment, or being harshly judged, or a form of betrayal?

❖ What is the one argument that would ensue if you were both experiencing those fears at the same time?

❖ Do you recognize that argument?

Prepared with your best guess about your one argument, you can now start tagging the other relationship when it grabs stage center. It will usually be easier to see the change in your partner than in yourself. Consequently, one method to catch the other relationship in the act is by noticing when your partner seems to be in the grips of such old fears. When this seems the case, ask yourself: Am I also under the spell of my old fears?

Self-diagnosis

As always, the key to change begins with awareness. Knowing when we enter our own versions of the stress-regress empowers us to apply the strategies we will soon review to break out of it.

The problem is that the stress-regress reduces awareness significantly. Along with causing regression to old and outdated responses, distress produces a type of tunnel vision. Just as the structure of a tunnel is not apparent from inside it, we are usually unaware of the switch into rigid functioning in ourselves. Still, there are ways to notice when it is happening. People have three hints:

❖ *Overwhelming feelings.* Unless we are literally and physically overwhelmed, intensely negative emotions supply a good clue that our reactions are coming from the stress-regress.

❖ *Perseveration.* This is the psychological term for the AA definition of *insanity* as doing the same thing and expecting a different result. This inability to change strategies is caused by the stress-regress.

❖ *Either-or thinking.* If we cannot think of more than two options, and neither is helpful, we are probably stuck in the dichotomous thinking that goes with the stress-regress.

Any one of these three is sufficient to alert us that our responses are not present-based. Some of us are better at noticing when we feel overwhelmed. Others are better at noticing repeated ineffective behaviors. Still others are better at counting the options that occur to us. Any of these methods tells us what we need to know. Then, we become more ready to resolve the problem of colliding childhoods.

Section D: Resolving the Argument

Of the three options below, the first method aims to prevent the one argument altogether, the second ameliorates the harmful effects of that other relationship, and the third exercise is a quick rescue for when you are both just stuck in it. Together they comprise three effective ways to get the "dogs" of our previous story to play nice.

The prevention method consists of effective reassurance of each other. This itself is simple; the challenge is realizing when it is necessary.

What is so difficult about remembering to offer reassurance to someone you love? Our partners are the most important peer relationships we have. It should be easy to let our lovers know we love them, that we care

The reassuring "prevention recipe"

about how they feel, or that we want to make their fervent wishes come true.

Here is where we can discern the powerful barrier posed by the one argument and the *other relationship* it reflects. Within the grip of colliding childhoods, we will not know, without preparation, that the other person needs or even deserves such reassurance. We know that we do, but the other person seems too powerful to need anything. How do we convince ourselves of the illusion of this great and threatening power? We know we are hurting and believe the other person is the cause. Of course, the other person, who is also responding from the distant past rather than the present, is similarly convinced.

This interaction results in a pair of mutually self-fulfilling prophecies. *My fears about you cause me to act in exactly the way you fear.* Imagine if I were hit often in the past, so according to my expectations your upraised hand could only signal an attack. Actually, you mean to hug me, but instead I put up my guard and raise my fist. Horrified by what looks like an attack to you, it is natural for you to defend yourself. The next thing we know, we are fighting, but neither of us started it. Verbal arguments are much the same: Each person engages in self-defense, but each act of defense appears to be an offense to the other.

Worse, after the other relationship has crowded out the loving one, arguing can become the most intense activity we share. This is sometimes called the *soggy potato chip theory*. Imagine you are

Settling for the soggy

quite hungry and wander into a room, where you notice two bowls. One has fresh, crisp potato chips just poured. The other contains old, soggy ones that no one threw out. Most likely, you will enjoy the fresh snacks and discard the old ones. On the other hand, suppose you are just as hungry and encounter only one bowl, which contains the soggy chips. The theory suggests that you will pick up a chip, wonder if it might not be that bad, and take a nibble, then finish the bowl. The relationship counterpart to the old, soggy bowl is the stress-regress relationship and its old, soggy argument. Our hunger is our loneliness, and we fill the hole left by lost loving through increased conflict.

Couples can truly become addicted to their one argument. They both hate it, but they love to hate it. This is easy to discern in my office, to both my clients and me. When the argument has become addictive, neither party can resist jumping in while the other is speaking. True to the nature of addictions, both people indeed want to wait their turn, but just cannot do so when heated up. To address this at home, I suggest that people agree they will have no spontaneous arguments. Really, I would rather that any conflicts be tabled altogether, so I can do the work instead of them in the session, where it likely can be resolved less painfully. Yet, because couples addicted to conflict cannot wait that long at first, I instead ask them to agree to reschedule the argument. Sitting down for a *scheduled argument* is rather funny, which often breaks the argumentative mood.

Now that we see why motivation to offer reassurance is sometimes elusive, we can learn how to break through the resistance to offering it. Of

Retrieving reassurance

course, you would prefer your problem be the two-relationship challenge, in which case reassurance would help. This is a much better prospect than the argumentative impression that the other person is impossible to deal with. To convince yourself to believe the better prospect, I suggest the following analysis.

Each person is aware that the other person has misperceptions about him or her. In other words, "how my partner is characterizing me in this conflict is not accurate to who I am, how I feel, or what I want." This is no question. Accordingly, the real question is whether the other person is sincerely deluded — does he or she really believe this? In response, I have always received agreement that, yes, although the other person is wrong, he or she genuinely believes sincerely in the mistaken perception.

The next question is whether their wrong beliefs could explain their unpleasant behavior. Could believing what they believe produce the negative reactions one is witnessing? Because the answer to that is also always *yes*, we now have two hypotheses. The other partner could be acting out because of bad intentions and a lack of caring, or it could be caused by mistaken beliefs. As it turns out, the first hypothesis is a stretch in light of the good times in every relationship, and the second one is much more likely.

I often justify this better conclusion in terms of the *law of parsimony* (also known as Occam's Razor). A scientific model offers the simplest explanation of the data. In our case, *the mean-person hypothesis cannot explain all the nice things the other person has done, and the confused-person hypothesis can explain both the good times and the argument.*

Having two people in the room at such a moment has advantages, because I can ask each whether he or she is feeling confident and powerful or diminished and hurting. After both people respond, I ask, "In that case, who is running the argument?" As I have already noted, no one is. Neither person is the big bad wolf. At this point, both people finally see the situation as I do.

Keeping this in mind, a much better option arises: For five minutes, offer reassurance to the other person about your intentions, long enough to break through the stress. Again, the reassurance itself is simple. "I love you, I want you, I care about how you are hurting, and I want you to feel safe with me." We can say those words; the first challenge is realizing it is necessary, and the second is being prepared to offer reassurance before you also need it too much to give any. Because the one argument can escalate quickly, some couples write down their most effective mutual reassurances in a notebook. Either of them can pull it out when feeling stuck, for help in remembering the way out.

A second strategy, which corrects for the effects of the one argument, consists of an exercise for remembering why the couple is together in the first place. If we go back to the dog-fighting metaphor, it would be as if the two people said to each other, "Hold on. We were having a great time. The problem is not the two of us, but these silly dogs. Let's separate them, tie them up, and give them something to chew. Then we can come back and get to know each other."

"The Homework"

When I learned this exercise, the counselors provided it to couples so often that they simply called it The Homework. It progresses from self-appreciation to appreciation of the other person and the relationship. In this way, it fits the perspective of Part II — that one's relationship with oneself precedes and influences one's relationships with others. Following are the instructions I suggest:

❖ Write down four recent enjoyable events not involving the other person. (They can be either big or insignificant, just enjoyable.)

❖ Next, add four qualities you enjoy about yourself. These are adjectives, characteristics you have ever evidenced. (For help with this, see chapters 8 and 9.) Use examples to fill out the picture.

❖ Now, identify four qualities you enjoy about your partner. They are not the only four or best four, just any four. Use examples; this also allows your returning to favorite qualities without sounding repetitious.

❖ Finally, recall four memories you have ever enjoyed with this person from any time, even the first five minutes you met.

There is no wrong way to do this, except to unnecessarily limit it. It already goes without saying that none of these positive events or qualities occurs all the time, so you don't have to say that.

It is a lot easier to write this in advance so there is less performance pressure. Just set a time to read it to each other. Prepare to be embarrassed, maybe to cry. When you are listening, do not say a word. Just experience the gift.

Doing this exercise can be a fantastic way to make the transition to couple time, after work or family responsibilities have kept you apart. It provides an effective counterpoint to whatever is keeping you apart, whether life circumstances or the one argument.

Finally, a third and unusual strategy can transport a couple out of the other relationship when words fail them. Sometimes, people can become so stuck inside the one argument that they misunderstand anything the other says. In such a case, I recommend stopping the conversation for a while. Fortunately, the silence itself can become a powerful aid if channeled into the following activity, which takes them beyond the interaction of their childhoods and all the words of misunderstanding.

A transporter beam out of the one argument

❖ Just take hands and look wordlessly into each other's eyes. Look closely.

❖ See the pain, longing, fear. Noticing any of these will help, because it shows that the other person is no threat.

❖ Feel the reality of the other person's hand. Notice that this is a unique hand, one of the hands of your only partner. All other hands, even ones you love, are different.

❖ Any words that come next can only be either loving or vulnerable, but not judgments or analyses.

❖ Do this until you cannot help but hold each other.

No one feels like doing this at the time it is most necessary, because neither person feels safe. To correct for that, I ask people to agree beforehand that either partner can request this activity at any time and the other person agrees in advance not to refuse. This *transporter beam* is too good an offer to pass up.

Following the guidelines above, we can accept that, like all couples, we have two relationships. Anticipating this, we can learn to predict our one argument and spend less time in it. In this way, *progress in a relationship is a quantitative improvement that produces a qualitative one.* Both relationships already exist, including the one we want. We are just learning how to spend increasing amounts of time in the present-based relationship.

Although the pitfall presented by the mutual influences of our respective childhoods presents an important hindrance to adult relationships, few people are surprised to learn that it is so. We all recognize that we were certainly unprepared as children to manage adult challenges of all sorts. Children have fantasies about their eventual marriages, but are not ready to understand what is involved. The influence of our childhood relationships on our adult relationships has to be tricky. On the other hand, the pitfall of the next chapter is more surprising. Who would expect that our similarities could destroy our love relationships?

CHAPTER 18

Missing Ingredients

Psychotherapists sometimes claim that couples break up for the same reasons they originally got together (which consist of their differences). It seems obvious to the rest of us that opposites both attract and repel. Initially, our contrasts intrigue us into exploring a connection, but later we in fact argue about them. This is the common wisdom on the subject, that our differences supply the essential fuel for our relationship conflicts.

Our perspective in this chapter will be the opposite. We are about to see the reasons that our inevitable similarities, not our personality differences, actually lead to conflicts. *Although the literal content of these conflicts consists of our differences, the causes of our conflicts are rooted in what we have in common.*

Section A: A Final Way Not to Blame the Relationship

First, an image: Picture a mosaic design. You see an intricate pattern, much of it filled with pieces of colored glass. It is beautiful, but incomplete. There are gaps. Not to worry, there is a second mosaic, with the same design pattern, which fits perfectly on top of the first. The design is now even lovelier. The second mosaic supplies most of the missing pieces in the first. In areas that both mosaics possess, the layers are now doubled, filled by both patterns, revealing deeply enriched hues. In this way, the differences in one fulfill the other, while the similarities strengthen both.

Yet, the story is not over. One or two of the pieces are still missing, neither design filling the gap. This mosaic is our relationship story; we compensate for each other's deficiencies easily, usually without even knowing it. In other areas, neither of us fills in, also without realizing. No couple is completely different. The ways that we are similar leave *couple-gaps*, areas of life where neither partner is facile at filling in for the other. I term the problem of such similarities common ground, because it can take a soaring love and drive it into the ground. Common ground is the third of the inevitable and universal pitfalls to happy relationships.

An always incomplete mosaic

The discussion immediately begs a question: If this is the last pitfall, when do we discuss the danger of our differences? After all, these are indeed the subjects of most of our arguments. Nonetheless, other than the values and lifestyle differences outlined in the fifth chapter, differences are not the problem. (For more on the types of differences that draw us together, see the sidebar.)

People seem to choose nonromantic friends who are similar to them in personality, and are attracted to loving mates who complement them. Accordingly, when psychological theorists differentiate personality types, no sooner do you understand the typology when you begin to think of couples who display marked contrasts in type. For example, the Myers-Briggs Type Indicator divides introverts from extroverts, intuitive types from external data-driven types, those who make decisions more by thought than by emotions, and spontaneous types in contrast to planners. You probably know few couples who have most of these in common. Similarly, David Merrill's (1981) system, which is oriented for understanding personality contrasts in work style, also applies to couples. He contrasts "drivers" (bossy types) to "analyticals" (techie types) to "expressives" (sales-pitchy types) to "amiables" (loyal, assisting types). Teams too similar to each other can have trouble getting much done even at work, let alone a in a relationship. It's no wonder that opposites attract.

Regardless of the content and context of a couple's conflicts, the problems they encounter are mostly driven by the three pitfalls. In that case, why do

No laughing allowed

we argue about differences? We have to. When we are feeling pain that we are voicing with anger, we need a subject. The actual pitfalls do not work as argument fodder. They would make us laugh. Couples argue about differences because it is impossible to shout things like:

❖ "WHY DO YOU HAVE TO BE A DIFFERENT GENDER?" — Chapter 16 pitfall

❖ or "HOW COME YOU WEREN'T BORN AT THE AGE OF 21?" — Chapter 17 pitfall

❖ or "I HATE IT THAT YOU ARE LIKE ME!" — the subject of this chapter

As far as I know, *common ground* is a completely innovative model for explaining conflict. The downside is that I have only anecdotal evidence for it. Apparently, no one outside my practice is yet talking about it, though this book will perhaps change that. In the meantime, you will have to kitchen-test it yourself. You will learn how to do so in the remainder of this chapter.

Section B: What Is the Problem with Similarity?

It is obvious that any couple will have some similarities along with their contrasts. What may be less clear is why this must lead to deficiencies in the relationship. Why can't couples have some similar strengths without similar weaknesses, or at least without sharing any costly weaknesses?

The short answer is that strengths and weaknesses are situational. All the personal traits that are typically viewed as faults have certain circumstances where they are quite appropriate. For example, there are sadly certain life situations, such as war, in which even a vicious response may be best. In contrast, every virtue can become totally out of place at times. Thus, there are situations, such as when extricating oneself from the addictive relationships reviewed in Chapter 11, during which a caring response would be a bad idea.

As a result, every personal quality has a front and a back. Each characteristic brings certain advantages and leaves certain deficiencies in its wake.

Two sides to every coin

Each mutual similarity between romantic partners also leaves some area in which there is no one to fill in. Specifically, to live happily this week, not to mention ever after, at least one of you has to perform certain couple tasks. For two people to make a life happy together, at least one party must be able to:

❖ make decisions

❖ reach out for affection

❖ both show and accept thoughtful acts

❖ look for compromise

❖ plan joint activities

❖ lighten the atmosphere and play

❖ show appreciation

❖ initiate communication

❖ say no to impulsive choices

❖ bring up problems

❖ place conflicts on a concrete level for solution

This may look like a long list and is probably a partial one, but most of this happens without thought for many couples. Various types of personality are more or less likely to do each of these things, and usually one of you can cover many of these needs.

However, in areas of common ground, one or more tasks are left neglected by the couple. For instance, a very courteous couple may both be too polite to bring up problems; the assertive couple may not include a member who looks for compromise; the self-reliant couple may not have anyone who can reach out for affection. What happens instead?

As I pointed out, it is remarkably difficult for people to fight over similarities, so no one will complain at first. Instead, the spouses will feel increasingly irritated with each other, until someone runs out of tolerance and voices displeasure. Whether this starts a hot war or a cold war, the verbal content of the argument will center on differences, not similarities.

Section C: Examples of this Challenge

The members of a couple do not get to pick their common ground pitfalls. Each couple's version is inevitable and inherent to the similarities already present between them. Later, we will explore methods for filling in common ground. As usual, the first step is awareness.

See if you recognize your own relationship in the stories of the couples below. In each case, the essence of the pitfall consists of unawareness of its nature. In other words, if the couple blames the relationship rather than the similarity, no one will fill in. Yet, once the common ground is unearthed, lending a hand becomes a simple and encouraging option.

Their story is our story.

A powerful formula for success in a marriage is when two givers pair up. An even greater formula for grateful success is when two givers, each of whom had been previously married to takers, pair up. Deb and Mark are in

When giving feels lonely

this latter group. They are both nurturing people, very supportive of others. It takes one to know one, and when they met, they grew close quickly and married within the year.

Both are highly attentive to others' needs, but they tend to leave themselves out of all that nurturing. You might think that each of them would encourage the other to take better care of himself or herself, but neither is particularly tuned into self-care.

As a result, each views the other as unavailable. Deb's emotional style in stress is anxious, and Mark's is depressed. Morosely, Mark complains that Deb is never around. She avoids confrontation, but eventually loses tolerance and yells at him. This only adds to his expectation that she prefers to ignore him. Meanwhile, she views him as critical of her and a negative, difficult person. What they really need is to understand their similarity and to support each other in scheduling themselves in the picture of their lives.

A related difficulty plagues Meg and Tim. Both highly responsible, they are attracted to the responsibility and diligence in the other. This does not mean they are both dull and plodding. Quite the contrary, they are both vibrant, fascinating people who developed a strong attraction to each other.

Still, what they lack is play, and they are not alone. Play has become a lost art. Not just distraction, play consists of the discovery of places to laugh, people to wrestle with verbally or physically, and especially pointless activity. I often recommend that couples claim a little time to do things that have no goals at all, not even the goal of learning to play!

All work and no play

Meg and Tim are even more deficient than average on the playfulness scale, which is only the flipside of their laudable industriousness. Having such diligence in common, they do not notice the lack of playtime in their lives. It shows up as a lack of couple time, which Meg noticed first, as we would expect based on the 16th chapter on gender differences. How did she interpret it? She thought it meant Tim did not want to talk with her. How did her subsequent displeasure strike Tim? He thought Meg did not appreciate his efforts, as we also might expect based on gender-dynamics.

As I write these examples, I can think of scores of couples who have variations of each of these versions of common ground. In fact, although the examples I am providing are composites of many people, *I fear that every couple I know will think I am speaking about them!* I suppose I should call this *common common ground.*

Another common denominator is that of Steph and Rob, both awfully considerate people. In our work together, they are vocally appreciative of my efforts and even both apologized at different times for how hard they think my job is. (This always surprises me — I usually think I have a dream job, until I hear how terrible it seems to others!)

Both pride themselves on being easy-to-get-along-with, and they are. They each recognized and appreciated that in each other when they met. They

No drama, but no action

are not dull, either. Rather intelligent, they have great conversations with each other. They each enjoy that the other is low-drama, viewing their more dramatic acquaintances as a bit narcissistic.

Sometimes, however, it is possible to be too polite. Neither wants to intrude by expressing unwanted interest. Taking this too far will appear as expressing disinterest! That is Steph and Rob's story, two-way. Their relationship is in danger of being canceled due to lack of interest. There is simply no one to invite interaction, leading to the impression that the other does not desire it. Being no-drama people, neither brings this up, and both become even more careful to avoid bothering the other.

Such situations are poignant but unnecessary. How often do we hear of "everyone's favorite couple" getting divorced? Common ground is often the

Many versions of the same story

culprit, and the gossip always misses it. The couple with a great sense of humor has a full dance card for restaurant double-dates. Yet, privately, they may have no one to focus the conversation

at serious moments. The prominent power couple, so impressive to others, privately stumbles because neither has much skill in conciliation and compromise.

Such million-heartache misunderstandings abound. Sensitive and artistic, Chloe and Nate are accustomed to trusting their intuitions, so neither wonders about the inevitable misunderstandings every couples has. In the stressfulness of meaningful relationships, occasional misperceptions are unavoidable. If each partner is certain that his or her usual perceptiveness is impeccably reliable, each will live with hurtful distortions of the other's meaning, as the resentment grows.

Sue and Bobby have a common ground that seems to be one of the most prevalent, although this may be because I am similar to them. They are extraordinarily self-reliant. Again, this was an attractive feature to both of them. They are upbeat, independent people, both go-to people for others.

Excessive independence

Neither resents being the centerpiece of the pyramid for others, but each respects finding someone else not wanting to jump on top of the pyramid.

Vulnerability is essential to emotional intimacy. No one else expects or even wants vulnerability from Bobby or Sue, but they need to need each other in order to stay close. Neither one understands this. They are otherwise very different in personality. She is quite an extrovert, and he very much an introvert, but both are lonely in the relationship. As you would expect, they immerse themselves in other interests. The situation brewed that way until it boiled over. They came to see me because of conflict, and it soon became clear they had become addicted to arguing.

This is a common attempt couples make to fill the void left by common ground. *Self-sufficient couples, in particular, become addictively attracted to conflict, as it does not require vulnerability.* When couples are arguing, the rest of the world goes away (see Chapter 12). It is actually like sex that way (as we will see in Part VII). Their entire focus becomes each other.

Of course, the situation is agonizing, and no couple realizes that the excruciating conflict between them could be addictive. In counseling sessions, however, it is easy to demonstrate. Part of my style is to ask both partners to communicate through me most of the time. Couples hooked on fighting cannot do this initially. Each will jump in when the other is speaking, even though they do not plan or want to do so. They both fully understand why I want to speak with one at a time. As they notice themselves unable to comply, I can leverage that awareness to demonstrate that the conflict has become a void-filling addiction.

Often, as with Sue and Bobby, the void of vulnerability is the flipside of admirable self-sufficiency. This form of common ground is so prevalent that I have noticed four versions:

❖ In some couples, no one reaches out with affection.

❖ In others, neither can accept help.

❖ Although both are sounding boards for many other people, each keeps things to him- or herself.

❖ Both show anger but not tears, so neither can de-escalate the argument.

Many couples combine more than one of these. In some cases, it produces heated exchanges; other times the couple has a cold war. Both compete to demonstrate how unaffected they are by what they perceive as the other's lack of caring. Meanwhile, both of their hearts are breaking.

If Sue and Bobby embody a prevalent form of common ground, Lois and Stu's version is more rare, but still emblematic of its pain. Like Deb and Mark, they are both particularly caring people, and Lois and Stu even manage to keep the giving focused on each other. So what is their common ground difficulty?

Recall that every asset is also a liability. In this case, caring people can easily become *caretaking* people. The difference between caring and caretaking hinges on whether the person to be helped is actually working on whatever we want to help him or her accomplish. Otherwise, help can become disabling and/or annoying. In 12-step groups, the term for such disabling help is *enabling*, and the adjective for those providing it is *codependent*.

When enablers marry each other

Lois and Stu are each codependent in their own way. Lois wants to make certain that Stu is in a good mood at all times, and Stu worries about Lois's impulsive choices. Inside the pit of their common codependent ground, he often gets the impression that he has to either agree with her spontaneous choices or convince her to change her mind. Meanwhile, she has the impression that she has to put up with what seems to her as his arbitrary and impatient moods. The sense of pressure to take care of the other only increases their difficulties together. However, she would not feel insulted if he passed on some of her plans, and he enjoys an occasional emotional funk, finding it somewhat relaxing. Neither needs or expects caretaking by the other, but you cannot address a misunderstanding you do not know you are having.

I have saved for our last example what is probably the most common form of common ground. It usually coexists in couples along with the other versions. It may seem trivial when I mention it, yet I have seen several couples completely fall apart by not addressing it. I am referring to nonproblem drinkers.

Of course, drinking alcoholics have problematic relationships, but what about people whose lives have not been made unmanageable by drinking? These couples have heard that a drink or two is actually medically healthy for them, and they follow this advice when they go out together. So if it is not a problem, what is the problem?

The problem with not being an alcoholic

The problem is that light drinkers are more affected by drinking, and if there are any current struggles in the relationship, neither person will know what to do about them when drinking. Even if the couple has been making progress and learning new strategies, they will both usually forget what they have learned, although neither is intoxicated. Having the similarity of no experience with problematic drinking, neither will know to warn each other to watch for the effects of alcohol on attempts to resolve conflict. Making it even more painful, this breakdown occurs just as the couple has gone out or prepared a special meal at home, hoping to have an especially good time together. For this reason, I practically beg couples not to discuss anything serious if they have had anything at all to drink.

Section D: Getting Past this Challenge

As with all pitfalls, awareness itself is halfway to freedom. Rather than blaming your relationship for an inevitable challenge, you can begin to apply your energy toward addressing it creatively.

People are complex, and my delineating these pitfalls, while accurate, may be misleading in a way. In your life, several may tend to merge, sometimes creating a figurative black hole, sucking the life out of your love. As we have noted, similarities leave painful gaps in the mosaic, but couples argue about differences instead. Gender differences and differences in childhood experiences simultaneously fuel those arguments.

Happily, we do not have to decipher which particular elements of our conflicts stem from each of the pitfalls. Rather, in each of the previous two chapters, I showed how to notice each pitfall's effects and how to resolve it. We can proceed the same way with the last, that is, with common ground.

The most simple procedure to unearth your version of common ground returns to the couple tasks I mentioned previously. *Taking another look at them, ask yourself whether either of you are good at them.*

❖ Make decisions.

❖ Reach out for affection.

❖ Both show and accept thoughtful acts.

❖ Look for compromise.

❖ Plan joint activities.

❖ Lighten the atmosphere and play.

❖ Show appreciation.

❖ Initiate communication.

❖ Say no to impulsive choices.

❖ Bring up problems.

❖ Place conflicts on a concrete level for solution.

Some of these are probably difficult for one of you, while the other more easily fills in. Others lack a champion in either of you. These are the gaps in your relationship. *Having identified the common ground, look for the virtuous flipside of each weakness.* I have supplied an example below of positive qualities that can lead to a deficit in the couple task.

❖ Make decisions: Both may be cooperative, accommodating, and/or supportive.

❖ Reach out for affection: Both may be polite, or considerate, and/or emotionally strong.

❖ Both show and accept thoughtful acts: Both may be self-maintaining, efficient, and/or practical.

❖ Look for compromise: Both may be decisive, self-assured, and/or confident.

❖ Plan joint activities: Both may be content, present-focused, and/or agreeable.

❖ Lighten the atmosphere and play: Both may be diligent, dedicated, and/or passionate.

❖ Show appreciation: Both may be industrious, independent, and/or individualistic.

❖ Initiate communication: Both may be self-possessed, pensive, and/or mindful.

❖ Say no to impulsive choices: Both may be spontaneous, playful, and/or easygoing.

❖ Bring up problems: Both may be accepting, patient, and/or trusting.

❖ Place conflicts on a concrete level for solution: Both may be intellectual, intuitive, and/or hopeful.

Any of the listed assets can show up in the relationship as a deficiency in the associated couple task, especially if the other person is the same. In practice, connecting the particular gift to the burden provides a more certain footing as we resolve the common ground pitfall. Not only are the two of you similar in this way, but it simultaneously reflects some of your strengths.

All this preparation has the purpose of preparing you to fill the hole together. Any relationship you might have chosen would have some version of this challenge. Solving the problem requires awareness that neither of you is a natural at this deficiency, and it just does not work to wait for each other. You are not likely to remember to integrate these new behaviors into your life without a plan. Fortunately, the plan can be a simple one.

How do you otherwise remind yourself of things to do or appointments? Some people use lists, others mark paper calendars, and others program their phones. Imagine adding a reminder once or twice a day to take a step toward filling the common ground gap. Sometimes, it is that easy.

You may realize you do not know what such a step would be, but remember: Our premise is that you do not have to be good at it. If you were, it would not comprise a form of common ground.

When you want a new result, it may be time to consult. When you want to enter new territory, find a guide who has already been there, such as a friend. Alternatively, maybe you will consult with each other, such as asking, "When I want to do something thoughtful that would make you happy, what are some things you would enjoy?" Other times, neither of you will feel confident that you have a good clue. In that case, check with someone else who is better at whatever it is. Try asking, "If someone wants to act more playful, what would he do?" Of course, your consultant might suggest you do something outside your comfort zone, such as learning to play by making faces in the mirror. Then again, maybe that is a good idea. As I have mentioned, comfortable equals stuck!

Couples can circumvent the inevitable pitfalls they will encounter on the path toward making a home together. To summarize it succinctly: *Gender differences benefit from translation. The one argument benefits from mutual reassurance. Common ground is helped by each person stretching into the areas of mutual deficiency.*

Thus equipped, you walk on, companions to and for each other. Your home comes into view. Once you arrive, find your way to the kitchen, because you are ready to share a delicious reward. Your journey has freed you to prepare the recipe for a vibrant and resilient love.

PART V

The Gold Medal Recipe

CHAPTER 19

Why You Might Forget this Recipe

This chapter provides the essential formula for an indestructibly vibrant love. It is a very simple recipe. Earlier, I suggested that, *while it is actually impossible to make someone else happy, two people aiming at the same time to do exactly that provide the formula for a terrific relationship.* Two people who are good to each other stay in love — it is that simple. This formula provides the *gold medal recipe* for love.

Yet, as I mentioned in the introduction, *simple* and *easy* are not the same. In this chapter, our question will be less what the recipe is, but rather why we forget to prepare it whenever we enter the kitchen. If it is so simple, why don't we remember to do it?

Actually, it is my fault. Well, not mine alone, but it has a lot to do with my generation, known as the Baby Boomers (because of the rapid expansion in population following the Second World War). As social researcher Daniel Yankelovich explained (1981), the World War II generation's definition of duty was *self-sacrifice*. Baby Boomers replaced this ethic with an obligation to *self-fulfillment*. (For the history of this surprising transition in values, see the sidebar.)

The greatest versus the *me*-ist

The World War II generation has become known as "The Greatest Generation" (following the book of the same name by journalist Tom Brokaw). As explained by Yankelovich, the WWII generation lived and died by an ethic of self-sacrifice.

This moral stream carried them through many trials, as the hardworking children of immigrants, and it considerably strengthened as they tumbled through the Great Depression and the worst of wars. Bathed in this stream since birth, they were often ready, not only to give of themselves, but to give their very lives.

Robert Leckie, a U.S. Marines veteran of the Pacific campaign in World War II, wrote of being challenged to describe what he gained from his foray through hell. He responded (2010, p. 304):

> Now I know. For myself, a memory and the strength of ordeal sustained; for my son, a priceless heritage; for my country, sacrifice. The last is enough for all, for it is sacrifice — the suffering of those who lived, the immolation of those who died.... It is to sacrifice that men go to war. They do not go to kill, they go to be killed, to risk their flesh, to insert their precious persons in the path of destruction.

This generation understood sacrifice intimately. Their relationships largely reflected this ethic, too, imbued with ideals of giving rather than taking. Indeed, if the simple formula for a marvelous love is to combine two givers in the same marriage, most of this generation's marriages should have shown brightly. But these relationships often did not inspire, as their children noticed. Of course, not all of the Greatest Generation followed their generation's ethics, but the problem somehow went deeper than that. To their children, including me, their relationships did not seem particularly close or worthy of emulation. We had our own ideas.

The differences between these two generations were so large as to be coined The Generation Gap, and led to the Baby Boomers becoming termed The Me Generation. The challenge to our elders had been their terrifying hardships, from the Great Depression to the Great War, struggles they met with courage. In contrast, our relatively small challenge consisted of a world of contradictions, which we met first with confusion and later by turning that world upside down.

To the adolescent and 20-something Baby Boomers, the "greatest generation" didn't seem so great. First we became distrustful — then we became angry. Eventually we started seeking a cultural revolution. Our presidents had told us we were on the verge of a New Frontier (JFK) and a Great Society (LBJ), while we were frequently stashed in the hallways of our grade schools in drills preparing for nuclear bomb attacks that promised "mutual assured destruction." We were told that we were the generation to pursue our dreams in the new world that our elders had made safe, and then we received orders to register for the

> draft to fight a very ambivalent war in Southeast Asia, which would prove politically impossible to win. Those under 30 mostly saw the reason for that quagmire in ethical terms, thinking it a "wrong war," while those over 30 mostly saw it as a practical result of a divided country. We also felt encouraged to explore our individual potentials by our parents, but then met with much resistance for the rule-breaking nature of our explorations, as well as our self-indulgence.
>
> My counseling mentor, Tom Sargent, himself a countercultural refugee from a very wealthy manufacturing and banking family, saw the Baby Boomer ethic as an infusion of economically upper-class values into the middle class. The doctrine became one of self-fulfillment. As Yankelovich explained, we replaced the previous duty to self-sacrifice with a duty to fulfill one's own needs.

The Baby Boomers were the first generation to feel guilty if they did not sufficiently pursue self-fulfilling experiences. People were a collection of needs, and if a spouse did not meet enough of these, there was an ethical obligation to end the relationship. (Many years have passed since this generation gap, but I still see occasional self-sacrifice relationships in my office, and I see even more people leaving marriages to fulfill themselves.)

As you may have surmised from the above discussion, the WWII generation was closer than the Baby Boomers to the gold medal recipe of mutual giving. However, their ethic of self-sacrifice prevented their including two essential details: First, one must be able to show emotional vulnerability when one is not capable of wholehearted giving.

Close, but no gold medal

The WWII generation thought the expression of emotions was self-indulgent. Second, one must be able to receive what others give. This detail hits a snag within an ethic of self-sacrifice.

We Baby Boomers were way off the mark. We craved love as *experiences*. As noted in Chapter 2, all the commonly sought-after experiences — including meaning, happiness, love — are only achieved as by-products of living well. When one seeks to find them directly, they rapidly evaporate.

I call this mistake *emotional spectatoring*, a metaphor I adapted from the field of sex therapy. When men are anxious about their sexual performance, they worry they will not achieve or maintain a sufficient erectile response. As a result, during sex, they may engage in spectatoring, in which they keep monitoring their own physical state. Naturally, the result is increased anxiety and decreased attention for mental and physical erotic stimulation. Similarly, *when one seeks love as an experience, the result is another kind of spectatoring, one that similarly robs the potential benefits that one seeks.*

Instead, we have to redirect ourselves toward the mental and physical acts that promote loving. The next chapter begins that process with a story.

CHAPTER 20

Learning the Recipe
by a Story about
Angel Food and Devil's Food

This increasingly popular story has to do with a man who lives a full life, dies, and finds himself in the final, heavenly interview.

The angel smiles at him, saying, "Welcome. We have been expecting you. You have lived a good life, and I can tell you right now that you are heading toward the eternity you have earned."

"Thank you," the man responds. "I had hoped for that, of course."

"There's just one question I want to ask you," the angel continues. "Would you care to take a short look at the fate you avoided?"

"You mean Hell? Oh. Well, I will take a look, if you recommend it."

Heading down a hallway, the man spots a large, thick door. Then he hesitates, because he hears horrific wailing. After some encouragement to proceed, he approaches the door and sees that it has a window. Relieved, he peers through the glass.

At first, he feels astonished by a beautiful scene. Inside is a massive banquet, its tables overflowing with a delicious-looking feast. The hot foods steam, and he can almost smell their fragrances. The cold dishes appear as fresh as if they were prepared only a moment before. All the textures and colors look vibrant and inviting.

Yet, the people appear to be starving. They scream their torment, and he wonders why. Then, he sees it. They are bound to their chairs, and strapped to their arms are utensils much too long to be of any use. Their tearing eyes bulge as they stare at their plates in total desperation.

The man cannot stand the horror and asks to leave. The angel smiles again, offering, "Certainly. I'm sure you would like to see Heaven now, so please follow me."

Eagerly complying, the man accompanies his celestial guide down another hall. Happily, he can hear the contrast immediately. Instead of torment, people are singing and laughing. Relieved, he approaches the end of the hall, finally reaching a golden door. He peers through its window before entering.

Now, he feels astonished once again. Before him is the exact same arrangement. Not only does the food seem identical, but also the people are similarly restrained and bound with those long utensils. Yet, they are all smiling broadly, and their eyes shine warmly. Quickly, he understands: They are all doing what he would do in such a circumstance.

They are feeding each other.

Our fictional Heaven and Hell is exactly like Earth. As I write this, you and I live in a world in which people, every day, must decide how much to grab and how much to offer to others. *The outcome of our choices will be predictable: Our physical pleasures come from taking, and our emotional joys come from giving.* A grabby lifestyle can bring many opportunities for pleasure, but this approach ultimately backfires because of how the brain works.

To experience this, sample several types of cologne. You will have difficulty discerning the latter fragrances, because pleasure desensitizes rapidly. This numbing applies to most sensations. Many have had the experience of gradually increasing the volume of music in an automobile, later finding it too loud upon restarting the car. Even more commonly, we desensitize to the feeling of the clothes on our bodies, shortly after putting them on.

When repeatedly stimulated, the senses protect themselves by dulling. When this diminishes pleasurable feelings, it is called *tolerance*, and leads to needing more of the pleasurable behavior to match the previous effect. The senses also naturally track toward novel stimuli, which adds to the desensitization effect. Later, the brain literally reduces its sensitivity to pleasure (we will explore this process more fully in the Chapter 31).

None of this happens when one leads a balanced life, but a life of taking tends to become a life of addiction, as one seeks hopelessly to regain the initial paroxysm of a preferred pleasure. A life that leans toward giving includes plenty of pleasures, especially if one chooses the company of other givers. *Yet, these delights are just the high notes in an ongoing symphony of shared devotion, written in the key of joyful contribution.*

This is how things work in our world. If the Heaven-Hell story explains how the choice of unrestrained giving plays out, the story in the next chapter explains the psychology of why it works this way.

CHAPTER 21

Becoming the Chef

Imagine you have an uncle who has become a world-renowned chef. One day, he calls you on your phone. You are surprised to hear from him, because, the last you had heard, he was living in Italy. He says he has recently moved to town.

Because of the fortunate turns of his career, he can now live wherever he wants. He goes on to explain that he has not seen much of you during his journeys, but he would like to make it up to you, because you were always special to him. If you would allow him, he would like to come to your place tonight and prepare a fantastic meal for you and your spouse.

After you accept, he tells you that he would like to make your most favorite meal. You tell him your preferred dishes for every course, and he brings all the ingredients and equipment. When he serves it to the two of you, it seems as you have gone to the Heaven of the previous story. Not only is every course your favorite choice, but you have never tasted each dish so well prepared.

As you express your gratitude, he reassures you that it was indeed his pleasure, and he would feel honored to come by every week and repeat the performance. So, every week, that is what he does. At first, it is an amazing repetition of a great night, but after a few months, the novelty wears off. Privately, you rehearse how to suggest that, if he ever wants to make something different, it would be fine.

What is going on? If even your all-time favorite items, prepared perfectly, become tiresome, what chance does a relationship have? After all, had he prepared that same menu every single night, rather than once a week, you would have tired of it even sooner.

But we have not mentioned the most important part of this story. You are bored with his menu, and so is your partner. Who is not?

The chef is not bored, which is why you have to tell him if you want to change the menu. He is having a great time as he cooks up the recipes for you, thinking, "Here is the amount of this herb I bet they'll like.... Maybe I'll add a different wine to that sauce...." The same dish is forever new when prepared with warm feelings and creative attention focused upon the recipient. The best teachers say the same thing about repeatedly teaching the same subjects, but a bit better each time.

This is our take-home message: *Be the chef.* The chef does not tire of the recipe of love. Be the chef in the kitchen, in the living room, in the bedroom, when you reenter your home, when you call each other for a moment during other tasks, and whenever you get a chance to reach out for each other.

This short chapter may also be the most important. Choose to be a chef, but also pick another chef to love. Let her or him cook up a delicious life for you, too. Just as in the previous story about Heaven versus Hell, *feeding each other, you will not have to wait to taste some Heaven at home.*

CHAPTER 22

Can You Really Learn to Cook the Gold Medal Recipe?

Now that you know the recipe, can you really learn it? Can a person who has lived as more of a consumer, at least in romantic relationships, transform into the chef?

We will accomplish this in two ways. In this chapter, I will explain the power of building a new mental pathway and help you establish it. In the next chapter, you will learn a system of simple strategies to stay on track with this delicious recipe.

When you learn something new, what actually happens? In fact it is a physical process, because the conscious mind is a function of the brain.

A neuro-mental journey to love

Neuropsychologists refer to *neural pathways*, which we establish through repetition. This is currently a developing scientific model, so we cannot be certain how literally to take it. Nonetheless, it fits experience perfectly.

When people learn new options, they seem foreign at first. After some time, the new direction becomes familiar and available. If you repeat them and thus strengthen them in your mind, you will weave this new path into your life.

To reach the gold standard, leave work and come home. Your relationship is not a business, and it is not about negotiation. The taking relationship is a

Contribution not negotiation

negotiation about demands. *The loving relationship is a communication about contribution. The bottom line is endless mutual contribution. The rest is commentary.*

A high-quality relationship is about love and connectedness. We have heard that "love makes the world go 'round" so many times that it has sunk into the soporific ditch of a cliché. Look at it again: It is truly what the quality of life is made of. Connection may be the basis of what truly matters in all dimensions of life. In the realm of the intellect, knowledge connects people with the eternal reservoir of learning. In the realm of spirituality, expanded consciousness connects people with a sense of the infinite cosmic ocean. In the realm of love, a giving heart connects people with the endless potential for communing with others.

The word *family* derives from the Latin *familia*, which refers both to those who live in a home together and those who serve the family. Does this refer to a household member or a servant? It is actually the same: A family is the loving connection of those who serve each other.

Similarly, the Hebrew word for love is *ahava*. The middle of the word, *hav*, means *giving*. A giver is a lover. A giving lover lives in love. A home filled with love is a family.

Accordingly, home is the one place that Karl Marx was right. His ideal was "from each according to his ability, to each according to his needs." The functioning family is exactly that.

One night in my office, I was explaining to a couple the magic that happens when two people spend their time aiming to make each other happy.

How and why

The husband looked at me, honestly perplexed. He knew this would be new territory, and asked, "But how do you do that?"

I thought of the happiest couples I knew and considered the glimpse they had allowed me into their attitudes toward each other. "Whenever you are together," I responded, "ask yourself: *If I just wanted to be good to you, what would I do next?*"

You do not have to guess. This is about contribution, not about performance. Say with a smile, "I'd like to do something nice for you right now, but I am not sure what you would like. Give me a hint."

Filling out this picture, marriage counselor and author Gary D. Chapman (2009) writes that a person's most preferred way to receive love will probably fall into one of five categories, or "love languages." In addition, he observes that most people will marry another who speaks a different one of these languages. This result is the need to ask what the other person prefers.

As I often put it, loving attention does not mean the same thing to everyone. For some people, the most meaningful kind of attention is devoting some one-on-one time, what Chapman refers to as "quality time." For some, it consists of thoughtfulness in offering tokens of love, such as cards, flowers, or other gifts, while for others it consists of thoughtful acts of kindness. These may be tasks, projects, or little gestures that help the other person. Sometimes I will explain to a married woman, "You know your husband loves you when he spontaneously clears the snow off your car." Usually, she had not seen it that way. Physical affection is the most precious sign of love for some, and still others look for affectionate and admiring words. Chapman refers to the latter as "words of affirmation."

Most notably, he includes simple and helpful strategies to help discern one's own "language." How, he asks, do you tend to show love yourself? What do you ask for most? Conversely, which of these are you most likely to complain about not getting?

If employed as rote techniques, insights such as these will go flat in time. The essence of relationship recharging is all about the gold standard. It is not about practicing a particular behavior. No one wants to feel managed, but most of us would like to feel loved. Yet, in service of the recipe, the "love languages" can sharpen our skills in the kitchen.

In actuality, most of us would probably enjoy all five of these categories of contribution, so by no means limit yourself to the other person's specialty. In fact, Chapman proposes a profile of preferences, where a secondary language accompanies the favorite one, and so on. As you will recall from our story about the chef, the exact same meal can become a little predictable, so have fun with it and experiment. You can also ask for a hint.

In a relationship where you are working together, your efforts will be noticed and appreciated. There are just a few more details to the gold medal recipe, but truly just a few: one corollary, one motivation, and one backup plan.

The corollary is a detail that the WWII generation could not include because of their ethic of self-sacrifice. *A relationship is more than one person, of course, and therefore we require two givers who are also both receivers.* For the simple recipe to work, the other person must say "yes" and receive the contribution. Either person refusing subsequently ruins the dish. If "What can I do to be good to you?" is the best question, "Thank you" is the preferable answer. For instance, using our last example, if one's partner says, "I'd like to do something nice for you right now, but I am not sure what you would like," the best answer is not, "Thanks, but I'm fine."

As for the motivation, while we might wish it were innate, it often is not. Many of us could benefit from a motivational method to overcome this limitation. Otherwise, we confine ourselves to a lonely space, the results of frequently assessing whether we are getting enough of an emotional high from love. Another emotion fits the bill perfectly to fill that space: gratitude.

Gratitude is the connection between taking and giving. Yet, sometimes it comes too late. Common wisdom is correct that we only realize what we had after it is gone. When eternity takes lovers from each other, the room often fills with a blazing, loving gratitude that could nearly rip one's heart apart. Indeed, the heart does not always survive, and broken heart syndrome is a real and sometimes fatal medical condition.

Losing a beloved person through death feels like an emotional amputation and throws the survivor into a seemingly bottomless chasm of grief. The feelings of suffocating loss are amplified by guilt over the many missed opportunities to cherish the person now gone. Not only those bereaved by death suffer such guilt, but also those who lose their loves to neglect.

After such a break-up, your heart screams out in regret, knowing that the other person was always on your mind but you never said it. Some of the most poignant love songs decry the ache to have just one more chance to show love to someone who has given up on you, because you failed to know what you had.

Often it is the dominant person in the relationship who is left behind. Thinking he or she was on top, all the previous loving felt like an entitlement. The needs of the more compliant member of the relationship seemed so unimportant, until that fully discouraged person walks out. Complacency gone, the neglectful partner now begs for any opportunity to give love to, shower attention on, and hang on to the person who has finally given up.

Whether through the finality of death or the futility of failure, lovers left behind love deepest and cherish most fully the chance they had. They overflow with excruciating but profound gratitude. You do not have to wait for this.

The bottom line is that our years are the most scarce and valuable possessions any of us has to give. When someone gives you his or her years, it is imperative to notice the gift. Yet, as much a gift as it is, the time bestowed upon you is just the beginning of innumerable kindnesses and favors. And, speaking of beginnings, let us move our focus from last moments to first moments. If you are in a long-term relationship, do you remember when you could not believe you had finally found each other?

This is what great loss and great gain have in common: shock. Both joyful beginnings and sorrowful endings are typified by astonishment. In both cases, the event is much too massive to absorb quickly. When it comes to love, the message of such beginnings and endings is the same: We feel grateful beyond measure. But we cannot return to the beginning and no one wants to wait until the end to express such gratefulness. Open your eyes to each other now. If you have someone to love, you are living with a blessing. Upon noticing this, the first response must be "thank you," and the second will be "I want to be good to you."

Shocking love

There you have it. So, why is there more to this chapter? We have a simple formula: *two people aiming to make each other happy.* Protecting the formula, we have a corollary that the two people mutually give and accept the giving. We even have a motivational method, the emotion of gratitude, which simply requires attention to regenerate. So, why do we need a backup plan?

None of us is strong enough to give all the time. Sometimes when we are hurting, our gratitude feels temporarily occluded and our capacity for giving becomes weakened. When we feel barred from contribution by exasperation, sometimes the most loving approach we can manage is to spare someone else the fiercer versions of our emotions.

When life hurts (whether or not the source of the pain has to do with our loving partners), it hits us several ways emotionally. The sense of deprivation creates painful feelings of loss, the attributed cause brings anger, and the worry that it may continue provides fear. All three feelings are primary to human life — even babies have them.

The backup plan: vulnerability

We have a choice which of these, if any, to share. Showing pain or loss is the most accurate expression, because it is the basis of the other feelings, as above. And inside an intimate relationship, vulnerable feelings are the easiest to hear.

Such softer, more vulnerable emotions open up caring attention in the other person. In contrast, anger brings down an impenetrable iron gate. Further, vulnerability inspires vulnerability in return, while displays of anger engender either intimidation in others or angry retorts, sometimes both sequentially. If we do not show vulnerability, our partners are likely to misinterpret the times that we are not able to act loving, and instead think of us as uncaring.

It is worth noting that anger, like all emotions, has a valuable place in our emotional repertoire. In fact, chronic guilt, tears, or depression can all be caused by avoiding anger in oneself. All emotions have their place. I am only suggesting that this place is seldom with someone who loves you deeply, someone who is very sensitive to you and wants to stay that way. *Love has the effect of magnifying all of your responses to each other, whether inviting or forbidding.* In this way, my advice to lead with vulnerability rather than anger does not represent a blanket rejection of a role of anger within a healthy emotional range, but a recognition of what works and what does not in a relationship, especially as a backup strategy for the gold medal recipe.

Vulnerability is relatively easier to achieve than endless giving. Yet, especially during stressful times, it presents a challenge in itself. In fact, without attention to vulnerability, few of us will achieve it.

Vulnerability consists of tears, fears, and tender hopes. When people disclose what breaks their hearts, what frightens them, and what they deeply wish for, they are showing vulnerability. Simple though that sounds, vulnerability can sometimes be elusive to identify. Let us listen in on an argument between Miriam and Ben. Like most couples, their fights follow a repetitive script. In the middle, you can hear them interacting as follows.

With a wrinkled brow and lowered eyes, Ben complains, "You know, I'm feeling very concerned about this. We've gone over it many times, but nothing changes."

Miriam, tears streaming, retorts, "You just hurt me and hurt me, and I can't stand it anymore."

Thereupon, they look at each other, he irritated and she exasperated, as they spar by successively repeating, "This is what I *mean!*" "This is what *I* mean."

Which of them is showing vulnerability? In fact, both Miriam and Ben believe they are doing so, but neither actually is. As different as they are acting, they have something in common: Both are engaging in psychological assessment of the other person.

This is why therapists talk about "I-statements," such as, "When you say 'nothing changes' or that you cannot stand it anymore, I feel afraid, because I want us to be together." The formula for an I-statement is: *When [some observable behavior happens] I feel [an emotion, not an opinion], because I want [preferably some joint interest rather than a demand].* The key, however, is not the technique, but the vulnerability it expresses. *Vulnerability does not appear in various versions of blaming others, but instead is revealed in our own positive and cherished hopes.*

Some people, typically men, hide vulnerability with emotional distance and criticism. When people do this, but think they are expressing vulnerability, they often say, "I'm concerned," rather than a more direct expression of hurt. Other people, most commonly women, hide vulnerability with a different type of criticism. They may be crying, but the words center on blaming the other person. Both varieties mimic vulnerability, even to the point of convincing oneself, but they are actually both passive-aggressive.

If we define vulnerability as tears, fears, and tender hopes, this simplifies the process of knowing it when we see it. Showing vulnerability is quite simple:

❖ Tears, as in, "I'm hurting about this," "I feel like crying," "I'm torn up about it."

❖ Fears, as in, "It terrifies me," "I'm so scared about this," "I feel shaky about it."

❖ Tender hopes, as in, "This is what I wish could happen…" "I so want it to go this way…" "I would love it to be like this..."

Here we see another way that the World War II generation, so close to the gold standard of relationships, were ill-equipped for intimacy, which convinced the Baby Boomers that their parents had it all wrong. Vulnerability requires knowing and sharing your feelings, and the ethic of self-sacrifice suggests the stiff upper lip. In contrast, vulnerability is emotionally brave and honest, because it tells the full truth about our feelings, and it is powerfully useful *because it shows our partners how to come closer even when we are feeling too weak to bring them closer.*

Vulnerability is so important as a backup for the gold medal recipe of mutual giving that it would be valuable to simplify it further. Next, we will consider a straightforward vulnerability strategy as well as a gauge to test if we are on track, rather than falling into the passive-aggressive faux vulnerability that Miriam and Ben were struggling with.

A useful strategy for finding and displaying vulnerability is the request for reassurance. When people weaken in their ability to give, it usually means the inner child, about which I wrote in Chapter 9, is hurting and needs to know he or she is loved and safe. When we do not seek that reassurance, we protect ourselves by displaying the somewhat older *controlling child* we created to lessen the pain of the younger hurting child. The arguments we explored in Chapter 17, in which childhoods collide, consist of the two controlling children fighting with each other. As adults, we can solve the need for reassurance in a better way — by asking for it.

A backup strategy for the backup strategy

In Chapter 12, I wrote about a method to practice new strategies so they will be available during stressful times. I recommend that here as well. Recall past episodes when you did not show vulnerability, which probably lead to misunderstandings, and replay it *once more, with feeling.* Imagine future such incidents, and practice disclosing your feelings.

You may be unsure whether you are achieving vulnerability. Remember Ben and Miriam — they thought they were, too. Accordingly, the next recipe is a vulnerability test. I call it the *jump in a lake* test.

The jump in a lake test

Suppose you make a statement like "I love

you" to someone you care about, and he or she says, "Go jump in a lake!" How much does it hurt? The amount of subsequently imagined pain accurately measures the level of vulnerability shown. If I say, "I love you and I want you," and then I hear "Get lost!" — it hurts a lot. If instead I had said, "I can't stand you" beforehand, the "Get lost!" response does not hurt much at all. It is a surprisingly precise indicator, given its simplicity. Putting it metaphorically, if your arms are open, then a kick to the middle will hurt a lot more — but if your arms are always closed, you never get hugged.

Renowned psychiatrist and rabbi Abraham Twerski has said that the secret to a successful marriage is learning how to say "Thank you," "I admire you," and "I'm sorry." What these all have in common is the vulnerability of sincere acknowledgment: I feel gratitude toward you, I look up to you in certain ways, and you deserve better than some of my treatment of you.

Such vulnerable acknowledgment opens people up to deepening their capacity to contribute to a loving relationship. In Chapter 5, when we spoke about the tendency for most people to look like givers during the beginning of a relationship, we specified the criterion of endeavoring to find out what the other person would actually like. The need for similar openness came up again in Chapter 18, when we learned about utilizing the other person as a *consultant* to learn what makes them happy. That focus continues here. Being a giver means learning what constitutes giving for the other person, which in turn requires the vulnerability to admit that, many times, we all miss the mark.

In this way, *an essential element of the gold medal recipe is the capacity to grow.* Living things are always either growing or dying, and this includes the love in your life with the love of your life. You can learn to be the chef, and then learn to be a better chef. Not only can you learn what vulnerability is, but you also can become less afraid of it.

Part of overcoming the fear of vulnerability is accepting the apprehension about getting hurt by opening our arms wider. Most of us have had the experience of regretting showing our feelings in unsafe situations, with people who took advantage of our trust.

Vulnerability phobia

People who have learned, especially as children, to fear the painful consequences of misplaced vulnerability will hold back emotionally, as if it will protect them. They may believe it is too difficult to overcome this fear.

There is a shortcut, however: Rather than trying to learn to be vulnerable, the quickest path to vulnerability is understanding it is too late to avoid it. *If you love your partner, you are already in much too deep to protect yourself.* You truly have nothing to lose. You are already highly vulnerable to the other person. That horse is already out of the stable. Now is the time to just admit it, let it be true, and learn to enjoy it.

As you both internalize this redemptive reality — the indisputable fact of your inherent vulnerability to each other — it transforms the conversation. We are very gentle, and we know that we have to be, when we are mindfully with people who love us. We hate to hurt such people. We hear that "you always hurt the one you love," but mostly when we do not really believe the other person cares as much as we do. Keeping in mind your partner's vulnerability toward you in turn inspires your showing the same emotional openness. Knowing that you are already vulnerable eases the process.

To overcome the anxiety of showing vulnerability, I have suggested three strategies:

❖ For motivation, apply the above *already-are* factor.

❖ For confidence, keep in mind the vulnerability of your partner to you.

❖ For readiness, aim for a 5-out-of-10 level of anxiety, as below.

People will seldom voluntarily subject themselves to a level 10 anxiety (on a scale of 1 to 10). However, with a purpose, most of us will allow a level 4 or 5. For example, showing increased vulnerability when someone is in a more placid mood is less emotionally risky than starting when someone else is agitated. Another example of a lower risk vulnerability exposure arises when you share openly about your days.

Therapists sometimes term such open sharing *self-disclosure*, though I often refer to this kind of conversation as the difference between the news and the weather. It does not take much vulnerability to share "news" events from one's day. Even if it was not an easy day, complaining does not require vulnerability. We can easily do this even with strangers. The more vulnerable sharing about "weather" refers to how it felt — how our day affected us, the victories, the disappointments, our moods, and other moments that influenced how much our work matters to us. For more on conversational vulnerability, see the sidebar. Perhaps no one else you know cares as much about your daily experience as your loving partner, because this other person cares about you. And if this person lives with you, he or she is personally affected by it. Say it like it matters to you, because it does. *Say it as if it matters to the other person, and it will.*

In order to experience the intimacy-enhancing effects of conversational vulnerability, imagine the following scenario. You receive a phone call from an old friend, someone you have not seen for a long time. Depending on your age, "a long time" might be two years or 20. This person is in town and suggests getting together for lunch, and you readily agree. After this lunch, when you speak of it, you may say, "You know, it was like we picked up where we left off, like it was just yesterday when we last saw each other." Alternatively, you might say, "I don't know if one of us changed or both of us did, but we really had little to say to each other." What determines the difference between these two reactions? It is not about whether you hugged hello. Whether you did or did not embrace, you may still have had either reaction. Neither do the actual words spoken determine whether you think you had little or much to say to each other. Rather, it has to do with the openness of the sharing. If your old friend describes a perfect life, ready for mass-publication, you may have offered congratulations but wanted to get out the door. On the other hand, if you heard about the whole picture, both the successful quests and the disappointments, you know you are still in this person's intimate circle. The fewer the people you would both tell these confidences, the closer you are. We call such an inner-circle person a confidant. In a marriage, the most inner of circles can be a circle of two.

Now you have the full recipe for reaching the gold standard in a long-term relationship: a lot of unreserved and mutual giving, an ongoing conversation about contribution versus negotiation, and a backup position of vulnerability for the times you are just not strong enough. Yet, we have left out an important question: What about the beginning of a potential relationship, when you start dating? This person may end up becoming the love of your life, or you may not even get to know each other. At what point does it make sense to begin cooking up the gold medal recipe dish?

The difficulty in conducting a new relationship is that it is tentative, which can be self-fulfilling. Two people meet, both looking for a relationship based upon contribution not negotiation, but they are both naturally in the fifth chapter's evaluation mode. *Conduct it the way you would like it to be if you both ended up together, according to gold standard guidelines.*

This way, while being aware you are in the evaluation mode, you both model the kind and nurturing interest that would intensify in a full relationship. If you play it safe and reserve or refuse vulnerability, you don't find out what's possible. Instead, model the possible future with the other person. The right person will recognize you as a giver, and the wrong person will show that by not reciprocating in kind. This is not *leading the other person on*, as long you are both clear that this is the evaluation period. *Begin the relationship on the right foot, so if you get beyond the evaluation mode, you are accustomed to acting mutually giving.*

From the very start, right through the move into commitment, and all the way into forever, make your love into a self-renewing resource, based upon the gold medal recipe:

❖ one endless conversation

❖ three parts giving — morning, noon, and night

❖ two-part faith in each other

❖ and a whole lot of showing up loving in each other's lives

The potential to love like this exists in each of us. Nothing can destroy it.

Simple formula

This book does not have to provide the potential to love, because it comes with the original equipment. Instead, we can point to it, as a poem does.

I care for you; you care for me.

I look out for you; you look out for me.

I treasure you; you treasure me.

I rely on you; you rely on me.

I talk true to you; you talk true to me.

I protect you; you protect me.

I respect you; you respect me.

I comfort you; you comfort me.

I listen to you; you listen to me.

I hold you; you hold me.

I laugh with you; you laugh with me.

I heal you; you heal me.

I look within you; you look within me.

I soothe you; you soothe me.

I teach you; you teach me.

I reassure you; you reassure me.

I long for you; you long for me.

I love you; you love me.

Such mutual giving is a straightforward formula for an indestructible relationship. It is also the *sine qua non* (literally: "without which — nothing"), the essential ingredient of romantic love. Any other recipe leaves you hungry. Fortunately, the gold medal option remains available to the two of you as long as you are still together.

With so much at stake, we could make good use of guidelines to determine whether we are each on track on our mission of unreserved loving. The next chapter provides this gauge.

PART VI

Freshness and Preservation

CHAPTER 23

Do Communication
Strategies Work?

This chapter is about communication strategies. How could our recipe be complete without them? Indeed, they are the best methods I have found throughout my training, after 10 years of training others, and over 35 more years of experience in my office, during which I learned from my clients' results. I should also tell you that such techniques usually do not work well.

First, let's understand the problem: The limitation of communication strategies is that they can be (and often are) easily subverted. Any form of communication can become argument fodder.

Imagine a simple, straightforward response to a request such as, "Yes, you can borrow my pen." This seems to be a friendly, positive statement. Now, watch what emphasizing some of the individual words does to its meaning:

Yes, *you* can borrow my pen. (Don't give it away!)

Yes, you can *borrow* my pen. (Make sure you give it back!)

Yes, you can borrow *my* pen. (You wouldn't give me yours!)

Yes, you can borrow my *pen*. (Don't ask for anything else!)

With such richly passive-aggressive potential, even such a short statement of agreement can become ruined with as small an error as the wrong inflection on a single word. Can you imagine the destructive possibilities with complex statements, such as communication strategies? Research has shown that communication techniques can be somewhat beneficial, but they are rather limited in their benefits. As often as not, people will sabotage them when feeling upset.

So why do we have this series of strategies for improving communication? What possible use can we have for them? After all, our goal together has been to make relationships simpler. Instead, such techniques seem tricky to apply.

What's the point?

As it turns out, communication strategies can be simple and highly useful, but not best applied as formulas for improved communication. Rather, *they are marvelous as both guides and gauges for whether or not we are on track in applying the gold medal recipe.*

As a gauge, communication strategies provide a self-check. I can tell myself, "If I am living and loving according to the recipe of mutual giving, these are the kinds of things I will be doing." As a guide, the same techniques give me a clue about how to get back on track, if I have veered away from my loving objective.

Love gauges

Use the suggestions below as a kind of checklist. They will allow you to assess quickly the state of your love today. Happily, every day is a new choice and a new chance.

Here is how communication strategies can fit within the gold medal recipe:

❖ The gold medal recipe sustains love in a relationship. This is what works.

❖ When techniques work, it is because they alert lovers back to this gold standard.

❖ In this way, love is like all the desirable states that are by-products or side-effects of taking the best approach, which in this case is the gold medal recipe.

❖ Our strategies will help us gauge if we are on track or guide us back, when necessary, to the most loving attitude.

Now, equipped with the right perspective on applying them, we can explore communication strategies in the next six chapters.

CHAPTER 24

How People Ruin the Dish

If the recipe for a lasting love is the attitude of mutual contribution, is there a similar recipe for reliably destroying a relationship? Evidently, such a simple formula also exists. According to psychological researcher John Gottman (1994), he was able to predict with 90 percent certainty those marriages destined to fail by scanning for the presence of this marriage-killing feature in new, loving couples. He surveyed these couples' conflict style and reported that he could locate this poison well before it destroyed their affections.

The insecticide of the love-bug is an emotional state that we call contempt. It consists of the common desire to look down on others when we disagree with them. If indulged, it engenders the same scorn in return, and our celebration of love becomes rained out.

Howard Markman's (1994) research showed that contempt is a tragedy in four acts. He identified four behaviors (he called them "the four horsemen of the apocalypse"), which express and extend the spidery hold of contempt inside a relationship.

His terms are:

❖ *escalation*

❖ *invalidation*

❖ *withdrawal*

❖ *negative interpretation*

Escalation makes small items into large, global conflicts, with the help of words like *always* and *never*. In its emotional expression, escalation ratchets up the upset, well beyond what the subject would seem to merit. The second horseman, invalidation, verbalizes contempt with screwed up facial expressions and words like, "How could you possibly say that?" As the third relationship destroyer, withdrawal turns the fight into a spiteful cold war, building a mutually punishing wall of emotional isolation. Finally, negative interpretation consists of taking ambiguous statements, found plentifully (especially in unedited, stressful communications), and hearing them in the most uncaring and hurtful ways.

As these four actions both show contempt and encourage it in others, it is not surprising that Markman also reported he could predict future relationship demise under the lash of these four horsemen. Yet, everyone I know has jumped on these destructive rides from time to time. Just as I previously described the pitfalls as "unfortunately normal," these are also. No psychological pathology is necessary for cancerous contempt and its four expressions. Similarly, no personality flaws are required for the pitfalls I described, which all supply the motivation to take the ride toward contempt. Further, these horses start at a trot and end up galloping. This is why most of the couples you know are not happy.

To address this, Gottman and Markman do more than warn us about the methods of mutually assured destruction. They also provide their own formulas for reversing these contempt-laden bullets before they can hemorrhage all the love out of a relationship. Nevertheless, if employed as techniques, they would be demonstrably helpful but still limited in their effectiveness.

Yet, *as guidelines to assess the habits of loving, such strategies can serve us.* It is from this perspective that we will review my favorite love-gauging tools. Many of them were taught to me by my clients, as I watched how they best expressed heartfelt affection. I also noticed that, by acting these ways, they usually inspired similar kindnesses in return from their partners. Every couples session has been an opportunity for me to fine-tune them and experiment with variations.

CHAPTER 25

Assessing Your Daily Diet of Love

All the guidelines in Part VI comprise a resource of suggestions for how to actualize an attitude of unreserved giving, in the context of everything life throws at both of you. Some of life's stress-casting will hook the two of you into conflict, and other days will sink you both under the waters of boredom. In the discussion of evaluation strategies, I mentioned that getting along during such low stress is one of the unanticipated challenges in marriages.

We read and hear lots about managing arguments in a marriage, but relatively little about routine days. One exception to this disparity is the advice on how to spice up a humdrum sex life, as if a couple who is bored with each other emotionally will sustainably respond sexually.

Instead, you can assess your daily diet of love by applying the following guidelines:

❖ The One Question: If I just wanted to be good to you, what would I do next?

❖ Some examples are:

- assistance in his or her missions in life

- affection

- learning what makes him or her feel loved and happy and doing it

❖ Active Listening: If I wanted to be 100 percent certain that I understood you, what would I do next?

❖ Vulnerability: When I am hurting too much to contribute in either of the above ways, what can I share instead?

- tears or words that speak of pain without blame

- fears of getting hurt

- tender hopes — what I would most want to happen

The guidelines above take the recipe (If I just wanted to be good to you…)

and provide some more specifics. For example, even when couples are both busy, so they literally pass in the night like two ships, they can insert brief and stolen seconds of loving. These moments may be squeezed in, and yet be precious moments of squeezing each other. Similarly, thoughtfulness goes a long way, but even further when two people notice what the other really likes. There is also nothing wrong with using a smartphone (or the counterpart device of the future) to remind you what these thoughtful things are and to do them. Remember that all five "love languages" send delightful messages. Finally, nothing warms a person's heart more than finding ways to pitch in with help for that person's missions in life. I know it well — my wife is my First Editor and Encourager-in-Chief for my writing projects, which is the legacy I want to contribute to others.

The next item on the list guides you toward effective listening, which is a huge gift in itself. One can get free advice at any Dunkin' Donuts, but some people originally come to see me just to experience someone else really listening to them. At the same time, of all the communication strategies that do not work well as techniques, listening is probably top on the list. Formulaic listening comes across as techniquey. Instead, *one can achieve instant high-quality listening simply by the intention not only to understand, but also to make absolutely certain, as if your life depended on it, that you understand the other person.* If that were your goal, you would naturally paraphrase to check out your understanding or perhaps ask questions to clarify the other person's meaning. *Offering this level of listening is love-making.*

Other than the spontaneous results of making 100 percent sure that you understand someone, there is not a specifically recommended technique for quality listening. However, there is a kind of method. Actually, I mean *method* in the sense of the Method School of acting. In this approach, the actors write notes along the margins of the script about related experiences from their own lives. As they say the scripted lines, they are reliving parallel emotions from their counterpart incidents in the margins. During listening, one has neither a script nor margins, but often does have comparable experiences to access. This does not mean you will know exactly how someone else feels, and it does not take your attention away from the other person's words any more than the actor forgets the script's lines. *You are just feeling your version of what you felt, at the times during which you went through the most similar events that come to mind.* Your emotional state is not identical with your mate's, but becomes naturally and noticeably congruent.

The last guideline reminds us about the *vulnerability backup* described in Chapter 22. This is the best place to go when the previous two items, the one question and active listening, become too difficult because of emotional distress.

These items can be a checklist for the gold standard of love. If you are wondering if you have been contributing toward your relationship today, scan down the items and gauge your gift. Another contribution you can make to your partner and your romantic partnership is to vaccinate the relationship to lessen the frequency of misunderstandings and conflict, and we turn to these guidelines in the next chapter.

CHAPTER 26

Preventing Indigestion — Strategies for Argument Protection

I once heard (from Tom Sargent) that there are two ways to relate to another person completely conflict-free. The first is for one person to stay in the role of a nurturing parent and the other to stay in the role of a helpless child. The other way is to be side by side in a grave.

Otherwise, living together includes some times of conflict. An occasional argument does not have to be cause for despair, but neither is it cause for celebration. The mutual-giving recipe is the best relationship nutrition to minimize the time spent in conflict, and the guidelines below provide a checklist on whether you are bringing its benefits home.

One of the ways the gold standard limits the frequency of arguments is that it gives us somewhere better to go. In many relationships, verbal fights fill emotional voids. Indeed, when couples successfully interrupt an argumentative pattern and return to my office, they often look relieved but a bit lost. If the simple formula for a vibrant, resilient love is mutual giving, then we could also say that the formula for conflict resistance is becoming too busy loving to interrupt it with an argument.

Three self-checks for the conflict-preventing aspects of the gold medal recipe are:

❖ expressing appreciation

❖ offering reassurance

❖ checking out understanding

Expressing appreciation is not only simple but easy. *The person you love is good to you, and you notice it to the point of mentioning it.* Chapman (2009) calls it "words of affirmation." Even if this is not your partner's main way to receive love, I recommend it for everyone. As obvious as this sounds, it can be easily forgotten. Couples tend to have domains of responsibility. For example, for some couples, the husband takes care of the yard and the wife takes charge indoors. For others, one person does the cooking and one does the cleanup. If such a pattern becomes habitual, the other person's efforts may become just part of the background of life. This guideline will correct that by reminding you to notice. If the words come to you, specify

Thank you

what you notice about other person's efforts and achievements. If not, saying something like, "Thank you very much for that," conveys appreciation too.

The next conflict-prevention behavior takes a little more practice, because most of us are more accustomed to showing gratitude than to anticipating misunderstandings. Nonetheless, it is useful beyond imagining. In fact, in counseling sessions, it comprises a lot of how I fill in for couples to help them increase their trust of each other. *Offering reassurance means, when possible, anticipating how ambiguous statements could be heard more negatively than we mean them.*

A little reassurance goes a long way

Examples of such reassuring statements include: "I have a different idea about this, but I'm very receptive to your point of view about it too." Or, "I'm feeling tired and a bit tense, so please don't think I'm disinterested in what you're saying. I'm just not at my best." Or, "I'm not thinking that you should have known what I wanted, because I didn't tell you. I just know that you care and would want to know."

Whenever you are able to anticipate the value of a reassuring statement, use it. But, what about the other times? We need a backup plan for misunderstandings, and fortunately, the next strategy corrects for this. Listeners know when they feel insulted. Rather than offending the other person in return, a gold standard response is to prompt the other person to offer the reassurance the listener needs.

The way I render this communication technique is, "When it doubt, check it out." *The checking-it-out strategy is based on our loving recipe, which includes a healthy infusion of what we call the benefit of the doubt.* One can contrast the benefit of the doubt with the destructive alternative, which I call *condemnation in doubt.*

When in doubt, check it out

How does one navigate from feeling offended to asking for reassurance? The compass is provided by remembering all the contributions this person has made to your life, after which you can ride there by considering the context. Maybe your behavior is affecting what you are receiving in return. Better yet, maybe the other person does not mean at all what you think.

The most effective, but more challenging, version of checking out someone else's meaning is wishful hearing:

❖ First, notice that you are starting to feel some offense.

❖ Second, remember that you can trust this person to care about you and not hurt you intentionally.

❖ Third, ask yourself what is the most positive way you could possibly take what you heard.

❖ Finally, ask the other person if that is what he or she meant.

One example of such wishful hearing would be, "When you said you hope we have fun tonight, you meant because you are feeling stressed from the day, right?" (as opposed to because I am not fun!)

Sometimes, it is too late in the ascendance of stress for wishful hearing, and one is already feeling too hurt and vulnerable to supply the confidence that strategy requires. At such times, a more accessible but still effective version of checking-it-out consists of ruling out the negative:

❖ First, notice that you are feeling uncomfortable and offended.

❖ Second, ask yourself what you would mean if you just did or said what the other person did.

❖ Keeping in mind that you did not pick someone with the same personality and childhood history that you have, consider that it may not mean the same thing.

❖ Ask the other person if she or he actually meant what you inferred, or something else.

❖ Last, believe his or her response.

The last step is quite important for a successful outcome. Sometimes, you may feel certain the person's meaning was truly negative, exactly the way you first heard it. You may even be correct. Sometimes, just hearing the negative meaning mirrored back can prompt the other person to reconsider and no longer mean what they originally meant. What is wrong with that? Just as I suggest you give the other person the benefit of the doubt, rather than condemnation in doubt, *the very act of checking out someone else's meaning can remind the other person to also give you the benefit of the doubt.* In such a case, the meaning has now changed, which means you both win.

An example of ruling out the negative would be, "When you said you hope we have fun tonight, it's not because I am boring, right?" If I am feeling even less confident at the time, a related question could be asked: "When you said you hope we have fun tonight, did you mean that I have been boring recently?"

In these ways, you can find a version of checking out meaning to fit whatever the state of your confidence or vulnerability at any moment. In each case, you are alerting the other person that this is a good time to offer some reassurance.

CHAPTER 27

Curing Indigestion — Strategies for Resolving Conflicts

When a couple is loving each other consistent with the gold medal recipe, one might wonder why conflicts are inevitable. Indeed, a mutually loving relationship can dissolve many potential conflicts before they even arise.

Specifically, there is a difference between giving to and giving in. *If my intent is to make you happy, and you have a strong preference in a certain direction while I have a mild preference in a different direction, I can happily assent to whatever you want.* Suppose you want to see a particular museum exhibition, which happens to interest me less. On my own, I would not go, because my limited interest would be outweighed by the details of travel, parking, and tickets. Still, perhaps the thought of going is not a miserable one for me, and you are excited about it. Saying yes to you is consistent with the kind of relationship we are creating together every day.

As you might expect, we will have other situations in which we both have strong and contrasting preferences. In such cases, the solution is more challenging to find, and just giving in might bring resentment, especially if it becomes habitual. Later, in Chapter 29, we will consider the love-toxic effects of such excessive resentments.

Of course, we can look for a compromise, and this might help, depending upon what kind of compromise. If you want a hot dog and I want a slice of pizza, we could both skip lunch and both be hungry. Silly though this sounds, it is not unusual for couples to settle for compromises that make neither of them happy, because they cannot untie knotty conflicts.

The kind of compromise that works better is the search for satisfying alternatives, so we look for a solution that supplies both of us the most important aspects of what we want. For example, we get the hot dog and pizza to go, and eat lunch together at the park.

When intimacy is the objective, winning is not the goal, unless it is a win-win. Recall that the tone of a loving relationship is not centered on terms and negotiations. Instead, we are aiming for a conversation about *contribution*. Still, the more successfully we love, the more surprised we may feel when conflict arises. The contrast can be painful.

This is something I witness in couple counseling. Renewed conflicts between appointments become more painful as a relationship improves. You cannot fall out of bed if you sleep on the floor. I frequently mention this emotional danger of improvement in a relationship in order to help prevent discouragement.

Part of the discouragement is the sense that *we are back to square one*, especially if the conflict escalates into an old-time argument. Indeed, if we keep in mind the premise that each couple has

How to make
conflicts worse

only one argument, it could hardly be otherwise. Whenever couples return to the argument, it will be the same one, the identical *square one*. Accordingly, if one were compiling a list of methods for escalating conflicts into arguments, *the first item on the destructive list would be to believe that renewed conflicts mean the relationship is unusually bad, if not hopeless.*

The second way to guarantee too many arguments is to label the differences of opinion as trivial, picky, or just nonsense. Couples often express embarrassment at the triviality of some of the items that hang them up. I suppose there are inconsequential conflicts, but those are usually about situations one does not care strongly about. When strong preferences contrast, no matter what the item, it is important to deal with it in order to not build resentment over time. Further, relatively trivial items can be a great place to start practicing conflict resolution, because less important items are relatively less stressful.

The third method for providing frustration when airing differences is to make a case. It seems that, during conflicts, everyone turns into an amateur attorney delivering a legal argument. Even lawyers turn into amateur versions of themselves. People are afraid to seem selfish by simply stating, "This is important to me." Bare requests seem naked and unadorned to us.

Instead, we make a logical case for why we are right to want what we want. This is very dangerous. The better the case I make for why I should get what I want, the more stupid you will feel for not having done it already. So, what do you do in response? You make a case explaining why I am wrong about my case! And the better job you do, the worse I feel. During all this case-making, *neither of us gets to talk about our wishes, just our reasons for having the wishes.* The frustration grows, and we settle for being right, which is essentially the booby prize in life. This leads us to the next rule.

The fourth method for extending conflicts is to obey the law of being right. It goes like this: During a conflict, one person must be right and the other person must be wrong. After the conflict escalates into an argument and eventually ends, when you regret how you treated each other, it is allowable to both be wrong, expressed with "I'm sorry" and "Me too." However, *you are never allowed to both be right.* Of course, as you would prefer to lessen conflicts rather than increase them, it would be better to violate all these *conflict extension rules.* Instead, I have a better set of methods:

❖ Tell the good news first.

❖ Say *and* instead of *but,* leading into a request or an offer.

❖ Don't say *no.*

The guidelines for quickly resolving conflicts start with the opposite premise of the conflict extension rules. It is not only possible, but likely, that

Rapid and satisfying conflict resolution

you are both right. You both have valid concerns and wishes, and the job is to find an alternative that combines them.

For example, Aesop's grasshopper and the ant both had a point. If one of you is campaigning for long-term savings while the other is pointing out the need to enjoy life in the present, you are both correct. If one of you is promoting a chore checklist while the other wants to walk along a river, you have the potential to balance each other. During unresolved conflict, our differences polarize us into extreme versions of our positions, while resolving conflict allows us to complement each other. The potential to resolve conflicts proceeds from the insight that someone worth loving is worth listening to and learning from.

Accordingly, *when resolving conflict, I suggest that you each tell the good news first.* Specify your area of agreement before exploring where you differ.

The power of accurate agreement

Note that this goes further than the listening strategy mentioned previously. Even the most effective listening can seem passive-aggressive during conflicts, as if you are underscoring your disagreement, in effect saying, "I understand what you're saying , but it's wrong."

We can do better by telling the good news first. *Beyond only hearing, offer agreement where accurate.* This approach resolves many conflicts immediately, because both points of view are often valid, really flip sides of the same coin: Yes, Mr. Grasshopper, bopping around the field is a great idea. After all, who knows if we will still be able to bop tomorrow? Yes, Mr. Ant, preparing for the future is a great idea. After all, if we live to see the future, we want to be able to enjoy it.

So, *agree where you can, and only where you can accurately do so.* This is a great start, but causes a dilemma: You now have to construct a bridge to your own point of view, a perspective that you are not sure is being heard or understood. To accomplish this, you will need a conjunction.

The most natural conjunction to supply at this moment is *but*. It is also probably the most grammatical word in the context, as if you are saying, "I agree with these parts of your outlook, BUT here is where I disagree." *The problem with the word but in this situation is that it has the psychological effect of wiping out the power of what came before.* Psychologically, it comes across as saying, "I agree a little, but really I don't." The simple solution, though it will feel awkward at first, is to *substitute the word* and *for* but. This links the two messages as equivalent, indicating, "I agree with you, AND I have something to add."

And no buts

Once you have gotten past the conjunction *and*, the gold-standard challenge becomes *stating your perspective as a contribution rather than a negotiation.* Phrasing your response as a request is much better than making a demand, while making a helpful offer is the best way to express it. The sweet tone you are looking for is one of, "I agree with what you think is important, and I'd like to offer a way I think it could work even better." Sometimes, fine-tuning the other person's idea may be better ("Could we go to the beach early and leave early, to avoid the traffic?"). Or search for a way to make you both happy at once ("How about we go to the movie you want and then go to the dessert place I like?"). Because you care a lot about each other, both of your happiness is guaranteed to be a mutual goal.

Requesting and offering

If you do not yet have a creative solution in mind, suggest searching for one together. Using the spending example, you might say, "I'm not certain how to do this yet — maybe we can look for a balance where we save significantly and budget some discretionary money for us to play too."

Following the guideline that a request is better than a case and an offer is a better way to convey a request, this is a good time to mention apologies. When conflicts arise, our moods so naturally tend to flare into anger or sarcasm. At such a moment, it feels so vulnerable to admit mistakes. Wait, isn't vulnerability the protective backup of the gold medal recipe?

Before you offer any other solution, the first offering can be, "I'm sorry." Just as appreciation is most powerful when made specific, so is an apology. "I yelled at you before I heard you out," might be one of these, if you are like me. To take another from my own apology history, "I'm sorry. I forgot to give you the benefit of the doubt," is good to admit, when it is true.

The third guideline for quickly resolving conflicts, after telling the good news first and offering to find an alternative, is to avoid the word no. While saying *no* is an important skill to have in life, it works less well in intimate relationships. I call this *no no's*. You are sensitive to each other and want to stay that way. With the help of the above alternative search, it is seldom necessary just to turn the other person down. To anticipate Part VII, about sex, suppose it is just not the right time for one of you, when the other person comes calling. "Thanks, but no," is a painful response to hear. A more encouraging alternative would be, "That's a great idea. I'd like to take you up on it after I'm just a little more rested."

Just say no to no.

Telling the good news first, contributing helpful alternatives, and avoiding saying a flat *no* are guidelines that express how the wish to make each other happy helps resolve conflicts. Even so, now and then we will blow it and need to be ready for that as well. Next, we will see how.

CHAPTER 28

Putting Out Kitchen Fires — Strategies for Fair Fighting

Conflicting desires are a necessary part of any relationship, at least occasionally. While arguments are not theoretically necessary, they are not completely avoidable. Most couples experience them, either a fighting version or a cold war version, also known as the silent treatment. Frequently, one partner fights hot and one fights cold, and this combination can produce the largest conflagrations, as the emoting partner keeps raising the ante in order to finally provoke a hot response from the silent partner.

As you recall from Chapter 17 about conflict, anyone born under the age of 21 will have some leftover hot buttons. We sometimes bump into them and trigger upset in each other without knowing it, until we notice the heat and smoke. Some couples can even become addicted to such arguments because of the intensity of the attention. When you are angry with someone, he or she becomes your whole world.

Gold standard loving provides a better way to live, with both parties knowing they are at the center of each other's worlds, so they do not require fights to prove it. Because arguments are mostly silly, one way of interrupting them is to change them. *As rigid patterns, they will tend to self-destruct if toyed with.* A simple version of this is to reschedule the argument. Make an advance agreement that either of you can table an argument until later. Set an actual appointment to continue the fight. When you both appear for the argument, sometimes you will agree to cancel it. Other times, watching yourselves pumping up the anger intentionally will laugh you out of the fight.

Do play with fire

Another way to fiddle with a quarrel consists of breaking the argumentative rigidity by altering the pattern. As my counseling teacher, Tom Sargent, would tell his clients, *"Don't try to do it right; just do it different!"* He told the story of a client who followed these instructions by walking out on the argument and into the kitchen, followed by her partner. Reaching the refrigerator, he took out a bottle of seltzer and poured it on his own head. That ended the fight in a funny, if drenched, manner.

He told another story about a woman who followed his advice by simply staying silent, which was not her usual pattern. She told him how it went:

You know how you always say an argument is like a script? Well, it went like a play! If one person misses her line, the other person repeats her cue. So, he yelled, "I SAID, YOU ALWAYS [this] AND YOU NEVER [that]."

I still didn't say anything. Well, in a play, if someone still doesn't say her lines, what do you do? You fill in for her. So, he continues the fight without me. He goes, "I BET YOU'RE THINKING THAT I ALWAYS [this] AND NEVER [that], BUT ACTUALLY YOU ALWAYS…" And, he just went on without me. I started laughing and told him what happened, and then we both started laughing.

A different way to tinker with troublesome squabbles is by simply speeding them up. The biggest problem with nonviolent arguments is the amount of time they rob from life and loving. They sap precious leisure time, not to mention putting us in a bad mood at work. So, getting done with an argument has crucial advantages. Better yet, *intentionally and quickly moving through the sequence of your own script sheds both insight and humor on the situation.*

As arguments are repetitive, it is a simple matter to agree on the sequence, at least eventually. You are looking for the progression of scenes in the script, rather than all the lines. Because patterns tend to run in circles (we call them *vicious* cycles), you will both have the impression the other person starts it. To deal with this, it is helpful to agree that the starting place is arbitrary and does not attribute blame. It is even more helpful to exaggerate the behaviors and make them as ridiculous as possible. For instance, one couple's exaggerated and accelerated argument might proceed as follows:

"Everything that goes wrong between us is your fault because you don't care!"

"You always make everything my fault! It is never my fault and always your fault, because you like to start trouble."

"I do not have to accept this treatment!"

"Don't let the door hit you…."

[Both of them now storm out of the room.]

[Next, they walk past each other and ignore each other.]

[Then, they sit in two different rooms for 30 seconds, after which one of them stomps into the other's room.]

"Why do you want it like this?"

"I don't"

"I miss you."

"Me too."

[hug]

Thus ends the G-rated part of the sequence. Actually, some couples do have a repetitive pattern of make-up sex, which immeasurably adds to the addictive qualities of arguing. Once they realize this, most are willing to find another form of foreplay, because the pain is not really worth the pleasure.

Just as couples can record their fight sequence to speed it up and get past it, they can also write an argument solution sequence. The essence of the anti-argument notebook is to write down potent forms of reassurance that help a couple escape the pit they fall into when their childhoods collide.

All of these argument-enders are effective and often even fun, if we do them. Yet, we will not always be in the mood to have fun with it. Sometimes, the argument will take off before anyone thinks to end it, and we have to be prepared for that contingency, too.

With the help of three fair-fighting rules, we can prevent occasional arguments from hemorrhaging the love from your relationship. Keep in mind

Fair-fighting rules

that preventing an argument from doing much harm does not mean the argument is doing any good. On the contrary, it is best not to try to solve any conflict during an argument. In reality, *you usually cannot argue and resolve something at the same time.*

Basically, an argument is a venting experience, which at best is confined to that purpose. The fair-fighting rules guarantee this by preventing dirty fighting. The list below proceeds in the order of increasing pain, so each mistake is more inadvisable than the previous one.

❖ *Do not change the subject.* This is nearly a universal mistake. We think we are making our case with examples that prove our points. The result is to frustrate the other person by offering too much content to manage, especially during an argument. As a result, the other person is likely to do things farther down this list.

❖ *No aggression.* Violence is out of the question. I am referring to more subtle forms of aggression, such as:

- Painful volume — yelling so loud it hurts the other person's ears

- Name-calling or behavior labels like, "That was so inconsiderate!"

- Aggressive gestures — rushing at someone, hitting objects or oneself

❖ *Do not threaten to break up the relationship.* Though common, this is the most damaging of the list. It is better even to call someone names than to threaten to leave the relationship. Break-up threats are meant to make someone else care, but they backfire. Instead, the threat strongly motivates someone not to care about you in order feel less hurt by your threat.

If arguments have had a disturbing role in your relationship, I am assuming you will both accept these guidelines, mostly because no one has ever disputed any of them in my office. Once you agree to them, commit to them aloud to each other. Most important, *promise to keep them even if the other person does not.* In other words, promise the other person that, "If you forget these guidelines and make any of these mistakes, it is not a rationale for my making the same mistakes."

The best part of the fair-fighting guidelines is that they can prevent dirty fights even without the other person's cooperation. How? You can get there in three short steps:

❖ *Say what you would rather have* (a fair fighting alternative to the dirty fighting), for instance, "Please talk to me just a little softer"; "Let's argue about one item at a time"; or "Can you stick to how much you dislike what I did, rather than characterizing it?"

❖ If necessary (if the unfair argument goes on), *set a boundary for what you cannot be part of.* Although there are several ways to communicate this, the words most in keeping with the gold medal recipe are, "I'm not able to treat you the way you deserve when [I hear the names you are calling me], so please don't do that."

❖ If still necessary, *take a timed break.* Providing a specific return time is indispensable for this method of ending an unfair argument. If the other person cannot disengage, it is better to leave the house. You were not going to get any sleep anyway. Later, when you keep your promised time for the break and come back, return to the first of these three steps, starting nice. If you cannot, it shows that you did not leave soon enough after the dirty fighting began. In other words, if you break quickly enough, you don't need as much time away.

This sequence yields remarkable results because it gives the argumentative person something for nothing, but nothing for fighting dirty. As simple as it is, I have yet to see it fail, in time. If you leave soon enough, you will not build resentment and can stay positive. The only complication would be if the other person bars your way. If you forgot to follow the three steps, including having a time limit on the break, that might correct the problem. Otherwise, by being blocked you are dealing with violence, and I suggest exiting the situation as soon as possible, and for an indefinite period. See more about this in my discussion of violence in Chapter 12.

Following the strategy above, *you actually have a choice about whether to have unfair arguments, or any arguments, for that matter.* To apply the same three-step strategy to complete argument avoidance, just set the bar higher. Rather than only using the steps when arguments turn ugly, apply them to any arguments. For the first step, instead of suggesting a fair argument, offer the conflict resolution approach of the previous section, perhaps introduced with the following reassurance: "What you want is too important to me for us to argue about. I'd like to talk it through and help you get it."

Try using the same sequence of saying what you would rather do, followed if necessary by what you will not do, and a timed break if needed. This way, you have the freedom to avoid harsh arguments, or to circumvent any arguments at all, if that is your wish.

This is good news, but I have even better news for you. You read in the preface that love is a choice. In the next chapter, we will learn how to make the choice to love.

CHAPTER 29

Love Is a Choice

Love regenerates continually through the gold medal recipe, which provides the essential point that you stay in love by being good to each other. Part VI has provided details, guidelines, and checklists for keeping you on track. Specifically, below are insights into the inner psychological generosity that results in your staying in love. *Based on how you think about the other person, you are actually choosing whether to love him or her.*

Throughout the years, I have had the chance to watch and learn what people do that successfully recharges their love of others. These measures are effective and reliable, but they are not obligatory. For yes to be a free choice, no has to be an available alternative. Love is a choice in the fullest sense. *There are times to say no to love.* Indeed, just as there are ways to stay in love, we have reviewed effective methods to fall out of love. The strategies in this chapter are devoted to situations during which the right choice is to enhance the depth of your love. At the same time, we are obliged to notice the alternative. Otherwise, many of us may feel pressure to stay in love, no matter the circumstances.

This caveat registered, we will review four ways people choose to love. If you find your loving attachment continually renews itself, these guidelines probably comprise much of what you are already doing. Alternatively, if you have lost some of that closeness by letting one or more of these love enhancements slip by, each of them will reward you with a deeper connection.

The first method — keeping a positive focus — may be the most obvious.

Keeping a positive focus We feel most readily attached to those we think well of. As I noted in the 14th chapter, we turn ourselves on or off depending on whether we focus on attractive features or unattractive ones. Most people find this easiest, perhaps more automatic, at the inception of a relationship.

An initial turned-on process, sometimes called *infatuation*, automatically accompanies the joyful tumble we call *falling in love*. We have all heard that love is blind, and certainly, during the initial stages of romantic attachment, we often cannot find any meaningful flaws in a beloved.

Because of scientific advances in our understanding of the emotional reward centers in the brain's limbic system, this state of infatuation is sometimes called the *dopamine stage*. The hormone dopamine has a biochemical role in the brain's infatuation response. Another way of psychologically understanding this initial entrancement is as the *astonishment phase*. We can hardly believe our good fortune at the thought that our love may be reciprocated. Our awestruck hearts tell us simultaneously that we have never felt like this before and that it feels like we have known each other forever. Positive focus flows freely and naturally throughout this astonishment phase. It seems we are biologically and psychologically wired for obsessively amorous beginnings.

Unless your self-esteem is extraordinarily poor, eventually you believe your good luck, and your astonishment gradually diminishes. *If your positive focus exits along with the dopamine, then you also fall out of love.*

If love is initially blind, we could say the blinders come off as the astonishment fades. This is when we choose: appreciation or contempt. If we cannot forgive those we love for now having some flaws, we develop a different blindness. Now we begin to see only faults.

Enduring lovers choose appreciation, of course. Though aware that not every trait is delightful, we are delighted nonetheless. Every gift that enthralled you before is *made even more precious because these positive assets express themselves in a human being, not an angel, complete with failings and flaws.* The humanness in your beloved renders only more impressive and lovable his or her wonderful qualities.

This concentration on wonderful features in a loved one results in an emotional overflow of liking, an endless enthusiasm for choosing this person over and over, and an eagerness to repay this person for being in your world. This person brings a special light to this world and deserves all the devotion in your heart.

Such positive focus is an obvious boon to lovers. Yet, what about those less pleasant traits and habits in those we love? What do we do about the negative features, once we notice them? The second way that people choose love consists of linking, when possible, the negative traits to the positive ones. This is easier than it sounds, because every personal quality has a front and a back, a positive or negative expression.

Linking the worst to the best

Virtuous behavior depends on where you find it. As I pointed out, there is a time and place to be vicious. Similarly, there is a time and place where acting kindhearted would be a mistake.

Instead of imagining a person's qualities as virtues or vices, try thinking of them as *measures,* as in the amount of some personality feature a person has (Steinsaltz, p. 49). To fully understand this, think of a literal recipe. The amounts of sweeteners, oils, and spices vary depending on the context, that is, depending on the dish and on the consumer of the dish. The right amount of an ingredient will vary depending on factors like people's tastes and health concerns. Such considerations determine the measure of each item, what is too much and what is too little. In the same way, *positive or negative traits are a function of context — where they're shown, how much, and to whom.*

This provides a glimpse into how you can connect some of your beloved's bothersome features to his or her marvelous features. When a characteristic appears in too great a dose, we call this *too much of a good thing.* In the 18th chapter on common ground, we saw how couples run into love-threatening conflicts from sharing virtues like being highly nurturing, responsible, or considerate.

Similarly, unpleasant features in our partners may just be excessive demonstrations of one of their endearing traits. We rely on someone to be organized, but sometimes this seems controlling. We enjoy someone's playfulness, but sometimes he or she becomes distracted. We admire perseverance, but this can lead to workaholic habits.

Keeping in mind how the annoying behavior links to a trait we appreciate becomes a way to forgive someone. Doing this is a second way that people choose to love.

What about those troublesome qualities in others we cannot connect to enjoyable ones? We sometimes refer to such behavior as childish or immature,

Childish or childlike?

and we have a point. If you get to know people well enough, most everyone will display some babyish moments. Recalling the *Wizard Syndrome* of the 12th chapter, even anger-prone people are usually covering up childish vulnerability.

This brings us to the choice involved in this third way people choose to love. *We can choose to see this behavior as infantile and obnoxious or childlike and endearing.* After all, we more or less forgive children everything. As most parents can attest, behavior that would harden and embitter us, if inflicted by an adult, is soon forgiven in children. Squinting through the annoyance to see the child in our loved ones of any age provides the same resiliency.

Women and men, when not in the company of the other gender, both display this. Assemble a group of women in conversation and one likely subject is how men are babies. Men need to have the remote control, they whine and complain when they are sick, they yell like children for their favorite teams. Most of the time, wives who do this are not truly complaining about their husbands. They are forgiving them.

Men do the same thing. You cannot make women happy, they always want something else, whatever you forgot at the store is always the most important item on the list. Sometimes husbands are really complaining about their wives, in which case they are viewing the women as parental and bossy. Other times, they are rendering their wives as petulant children, and thinking they are cute.

Another way to keep your beloved's childlike qualities in mind is by remembering his or her actual childhood. An unfortunately normal manner in which childhoods affect people is through a process I call contextual assessment syndrome. *Whatever happened at home growing up seems to be the way it is with the world.* For example, if everyone yelled or everyone was quiet, then a raised voice means very different things. Especially when stressed, people will act more in accord with their early experiences.

Because you grew up somewhere else, you have the opportunity to forgive each other for having different stress-patterns. Your partner will act certain ways that seem odd to you, until you recall his or her childhood background. Seeing the context has the potential to soften your response to the behavior.

We will all choose whether to consider the childhood context, and we will make this choice more than once. Do you see your mate's less adult behavior as childish or childlike? Is it willful and controlling, or is it a junior moment? *When you view it as childlike, you have made the third choice that keeps people in love.*

These first three choices — positive focus, linking the negative to the positive, and connecting remaining negatives to the person's childhood — all comprise generous attitudes toward someone else. As such, they make immediate intuitive sense. The fourth is the surprise member of the team.

In Chapter 27, you read about conflict resolution guidelines. Part of the rationale is that it does not help the relationship to suppress strong preferences. It breeds resentment. This resentment may build up emotional pressure to the boiling point, and we explode in anger. In others, the same self-suppression initially simmers and then gradually cools into emotional distance.

Resentment prevention

Your relationship is better served if you take care of yourself at least enough to avoid building resentment. How can you tell when it is time to take care of yourself? The clue is tangible and physical. Feelings are in our bodies. If conversations with your loving partner cause a knot in your stomach or heaviness/burning in your chest or a lump in your throat, then you are having feelings about it. This signals it is time to admit, first to yourself, what your wishes are in the situation you just experienced or discussed.

This sounds like such an easy task — just know your own will. Yet, it can sometimes be quite tricky, so I offer a thought experiment to figure out your own desires in a situation. Imagine you had an ample supply of short-term amnesia pills. Everyone else involved in the situation will ingest one, so they will not remember how you handle the situation. They will not even recall whether you attended the event in question. You would garner neither accolades nor blame, regardless of how you resolve it. What would you do, in that case? This is probably the best way to estimate your own wishes.

The amnesia pill

Once you have an idea what you would like, one important distinction concerns how important it is to you. If you feel unsure, you can watch for the previously mentioned feelings as well as for any signs of resentment. A sure sign of resentment is irritability, even if unexpressed. If little things, like listening to someone chew, start to annoy you, this can indicate resentment (unless you always react that way).

Another important distinction regarding this aspect of choosing love is the tone you will have when you address your concerns. In the 1970s, *assertiveness training* was a very popular communication strategy. It had to do with taking steps for oneself and setting boundaries with others. It was popular with Baby Boomers. *Applying this fourth guideline accomplishes the same end as assertiveness, but with a much more loving intention, and it sounds like it.* You protect your partner from the love-sapping results of building up resentment.

Motivation to do this is a particular challenge for many women. As we noted previously, one particular strength of women as a group is their much-enhanced ability to anticipate the emotional consequences of choices. Men, instead, have a tendency to do what they think best at any moment. They do not look too far down the road at the way their decisions will affect people later, including themselves. The problem is that *women often do not anticipate the emotional consequences of excessive compliance.* Perhaps the pressure to accommodate others overrides awareness of the danger of future resentment. Yet, their overall aptitude to anticipate emotional consequences equips them to learn to compensate for this reticence, if they become aware of it, which is exactly my intention here.

As soon as you self-diagnose the potential for resentment, you can apply the conflict resolution guidelines to prevent it. In doing so, you are operating according to the gold medal recipe by making sure you can stay on target with your goal of contributing lushly to the person you love. In this way, self-assertion and loving responsibility are not at odds; beyond consistent, they are in actuality instrumental to each other.

A last strategy worth reprising is The Homework described in Section D of Chapter 17. It builds positive focus and even helps connect unpleasant traits to positive ones, because it provides practice in shifting from a negative to a positive focus. In doing so, it reverses the tendency of each person's past to swamp the couple's aspirations for closeness in the present. (Recall the story about the couple who meet in a park, walking dogs who get in a dogfight.)

Loving homework

Because of the stress-effects of knowing how much people we love can hurt us, it is the most difficult to be ourselves with the people who matter most. This bothers me a lot. It is a large part of why I enjoy working with couples, and it is most of why I wrote this book. For the same reasons, I appreciate this strategy. It directly and immediately reverses the problem. It allows people to tie the dogs to (different) trees and get on with getting to know and love each other.

To recall and re-experience why you first began to hang out together:

❖ Write down four recent enjoyable events, not involving each other (big or little events, no matter).

❖ Add four qualities you enjoy about yourself (adjectives, characteristics you have ever evidenced).

❖ Write four qualities you enjoy about the other person (not the only four or best four — any four).

❖ Recall four times you enjoyed with this person (from whenever, even the first five minutes you met).

❖ There is no way to do this wrong, except to qualify it. As you do this activity, you'll remember what the couple with the dogs forgot.

❖ Ask your partner to do this, too. Set a time to read it to each other. When you are listening, don't say a word. Just experience the gift.

You will both enjoy the fruits of this activity, as well as the strategies in the rest of Part VI. If communication techniques worked a bit better, I might suggest you memorize them, practice them, and keep them in mind frequently. You would be applying them toward the goal of intimacy. Instead, I recommend that you work in the other direction, which is also simpler to do. Start with the goal of intimacy, expect the best, and aim high. When you think your relationship is falling short, check the strategies.

If you are feeling more contempt and less love, if there is too little day-to-day closeness, if conflicts seem to be coming up too much, if arguments seem to ensnare the relationship, or especially if you two are fighting dirty, a review of Part VI will allow you to discern precisely where you are missing the opportunity for intimacy. You can thus diagnose where you are heading off track, correct your course, and return to loving.

Speaking of loving, we are ready to leave the kitchen. As a multidimensional experience, being in love includes a robust physical connection. Can our recipe augment that?

PART VII
Special Benefits

CHAPTER 30

Is there a Recipe for Sex?

My selecting sex as a special reward for the gold medal recipe for love will seem an obvious choice to some, but, as I write, it also brings a question: Does sex truly have the potential to comprise the culmination of a couple's emotional intimacy? Does it still have anything to do with love?

Post the historic sexual revolution in the U.S. in the 1960s, sex apart from committed relationships has been viewed increasingly favorably. Outside of traditional religious communities, female virginity is no longer expected in contemporary society; rather, it seems psychologically suspicious in many peer groups. Further, as the Baby Boomers insisted, sex can be a wonderful pleasure, and pleasure is good. Once upon a time, one could ask if there was any role for a sex life outside of marriage. As I write, in the early 21st century, one can equally ask if a committed relationship has anything at all to offer sex. Certainly, sex can be experienced as trivial but enjoyable. Can it also be anything else?

My perspective in Part VII is that sexuality indeed has the capacity to attain a special depth inside of your loving relationship. In fact, sexual experience is unique in its capacity to bring couples there. Thus, it is the recipe's special reward.

However, blending sex and love harmoniously seems a challenging notion, because each expresses a different dimension of human experience.

If I count the dimensions of a human being's experience, I come up with six:

❖ One of these dimensions is what I call *spiritual experience* (defined psychologically as an experience of self-transcendence — connection to realities larger than ourselves, which includes the capacity to love another person deeply)

❖ Another is the intellectual (by which I mean the endeavors of the mind — philosophical, aesthetic, and conceptual analyses such as history and economics)

❖ A third is the intrapersonal (psychological self-awareness)

❖ Fourth is an interpersonal aspect to experience, which consists of our relationships with people in general (outside of the spiritual connections above)

❖ Related to the other dimensions, the emotional realm consists of our experiences of motivational energies, which can direct our behavior toward any of the other five dimensions

❖ Finally and most tangibly, we have the realm of the senses, the physical dimension

I organized these as a continuum from those dimensions most associated with humanness to those least so. At the spiritual top of the continuum, we expect that only humans contain conscious connections to realities larger than ourselves, although the devotion of many pets for their owners might challenge that distinction. We also believe that only people have complex, abstract concepts about the world, which is the intellectual dimension, although animals certainly think. Similarly, we expect that only humans have self-insight, the intrapersonal dimension. On the other hand, other mammals display much evidence of both the emotional and the interpersonal dimensions. On the bottom of our hierarchy, even inanimate objects possess physicality. *The physical or material aspect of life, including sexual pleasure, seems the furthest removed from the spiritual aspect of love.*

Here is where the picture begins to seem confusing. Sex, being the most physical aspect of a relationship, simultaneously distinguishes a romantic relationship from other types. It can supply some of the closest moments of connection you and your partner will ever share, so perhaps something is missing from our hierarchical view. *The chapters to come will propose another way to look at sex and its delicious place as the culmination of the recipe for love.*

Speaking of recipes, as we have done before, we will benefit from starting our discussion at the endpoint, that is, at the goal. The ultimate "fact of life"

Starting with the gold standard

to know about sex is that its quality rises or falls according to the same factors as the rest of your relationship. If your sexual feelings reflect the gold standard of two people seeking simultaneously to make each other happy and accepting gratefully each other's efforts, your romance springs forth brightly and renews itself continually. Love has the potential to fuel your sex lives forever. *The point is to love each other in the arena of passion as you do in the rest of your relationship.*

So if the secret to a satisfying sex life is as simple as applying the gold standard to lovemaking, why do we need this chapter at all? Perhaps the previous paragraph could have been noted within Part V, as one of the benefits of a giver-to-giver relationship. It could have been an aside, as in, "By the way, all this helps your sex life, too." In reality, sexual sharing has some confusing aspects to it, and the spiritual/physical paradox above is only the beginning.

Extending the apparent contradictions, your time together body to body is fundamentally superficial, because it is literally skin-deep. Further, bodies

Deepening the superficial confusion

are common to all of us. Despite minor variations, we all have the same parts and do mostly the same things in mostly the same ways. Much of what we do sexually is even similar to other mammals. Yet, it is all so private that one of our euphemisms for the sex act is *intimacy*. Not only do you engage in sex with only one person in a healthy marriage, but in economically developed societies (read: those with bedrooms), no one else can even be present. Further, the anatomical parts most directly associated with sexual behavior are those socially and legally ordained as private.

Mixed messages about sex are prevalent. Some elements of our culture still guide us to consider sexuality a sacred part of a marriage, while other (commercial) influences display sexuality blatantly as a form of marketing, both of ourselves as desirable commodities and to promote the sale of products. Such self-contradicting societal messages persist generally but have been much more pervasive during certain historical periods. Consequently, I learned in my counselor training that, if you took all the contrary sex-related messages of America in the 1950s and put them together in one statement, it would be, "Sex is dirty; save it for someone you love."

Even well past the sexual revolution of the 1960s, we still receive differing messages according to gender. No matter what the age group and what the lifestyle, one usually finds some line that men can cross but women should not. The double standard boundary moves, but never fully disappears.

Speaking of standards, are you good in bed? This question is another example of a counterproductive cultural message about sexuality. The question implies performance, as in performance pressure. People usually hear about the importance of being a good sex partner before they have even had a sexual experience, so the worry precedes the pleasure.

Psychologically and even physiologically, anxiety and pleasure are mutually exclusive (Wolpe, 1968). As a result, sexual worry is self-fulfilling. People who worry about erections and orgasms tend not to have them. Even when all goes well functionally, grading sexual experiences usually diminishes them.

All the above ambiguities complicate the process of incorporating lovemaking into the gold medal recipe. *Our goal is nothing less than gold medal sex, which is not achieved by Olympic efforts but by getting out of the way of gold medal loving.*

The process begins with some very good news. Previously, I explained the recipe for self-renewing affection, and sexual affection is also perpetually re-freshed in a thriving relationship. I often recall a conversation with an older man, who decided to let me in on a secret. He began, "You know how you see old-looking couples who seem happy together, and they may be holding hands? You find yourself wondering if they still, you know, love each other and how far that goes?" I smiled and nodded. He continued, "I always won-dered about it too, and now my wife and I are one of those couples, and they do and we do." As I soon learned, he had done his own social research. He said, "I have friends who are just like me too, and our age doesn't make any difference. We love each other and we still want each other."

This is the power of the gold standard. When you live in mutual devotion with a spouse, you feel delighted to delight each other in multiple ways. Sex is just one of them. The secret ingredient is this: When it comes to gold stan-dard sex, turning on your beloved partner and bringing her or him a little bit of Heaven is a stirring turn-on for you as well. The next chapters provide a few of the details.

CHAPTER 31

What the Oldest Story Tells Us about Making Love

Long before psychological theories, religious systems devised methods of changing people's perspectives on life experiences. These strategies often utilize highly symbolic events as what psychology would later term *therapeutic metaphors*. Not everyone is comfortable with these kinds of metaphors, even when applied psychologically and not theologically, as I am doing here. We often learn biblical stories as children, and they may stay both cartoonlike and silly in our minds. Finding them uniquely helpful psychologically, I referred to their effects on consciousness in Chapter 9, while discussing the psychology of spirituality.

If sex indeed has the capacity to combine diverse elements of human experience, like the physical and the spiritual dimensions, human sexuality would become a lucid mirror of the essence of human nature. People are contradictory beings.

There are two of you and two of each of you.

This may sound abstract, but we struggle with dualities every day. At best, being human involves wrestling to balance the influence of the past with the goals of the present, egotism with love, and automatic habit with free choice. Such wrestling is *at best* because some of us do not bother to wrestle and instead rationalize mistakes, abdicate responsibility, and blame others. Those of us engaged in the struggle are aware of such dualities to experience.

Scientific research reflects this accurately, as we noted in the 17th chapter, where I mentioned that the brain is bimodal in operation. We saw there that our minds themselves work two very different ways, depending on the level of experienced stress.

In spiritual symbols, we frequently encounter one of the above dualities — the struggle between egotism and love — which is often described as the relationship between body and soul. In fact, both theistic (God-oriented) religions and non-theistic philosophies (mostly from Asia) have some way of framing this dual aspect of life as the contrast between a physical (fragmented) element of existence and a unified higher power. The ethical result of this duality is our internal struggle between a selfish side and an altruistic side. Every religious tradition will need to suggest a way of life to help us resolve this inner conflict.

One answer (Neo-Platonism and much of Vedanta) is to view the world as a prison for the spirit and therefore suggest that we transcend the physical plane, leaving it behind as we ascend toward the spiritual realm. Another possible resolution (much of ancient Chinese and Hebrew thought) sees the world as the lantern of the spirit. This results in a suggestion that we sanctify our physical lives through contact with the spiritual dimension. As you may have guessed, the groups with this latter perspective have a higher opinion of sex.

Nowhere is this positive version of duality more visible than in the Hebrew Bible. The dual nature of the human condition appears in the text almost immediately, in the second chapter, where we learn that people are the only element of the universe created out of two prior ingredients.

Every other element of the universe is described as being revealed out of nothing, but the recipe for people consists of two very disparate elements. One of them is the lowest aspect of the Earth, that is, the dirt under our feet. Understanding this, Adam names himself from the word for this earth, *adamah*. This is ingredient number one. The second ingredient is the opposite; it is the highest possible ingredient imaginable — *breath of God*. Although no commentator ever thought that God is in any way corporeal, the symbol of God's breath evokes that which comes from the core of God, so to speak, just as our breaths come from deep inside us.

In this way, we combine the lowest and highest possible elements of the world. The traditional commentators meant for people to keep this duality in mind at all times, simultaneously thinking (as Abraham stated) that "I am but dust and ashes" (Gen. 18:27) and "The world was created for my sake" (Talmud, Sanhedrin 37a).

Soon after humans enter the story, we receive a lesson in how this duality plays out in our sexual lives. The dual nature of our sexual relationships shows in the two reactions that Adam has to Eve (the following account follows the work of David Fohrman, 2013). He even gives her two different names, one the very first time he meets her and the other after they get into trouble together.

The first love story and the first lust story

The Garden of Eden story literally describes that God separates the first couple into two beings from one body. After deciding it was time for Adam to have a mate but before providing one, God next gives him the task of considering and naming all the animals, so he is especially impressed immediately afterward, when he first meets her. As Adam beholds her, separate from himself, he is astonishingly happy. He realizes that she is part of him, and he longs for closeness. Accordingly, the name he gives her is just the feminine tense of the word for *man*. (For more on this, see the sidebar.) She is the total mate, both soul-mate and body-mate, and he describes her as *flesh of my flesh*.

> *The Hebrew word that Adam first names his wife (pronounced eeshah) means both "woman" and "wife." This is the feminine version of the name for a man (pronounced eeysh). The two words share two letters, and each contains one letter not in the other. The word for man has a y, and the word for woman has an h missing in the other word. Put these two together and you get the word yah, which is essentially a nickname for God. Think halelu-yah, which literally means "praise God." If you subtract these same letters from both their donor words, the word for man and the word for woman are reduced to the same two-letter word (aash), which means "fire." It is just like the English word ash, but with a long a. The idea is that a woman and a man burn for each other when alone, but in a soulless relationship they burn each other up. In contrast, when connected deeply, they find the divine between them.*

Such a relationship is truly paradise, which is not surprising, because we are talking about the Garden of Eden, but we all know what happens next. After the first couple establishes a great emotional distance from their Creator, Adam consequently experiences a diminished partnership with the first woman, blaming her for his mistake. Not only is this the first time a husband blames his wife for his problems, but she also becomes the first sex object. Now gazing upon her sexual potential, this is when he gives her a second name: Eve (literally *Chava*, which combines the word *chaya*, meaning "life," with *yechaveh*, meaning "expression"). Instead of *flesh of my flesh*, he now exclaims that she is the *mother of all*. Psychologically, this correlates perfectly with male attraction to the female form. To a man, all the secondary sex characteristics signal fertility, whether or not that man wants to father a child.

Ever after, *future sons of Adam have faced the challenge to balance a woman's role as soul-mate with her role as sexual enchantress.* Perhaps in reaction to men, women have perennially struggled psychologically with their

Pleasure-pressure

body images versus the rest of themselves. Meanwhile, the surrounding culture has provided ample voltage to this struggle. From the preteen years, girls receive encouragement from media of all sorts to confuse feeling like a woman with providing allure to boys. Meanwhile, the boys are learning, from the same multimedia, a one-dimensional relationship with femininity, blurring for them the difference between sexuality and sex-addiction. This narrow focus hurts women, both through surface-based self-esteem and through normative displays of anorexic eating disorders. Shallow views of women lead men into problems like boredom, infidelity, sex addiction, and jealousy.

The problems seem to be accelerating, as I write. Girls, afraid to miss the train, jump on board to sexual relationships for which they are not emotionally prepared. Boys fall into sexually addictive behavior, usually involving the internet ever earlier, so related problems like erectile dysfunction are affecting even college-aged boys. This occurs in a similar manner to any other addiction, because excessive exposure to online pornography desensitizes the pleasure center of the brain's limbic system (the VTA, ventral tegmental area, and the NA, nucleus accumbens). A real, live partner cannot compete with addictive shocks to the system. The good news is that, as opposed to healing a cocaine-ravaged brain, which seems to take years, a month or two appears to be enough to re-sensitize a porn-intoxicated brain.

In pointing this out, I am by no means suggesting that sexual pleasure as a purely physical phenomenon must always be addictive. After all, all physical pleasures carry a risk of addiction. Rather, *we are just filling in some of the details about how sex can have nothing — or everything — to do with love.* Sexual interest can typify the most superficial relationships, render people only skin-deep, and even become the occasion for horrific violence. Simultaneously, it is the most miraculous aspect of human behavior, consisting of the way in which people create precious new life together.

Fortunately, we do not have to settle for an either-or dichotomy between sex and love, by choosing only one of Adam's two reactions to his wife. *Inside a loving relationship, sex has the unique potential to combine the duality of human nature into harmonic synergy.*

Indeed, any physical act, such as eating, can be elevated in meaning through an altruistic accompanying intention. We can inhale a meal too quickly to savor it, or we can break bread in deep gratitude, enjoying fellowship and strengthening ourselves for our life goals. By intending to do good with the advantage of good food, we can bring higher meaning to the activity. It is a choice, and a daily one. Yet, sexual potential exceeds even this. The act of eating can become intentionally sanctified by us, but sex can itself sanctify us just by virtue of loving our sex partner. As we will see in Chapter 33, sexual love is innately accompanied by psychological harmony between love and lust. *In the context of a loving relationship, sexual sharing broadcasts powerfully and clearly that soul and body are united.* Both are already present, intertwined as are lovers. It only requires our attention.

CHAPTER 32

What Swimming Pools Can Teach Us

Naturally, in order to benefit from the combination of affection and desire described in the previous chapter, a couple needs to have sex. In this section, I will help you understand and begin to correct the reasons that your sexual sharing may have stopped or become infrequent. One of these barriers returns us to the subject of gender differences, and another hindrance has to do with the effects of conflict. The first problem, however, is simply a function of daily stress.

During the discussion of the gold medal recipe, we considered the joys of the early astonishment phase of a relationship, as well as the wisdom of replacing it with gratitude later on, after absorbing the shock of finding each other. Feeling close to your partner during either stage, of course, often has a sexual benefit. Other times, however, an established couple may enjoy an emotionally intimate relationship, yet without the sexual advantages. A common cause for this infrequency consists of the effects of stress and fatigue on a person's appetite for sex.

The clinical name for low sexual appetite not caused by illness goes by the initials ISD, which stand for Inhibited Sexual Desire. To understand it better, render the same letters as the I'm Stressed Disorder. Most of us recognize the impact of mood on libido — thus, the expressions *in the mood* and *not in the mood*. I once heard someone say that all sex therapy could be distilled into one sentence: When you're hot you're hot, and when you're not you're not.

The relationship between distress and pleasure has also been the subject of research. The early behaviorists first showed that some feelings are physically incompatible with others. As I mentioned in

Reciprocal inhibition and you

Chapter 30 (Wolpe, 1968), pleasure and anxiety are two of these physically incompatible states. How was this demonstrated? It begins with Pavlov, the well-known Russian physiological researcher.

Ivan Pavlov is best known for his research on *classical conditioning*, where a natural, innate response becomes paired with a new event. In his experiments on such conditioning, he made some of his poor, experimental dogs hungry and fed them some powdered meat. Naturally, they salivated. Simultaneously, he conditioned them by ringing a bell as he fed them. Consequently, when he rang the bell they started salivating without his yet providing them with any food. However, he did not confine his experimenting on these un-fortunate pooches to ringing a bell.

He also utilized a device to deliver an electric shock, which the researcher could dial higher or lower. They started low. Instead of pairing the bell sound with feeding the hungry dog, a very mild shock was administered. Carefully and slowly, the intensity of the shock was raised. Eventually, the shock was strong. What were the responses of the dogs? They salivated. If a shock of the same intensity was applied to an unconditioned dog, it howled in pain and jumped about. In fact, if the strong shock was applied to the experimental animal but to a different leg, it reacted strongly to the pain. Yet, as long as the shock was to the leg they had used in the training, Pavlov reported that the dog voiced no anguish, just eagerness for lunch.

After describing this research, Wolpe explained the results as a case of *reciprocal inhibition*. Certain emotional reactions are physiologically incom-patible, he explained. Whichever of the two is higher will be the only one ex-perienced, effectively canceling out the other. *One of these physically incompatible pairs is pleasure and anxiety.*

Wolpe's reciprocal inhibition flows in both directions. As any therapist who deals with sexual issues can tell you, anxiety stifles pleasurable experi-ences. As a result, men with psychologically induced erectile problems can successfully address them by learning to trust their body's responses. If one imagines a chemist's scale with anxiety, fatigue, and resentment on one side and physical pleasure, attraction, and emotional closeness on the other, sexual responses in both genders will reliably reveal the predominant weight at each moment.

There is no need to argue with the body's readout. To change the physi-ological response, change the factors on either side of the scale, and preferably on both sides of the scale.

For people without specific sexual dysfunctions, but with little desire, the factors are the same. The difference is that the parties are not arguing with their bodies; they are just waiting to be in the mood. As a result, no matter how attracted a person is to the object of his or her sexual interest, enough anxiety will render pleasure temporarily uninteresting. To state the obvious: *Stressed-out is not a sexy state of mind.* This insight explains why you can be in bed with your beloved partner and just want to rest, even if you are as hun-gry for this person as Pavlov's dogs were for food.

Keeping Wolpe in mind, my favorite metaphor for the solution to this dilemma is a swimming pool on a hot day. Imagine you have the opportunity to jump in to a cool pool on a warm day. It sounds like a good idea, but it will

Getting back in the pool

not feel so good, at least not at first. The hotter the day, the greater will be the temperature difference between your skin and the water. If you go ahead anyway, here is the likely sequence:

❖ First, you will feel uncomfortable.

❖ If you stay in, it will start to feel OK.

❖ Then, you will get to like it.

❖ After that, you will not want to get out.

❖ Finally, you may think you should do this more often.

Having sex when stressed and/or tired is pretty much the same challenge and results in the same sequence. At first, it will feel unnatural, in the sense that you are not in a turned-on mood. After a bit, it will become OK, and then it will feel very nice. Not long after, you will not want it to end. Afterward, you will most likely realize that you could use more of this.

Like much of this text, the solution is simple, but not always easy. After all, we sometimes stare at that cool water for a while before we get ourselves ready to jump in. I call the reason for this the tyranny of mood, and it affects a lot more than our sex lives. To address it, I have reprinted, in the sidebar, a "Blum-blog" post (Blum, 2013) on the subject.

We often assume we should do what we really feel like doing. Maybe this rule seems obvious to you. Accordingly, we ask ourselves if we are in the mood to do this or that, which can be a very good idea if we like the current mood. Whatever we feel like doing both fits and maintains that mood. As a result, if we dislike the mood we are in but obey it anyway, we are being controlled by the tyranny of mood. Here is a different idea: Ask yourself, "Do I like the mood I'm in?" If the answer is yes, do what you feel like doing. It will tend to keep you in that good mood. If the answer is no, ask yourself another question: "What would I do next if I were in a better mood?" In other words, do exactly what you would otherwise do if you felt better than you do right now. Acting in that direction, especially if sustained, will take you toward that better mood. This is because feelings and choices produce each other in both directions. You can reverse the equation any time you want. For example, do you feel like smiling, like calling a friend, like taking a walk, like finishing a task, or like lending a hand? If the answer is no, and you are in a down mood, that becomes the best reason to do it. In this way, you will get a lot more done. By giving yourself the freedom to either obey or disobey your mood, you will most enjoy your life.

Another emotional challenge that affects the love life of couples has to do with gender differences, especially the question of how men and women achieve feelings of closeness. With exceptions, men connect through shared action while women speak to each other. This explains why sex has different meaning for each of them. *For men, sex is often the vehicle to bring closeness, while for women it is the result of closeness.* Unable to imagine this difference, husbands may think their wives are punishing them when their wives are just not feeling close enough. Equally unable to imagine the male point of view, women often think their husbands are just using them for a convenient sexual release. Meanwhile, he thinks it is the answer to everything. After she says no to him, he feels used too, as if he is just a paycheck.

Feeling used

This misunderstanding is a major obstacle in many marriages. As we learned in the discussion of gender dynamics, translation is the key: *He loves you — he just thinks that sex is a rapid superhighway for getting closer. She loves you — she just wants to know you cherish her as more than a warm body.* When I suggest to men that they ought to try showing affection without it leading to sex, they often respond that the progression from one to the other just seems natural. Once they understand how they are coming across to their wives, however, most are happy to comply with sending a different message.

Another common emotional barrier to an active sex life for couples is that sex usually functions as the "miner's canary" in a marriage. Before computerized air-quality gauges, miners brought a caged canary into an underground mine. If the air quality deteriorated, the canary was more vulnerable to it than the humans. If the bird

Don't forget the canary.

286

dropped over in its cage, the miners knew they had to evacuate quickly. In this way, the canary was the first warning that the workers were in trouble.

Sex is like this delicate canary inside a marriage. *It is often the first aspect of the relationship to drop away and the last to return.* The good news is that, if it was there before, it usually resumes joyfully once the issues have been resolved.

As a rare exception to this canary function, some couples have intense make-up sex, where both parties somehow channel their anger into passion. These couples have robust sex lives, but they can become dependent on raucous arguments as their form of foreplay, and these arguments can become intense and even dangerous. They need another form of foreplay!

When not blocked by stress, gender misunderstandings, or the canary syndrome, long-term couples' sex lives tend to fall into a bimodal distribution. There seem to be once-or-twice-a-week couples and once-or-twice-a-month couples. Interestingly, both types often express satisfaction. (Once-or-twice-a-year couples usually do not.) Compared to new couples, who may get together once a day or more during the astonishment/dopamine phase, this typical change in frequency might appear to signal the onset of boredom, but this does not have to be the case.

Accordingly, we are changing from the subject of quantity to quality of sex in long-term relationships. It turns out that one of the most powerful ways of maximizing the intensity of lovemaking is reserved only for committed, loving relationships. Physical joy can become not only compatible with, but also heightened through, the sacred connection of a couple's love for each other, as we will see in the next chapter.

CHAPTER 33

Is Anything Sacred
in a Hot Relationship?

Sexual love has the alchemical potential of uniting opposites, yielding an ecstatic alloy that transcends description. It is the most powerful way we know to join consciousness of the sacred and the ordinary (Blum, 2007). Emotionally, it brings together the experiences of lust and love. Psychologically, it unites head and heart. A wonderful symbolic metaphor for this appears during the biblical description of a moment of confusion for Moses in the desert (see sidebar).

The dilemma came up when the Children of Israel were building the tabernacle, the portable temple that was their spiritual center before entering the Promised Land. Finding the gold for the tabernacle was easy — everyone rushed to be part of the contributions. However, the problem came with the copper. A copper laver had to be built, a washing station that would sanctify the priests before they entered sacred space.

Here too, contributions abounded. As the text tells us (Ex. 38:8), the women showed up in a large gathering to offer their copper mirrors for the effort. The traditional explanation of the specific mention of the mirrors had to do with Moses' ensuing predicament. These were the mirrors the women had used to beautify themselves when seeking sexual attention from their enslaved husbands. The laboring men could not return home, but their wives found them in the fields and did their best, with the aid of the mirrors, to help the men to forget their exhaustion for long enough to join sexually. Could these items, used to inspire sexual hunger for their wives in the men, become part of the Holy Tabernacle?

Continuing the backstory, God's response was swift and clear: The Divine wish was not only to include the copper, but that these mirrors were in fact "more precious to Me than anything else."

The biblical tale presented in the sidebar provides a beautiful message about the biblical attitude toward sexual intimacy, but more remains to the story. The seductive behavior of the women was not only

Fully sacred and extremely physical sex

lusty, but also sacred, because it was directed to their husbands alone. The message is that sacredness is not about removing oneself from physicality and specifically not about removing oneself from sexuality. Rather, to be sacred means to be set aside as extraordinary, just as the portable temple itself was.

Clearly, there is an essential obligation to treat that which is special as special. Similarly, consciousness of extraordinariness is, in fact, what elevates sex to the sacred dimension. Sex in a marriage is sanctified, not by lessening or ignoring its physical dimension, but by staying mindful of the privilege of being invited where no one otherwise belongs. It results from staying mindful of the mutual gift of monogamy.

Accordingly, sanctifying your sexual union does not mean rendering it ethereal and incorporeal. Holy does not mean nonphysical, in this view. *It means rendering sex as awesome, recalling that the prospect of sexual time together is an astonishing opportunity to unify all the dimensions of existence, breaking the barrier between self and other.*

When a couple makes love within this honored space of unconditional commitment and appreciated love, the selfish side of the psyche is shocked into silence by the overwhelming pleasure of the moment. For once, there remains no conflict in the soul. *Every touch, glance, and embrace speaks of a breathtaking rhythm in which giving and taking are no longer distinct.* Within such a tabernacle, Heaven can dwell.

Whatever your previous sexual history, once you are in a monogamous relationship, your sexual sharing becomes eligible for this special kind of love. Even if your relationship has broken down sexually, you can begin again, gradually, as if you just met. Rebuild it the way you want it, starting with the touch of two hands, each to the other. Even holding each other's hands begins the process of sanctifying your relationship in the sense of the insights above, because with no one else do you touch hands this way. You have already entered extraordinary space, set aside just for the two of you.

CHAPTER 34

Talking About Sex

Few would disagree with most relationship-improvement guides that good communication is paramount. Our take on this has been to aim for the gold standard recipe. Useful communication in a marriage is not a negotiation about demands but a conversation about contribution. Bearing this in mind, we can turn to the art of sexual communication.

For sex to occur, someone has to initiate it. While this initiator can be either partner, more frequently the husband does so. Speaking heterosexually,

Giving cues
and reading cues

this seems to work for both partners. Men typically enjoy initiating and women enjoy feeling wanted. As a result, often a woman will wait for a man to reach for her, but she is far from passive. Most men in happy sexual unions are well aware of their wives' signals. It may be what she wears or does not wear, or it may be that she touches his chest rather than his back, or a different posture to her embrace. As a result, he feels safe from rejection when he starts things going.

Regarding such nonverbal cues, reading signals becomes even more important both at the beginning of a sexual relationship and when aiming to reintroduce physical lovemaking, if it is necessary to revive the aforementioned canary. Awkwardness is a good sign, actually, signaling sensitivity and a wish to proceed according to the partner's wishes. Yet, a path is needed to move past the caution.

I call this surefire method action-reaction. It usually eliminates the experience of rejection, while assuring that each is proceeding according to the wishes of the other. (See the sidebar for a separate method to treat those with a history of sexual trauma.)

A sexual trauma history presents a barrier to becoming comfortable with each other. When trauma recovery is needed, the key is to engage sexually together while lessening the impact of traumatic memories. The best way I have found to do this is for the traumatized person to run the encounter completely. She must know from her partner that her comfort is paramount and the pace will be totally hers. Accordingly, *she will do all the initiating at first. Further, the right sexual positions can do wonders to separate this consensual experience from the coercive history. Just the selection of a woman-on-top position can often bypass the past successfully.*

The nonverbal action-reaction experiment is a simple way to get things cooking again. Take a small step, then notice what the other person does. How small? This depends on the relationship, but aim for some act that, if not reciprocated, would not hurt or embarrass you. This may comprise taking the other person's hand for a few seconds. Or just touching the outside of the person's hand for a moment. The size of the step does not matter; what does matter is what happens next. Does she touch you back? Does she move her hand to grasp or stroke yours? If not, do not proceed until the next time. Move forward only if each step is soon reciprocated.

If reciprocity does not occur, it may be time to ask if the other person feels ready for such progression — in other words, if the canary needs more time in intensive care. Alternatively, you can just assume this for the time being.

Just as nonverbal communication can be a welcome addition to your love lives inside the sexual dimension of your relationship, verbal communication can also become a sweet addition to the dish. Too often people seem to consider it impolite to talk

Talk to me.

during sexual encounters. Discussing current events would be a bad idea, but talking about pleasure makes sense. If you were cooking an actual dish in the kitchen together, you might naturally ask the other person how it tastes to them and whether it could use more or less of some ingredient, but when lovemaking ensues, suddenly an unwritten rule says no one can speak. This produces too much of a guessing game. When someone jumps and gasps it could be from utter delight or complete discomfort. It is much better to find out.

Your goal is to become the world's greatest and only expert in pleasing this one person. To achieve this assuredly, you need help — specific assistance that only she or he can give you. The best such feedback is ongoing.

On one hand, a basic understanding of the anatomy of pleasure is simple because of our common physiology. Both the penis and the clitoris become erect, but the latter stays in position. The clitoris is similar to an erect penis, but upside down. As a result, a man and a woman can have expectations of each other based upon their own body's reactions. Strong pressure can be pleasurable at the bases of both a clitoris and penis, while direct stimulation is usually too sensitive at the tip of either. The sweet spot is usually right below the glans penis and right at the beginning of the clitoral hood. They are analogous to each other in all these ways.

On the other hand, people vary a lot in their physiologies of pleasure. Individual people vary at different times, too. This means that a person's state of fatigue, time of the month, and stages of arousal will all impact what feels too little, too much, or just right. To get it just right, we have to learn from each other. This element of loving consists of an easy back-and-forth communication and demonstration of how to please each other. Your message to each other is one of willing apprenticeship: You can show me, tell me, or both. Either way, I am eager to learn.

This is the gold standard at its ecstatic peak. During sexual sharing, giving and taking become one, as do the dualities we began our discussion of sex with. Spiritual and physical experiences become delightfully indistinguishable from each other. *Sexual love breaks through all the barriers, melting them deliciously into a climactic union, emotionally summarizing the entire relationship.*

Along the way, we have resolved the most notorious barrier to long-term relationships, which is romantic boredom. During the discussion of affairs in

Better than new, way better than new

the 15th chapter, I made the important point that no one, no matter how wonderful, can compete with newness. New relationships are charged with that feeling of astonishment that can render the sex addictive. Is boredom, in contrast, the inevitable price to pay for endurance, along the path of staying faithful to one person?

We have already begun to dissolve that myth. Long-term love has special powers that, once brought into the bedroom, fuel the exhilaration continually. We have already noticed that the unique (extraordinary=sacred) role of bringing special pleasure to your truly best friend is a profound and enduring joy. Further, I described that becoming the world's greatest expert in one person's pleasure is a scrumptious type of competence. In addition to the above benefits to long-term relationships, the melting of the physical/spiritual distinction is explosively enjoyable.

One way this may be expressed is through sexual playfulness. Sex play, such as shared fantasies, are much easier to share in the context of a long relationship because of the comfort of long association. Just as you share other secrets with each other, you can risk sharing fantasies. Whether these adventures take the form of stories you tell each other or safely act out together, they supply spice if your tastes run toward the hot. (Caveat: If they are not fully mutual, they at least cannot be distasteful to the other partner.)

For example, Mark and Annette would spontaneously slip into role-plays. Returning from the men's room, Mark would approach his wife at the restaurant table, with a sly smile. "Excuse me, but a lady as lovely as you should not be dining alone. Can I join you?" After she pointed out that she was ready for dessert, he suggested that he was available. On another occasion, bringing a bin of laundry upstairs to the bedroom and finding Mark there, she quipped, "Hello, Sir. What would you like me to do with all your clothes?" Without missing a beat, he suggested that she could remove them.

Their play was about pretending to be strangers, clearly, but the reality was that they were the most intimate of friends. The bittersweet blending of those flavors made for an exciting night. So it is for the rest of us. Inside a loving relationship, lust and love become friendly companions. Your sexual sharing can be hot and loving, passionate and sweet, familiar and renewed — a multidimensional expression of the deepest experiential knowing a couple can share.

Conclusion

We have often heard the expression that "you cannot live on love." This means that one also needs to make a living. But you can live *for* love. Indeed, love in all its forms is simply the most satisfying aspect of our lives. *The fulfilled heart is one fully filled with love.*

You now have an elaborated set of instructions for cultivating the love in your life, beginning in whichever circumstance you find yourself.

❖ If you are single and seeking, you have ways both to motivate and to refine your search.

❖ If you are single by choice or necessity, whether indefinitely or while recuperating from loss, you have options for the development of a love-filled life without a current romance. (The same approach also prepares you to be a complete partner.)

❖ If you are questioning the wisdom of staying with someone, you have steps to follow responsibly to determine the viability of the relationship.

❖ If you are strengthening a relationship, you have learned about three pitfalls (none of which invalidates the relationship) that are unfortunately normal, yet completely manageable.

❖ You know about the power of a self-rejuvenating relationship and its gold standard basis.

❖ You also have strategies not only to gauge if you are on this path, but also to get back on track when veering off.

❖ You have a path for sex and love to combine synergistically and passionately.

The next chapter will be written by you. I have compiled, tested, and presented the recipe, but the kitchen has always been yours. You will decide what to prepare next and what part this book plays in what you cook up. Related questions that occur to me include how familiar to become with this book, whether to receive additional coaching (relationship counseling), and how high to aim.

You may be holding some of the chapters in reserve for future use. For example, I have noticed that the break-up strategies are empowering emotionally for those people who are in painfully struggling relationships, but not yet ready to push the button. Such people feel strengthened to know they do have a way out, if necessary.

How expert at the recipes to become

They realize that their current partners do not have an unbreakable lock on their hearts. This, in turn, provides endurance and reassurance along the path to deciding.

Another issue related to single people is whether this is the time to go shopping. For some, temporary life circumstances may delay the search; for others, their young ages suggest they would rather meet their soul-mates later rather than sooner.

In contrast, many readers probably prefer the results sooner rather later. The summary below is a useful guide for where and when to review. For instance, if you are in a relationship for a couple of years and hope to keep love thriving as your astonishment phase passes, you could decide to focus on the Gold Medal Recipe chapter. A general gauge for review might be as follows:

❖ You are single or just met someone: shopping chapters (Part I)

❖ You are alone and want to feel complete: relationship with oneself chapters (Part II)

❖ You are feeling alone within a relationship, and may want out: reevaluation chapters (Part III)

❖ You just don't understand each other: gender dynamics chapter (Chapter 16)

❖ You are having the same quarrel over and over: one argument chapter (Chapter 17)

❖ The relationship seems to be running out of steam: common ground chapter (Chapter 18)

❖ You are both in love and want a love-life insurance policy: gold medal recipe chapter (Part V)

❖ You notice that the gold medal recipe is not natural, but an acquired taste for you: communication strategies chapters (Part VI)

❖ You like sex, or you want to: final chapters (Part VII)

Of course, you may be in several of these states simultaneously and consequently decide to review more than one part. At the same time, each of the parts is able to stand alone, and when they rely on information from another chapter, I refer to that specifically. This allows you to recognize whether the reference is fresh in your mind or not.

Another method to weave the recipe into your daily lives is a notebook strategy, which is a useful practice I mentioned previously, both when exploring the one argument and for conflict resolution. *The overall theme of the notebook is reassurance, written in advance so you can read it when you need it.* You may have already noticed that reassurance is a repetitive theme in cooking up a lasting love. Accordingly, it has been a subtext throughout all the chapters. For example:

❖ When single women are looking to attract the kind of gentle-men who read signals, we sought cues that would provide them reassurance.

❖ When single people are building their wish-lists, we reassured ourselves that we are not looking for too much if we meet the standards we hold for others.

❖ When building a robust single life, the development of an inner cheerleader provides an undercurrent of reassurance throughout life.

❖ When a nonsingle person runs into an emotional affair (whether or not it is also physical), we reviewed a plan to avoid any contact, in order to avoid any reassurance. In the case that the first relationship ends, this method allows the potential couple to reassure themselves accurately that no one left for the other.

❖ Conversely, in recovery from an affair, we applied the reassuring closeness that had once been absent for long-term assurance of fidelity.

❖ In all three of the pitfalls to relationships, we applied the normalcy and, indeed, inevitability of the challenges to reassure couples that their bonds are not fatally flawed.

❖ In terms of the gender pitfall, I suggested learning to translate between the genders as a way to overcome misunderstandings and provide reassurance.

❖ Reassurance is also the central method for overcoming the one argument. The first time I recommended use of a notebook was to prepare ways to overcome each other's greatest interpersonal fears.

❖ In describing the gold standard for relationships, openly requesting reassurance was an important ingredient of the vulnerability backup plan for the gold medal recipe.

❖ Reassurance also comprised specific steps both in methods for conflict prevention and for conflict resolution.

The notebook becomes a place to record any of these forms of reassurance for future reference. When you are writing it, you may feel that such preparation is unnecessary, because you obviously already know whatever it is you are recording. Ironically, this is exactly why you need to write it in advance. During stressful times, people forget new insights, no matter how useful. During such a stress-regress (as described in Chapter 8, and revisited often), the notebook may be all that remains to guide you where you want to go and save you from where you definitely do not want to go.

The question of how much expertise to develop with the recipe leads us to a related question: whether to seek professional instruction. Even people who love to cook also go out to dinner and may take lessons from a professional chef.

As I wrote in the introduction, there is a significant difference between *simple* and *easy*. Despite the fact that I work with

Whether to seek professional guidance

extraordinarily accomplished and capable people, virtually all would tell you that they get a lot further and do so faster when they (as I request of them) "let me do the work." The value of sessions that translate between couples' contrasting perspectives is itself a boon for trust and closeness, aside from tailored strategies for communication improvement.

To return to an AA analogy, even in such "self-help" programs, people need and receive guidance. Indeed, anyone who claims to be in a 12-step program, but without the guidance of a sponsor, is more or less without a program. Alas, it seems easier to find a highly qualified AA or Alanon sponsor than to find a highly qualified psychotherapist. I speculate about causes for this in the sidebar.

I am not sure why this is. Partially, it may be a similar problem in most professions. In a sense, professionals often become "too skilled" at their jobs, so they become habitual and perfunctory in its performance. It is easy to stop paying attention. When I consulted to the San Francisco Police Department, one of the academy staff explained that, "A police officer gets hurt when he handles a nonroutine situation in a routine manner." To my thinking, there are no routine situations. Averages are for statistics, but every specific situation is particular. Routine thinking produces complacency; it is bad for marriages and bad for marriage counselors.

It also may result from a problem with psychology not being a "normalized science." Normalized sciences such as medicine have a wide consensus on what competence is. Other sciences, like nutrition, have competing theories. As a result, the food pyramids have known large fluctuations, and widely disparate forms of advice are available. One expert's health food may be another expert's deadly diet. Similarly, many behaviors that I consider harmful in therapists, ranging from emotional detachment to advising couples to get divorced, can be justified according to one theory or another.

On the other hand, in some ways psychotherapy suffers from a typical problem in other sciences, which is the conflict between theoretical and practical scientists. In many fields, the academics see those in applied practice as intellectual lightweights, while those involved in practical applications see the academics as out of touch with common-sense realities. As a result, they benefit less from each other's contributions. This results in a large gap between the therapy being researched in the literature and standard practice in most communities.

Whatever the causes, the bottom line is that you should talk to any therapist before visiting. The way he or she speaks to you on the phone will usually be the way you will be treated in the office. Do not tolerate condescending or patronizing attitudes. Further, you can expect an active coaching style in any type of psychotherapy sessions. In the context of couple therapy, this may include having the two of you speak through the counselor, especially if there is conflict. During either individual or couple sessions, look for ample interjections of insights and/or strategies. Your overall impression should be that, if you know where you want to go, this person has the skill to show you how to get there. Along the way, if you feel a bit picked on sometimes, that can be part of the process, especially if accompanied with liberal amounts of respect and humor. Yet, during couple work, if only one of you feels targeted, especially more than once, the therapist may be biased. If you do not address this successfully, this person will not likely bring progress to the relationship. (For more on what to expect from therapy, along with some of the therapeutic insights it can produce, see my *The Tao of Your Psychotherapy Practice*, 2011.)

The final question you will be answering for yourself is how high to aim. In almost all endeavors, the highest results are reserved for those who follow

How high are you aiming?

through the most. In addition to traits like ability and inquisitiveness, effort is the greater part of success. How much attention you pay to growing your love will be influenced by how important it is to you and what you believe is possible.

As with most of this book, clients in my office have taught me what I have learned about relationships, and a part of this is that you should aim high. As I wrote in Chapter 15, the married couples who once loved each other, but later suffered through infidelity, tend to get the best results of all. I mentioned the wife whose friends asked her, "How do we get what you have without going through what you went through to get it?"

The answer to their question is now before you. The couples who endured infidelity know that the survival of their marriages depends upon seeking excellence together, much as those in AA know that "working their program" is not optional. Their lives depend upon it. Similarly, these couples know that their families depend on it. They do not settle for less than intimate intensity because they cannot survive on less.

I find these couples inspiring in so many ways. There is only one aspect of working with them that bothers me. Why, I wonder, should couples on such a brink be the only ones to soar off the ledge into glorious heights? This is the quest behind what you are reading. I am determined that they do not have to be the only ones. *Aim as high as they must, and you will ascend as high as you can.* Focus upward as if your happiness depends on it. Do not settle for less, and you will find much more, because if you pick the right person, your efforts will not be alone. Your mutual contributions will not only add to each other, but also multiply each other, and you will be flying astride and high. In your own wakes, you will carry whoever is watching, whether children, siblings, or close friends.

Besides yourselves, they are the ones to whom you most owe it. If you have children, you have proof that they miss little about what is going on. You know this because you were once a child and had a good fix on how the folks' marriage was going. I often feel that my clients and I are pioneering, because we did not see relationships around us that we could fruitfully model. Wouldn't you like your own children to be able to say the opposite — that they want to have a marriage full of love, friendship, and warmth like the one they saw at home growing up?

Otherwise, we become like the warring couple sung about by country music artist Kenny Chesney, in the song "Small, Y'all." While they go at each other, their children are nearby hearing every word. This leads to the song's title, asking if the couple feels "small, y'all." Here we have one side of the motivation to put our full hearts into a marriage. Our kids (or future kids) deserve better. Others who are close to us are watching, too. Have you ever noticed how nervous other couples get when another couple breaks up? Besides the sadness of it all, it calls into question whether or not any relationship will last.

Such is the downside of failure. Yet, just as compelling is the upside of success. I often think of the image of two dancers or two warriors who are touching each other, back to back. They literally *have each other's back* by virtue of their own backs, both moving in perfect coordination. They are each attending to their own activities, yet both are anticipating the movements of the other's body so precisely that they never come apart. This image is so sweet to me that I have felt moved when I see it choreographed, even in action films. In real life, it is even more beautiful to share this level of adaptive collaboration. I know what it is like to live without this, and I know what it is like to have it. The latter is very much worth your loving efforts.

The main point of all of this is that you have the opportunity to be both the chef and the diner. Your time in the kitchen culminates in your time relaxed at the table. As you will recall, you simultaneously serve each other, at least figuratively. Choose well, then prepare well, but most of all receive the bountiful gift before you. As the recipe takes shape, you will recognize that others have loved before, but no one has ever loved your mate the way you do, and no one has ever loved you so deeply and so well. *Bon appétit.*

References

Adams, J. S. Inequity in social exchange. In L. Berkowitz (Ed.), *Advances in experimental social psychology, II*. New York: Academic Press, 1965.

Blum, R. Don't Let Your Mood Boss You Around. Blog post at http://dr-rick.com/?p=1061. Accessed Nov. 14, 13.

Blum, R. The Most Sacred of Places. *Parabola: Tradition, Myth, and the Search for Meaning*, 2007;32(2):14-17.

Blum, R. *The Tao of Your Psychotherapy Practice*. Teaneck, NJ: The Paradoxical Press, 2011.

Brokaw, T. *The Greatest Generation*. New York: Random House, 2004,

Buber, M. *Between Man and Man*. New York: Routledge Classics, 2002.

Chapman, G. D. *The 5 Love Languages: The Secret to Love that Lasts*. Chicago, IL: Northfield Publishing, 2009.

Cloninger, C. R., et al. A Psychobiological Model of Temperament and Character. *Arch Gen Psychiatry*, 1993;50:975-990)

Csikszentmihalyi, M. Flow: *The Psychology of Optimal Experience*. New York: Harper & Row, 1990.

Fohrman, D. http://learn.alephbeta.org/school/catalog/course/genesis-unveiled-copy. Accessed May 8, 13.

Frankl, Victor. *Man's Search for Meaning*. Boston, MA: Beacon Press, 2006.

Gottman, J. *Why Marriages Succeed or Fail: What You Can learn from the Breakthrough Research to Make Your Marriage Last*. New York: Simon & Schuster, 1994.

James, William. The Varieties of Religious Experience: A Study in Human Nature. Radford, VA: Wilder Publications, 2007.

Leckie, Robert. *Helmut for My Pillow: From Parris Island to the Pacific*. New York: Bantam, 2010

LeDoux, Joseph. *The Emotional Brain: The Mysterious Underpinnings of Emotional Life*. New York: Touchstone Books, 1998.

Markman, H. J, et al., *Fighting for Your Marriage: Positive Steps for Preventing Divorce and Preserving Lasting Love*. San Francisco: Jossey Bass, 2010.

Merrill, David and Reid, Roger. *Personal Styles and Effective Performance.* New York: CRC Press, LLC. 1981.

Myers, I.B. *Gifts Differing: Understanding Personality Type.* Boston: Nicholas Brealey America, 1995.

Newberg, A. & Waldman, M.R. *How God Changes Your Brain: Break through Findings from a Leading Neuroscientist.* New York: Ballantine Books, 2010.

Phillips, D. & Judd, R. *How to Fall Out of Love.* New York: Grand Central Publishing, 1985.

Robertson, D. *The Sum and Total of Now.* New York: Berkley Trade, 2009.

Rokeach, Milton and Sandra J. Ball-Rokeach (1989). Stability and Change in American Value Priorities , 1968-1981, *American Psychologist*, 1989; 44(5): 775-784.

Royce, J. R. Metaphoric knowledge and humanistic psychology. In J. F. T. Bugental (ed.), *Challenges of Humanistic Psychology.* New York: McGraw-Hill, 1967.

Steinsaltz, A. *Simple words: Thinking about What Really Matters in Life.* New York: Simon & Schuster, 2008.

Tannen, D. *You Just Don't Understand: Women and Men in Conversation.* New York: William Morrow, 2007.

Wolpe, J. *Psychotherapy by Reciprocal Inhibition.* Stanford, CA: Stanford University Press, 1968.

Yankelovich, D. *New Rules.* New York: Random House, 1981.